Anger Management
FOR
DUMMIES®

by W. Doyle Gentry, PhD

BICENTENNIAL
1807
WILEY
2007
BICENTENNIAL

Wiley Publishing, Inc.

Anger Management For Dummies®

Published by
Wiley Publishing, Inc.
111 River St.
Hoboken, NJ 07030-5774
www.wiley.com

For general information on our other products and services, please contact our Customer Care Department within the U.S. at 800-762-2974, outside the U.S. at 317-572-3993, or fax 317-572-4002.

For technical support, please visit www.wiley.com/techsupport.

Wiley also publishes its books in a variety of electronic formats. Some content that appears in print may not be available in electronic books.

Library of Congress Control Number: 2006934834

ISBN-13: 978-0-470-03715-7

ISBN-10: 0-470-03715-6

Manufactured in the United States of America

10 9 8 7 6 5 4 3 2 1

1B/RX/RR/QW/IN

WILEY

About the Author

W. Doyle Gentry, PhD, is a clinical psychologist and Director of the Institute for Anger-Free Living in Lynchburg, Virginia. He is a Fellow in the American Psychological Association and was the Founding Editor of the *Journal of Behavioral Medicine.* In Dr. Gentry's four-decade career as a scientist-practitioner, he has authored over 100 publications, including eight books, and is a pioneer in the fields of health psychology, behavioral medicine, and anger management. He has previously served on the faculty of Duke University Medical Center and the University of Texas Medical Branch, Galveston. Gentry has conducted training seminars for lay and professional audiences throughout the United States, Canada, and Europe. He has also served as a consultant to major industry, where he specializes in conflict management, team building, and health promotion. Articles referring to Dr. Gentry's work on anger regularly appear in a variety of contemporary magazines, and he is frequently interviewed on radio and television for insights into how to create and maintain an anger-free life. He is the author of two earlier self-help books on anger: *ANGER-FREE: Ten Basic Steps to Managing Your Anger* (Quill, 2000) and *When Someone You Love Is Angry* (Berkley, 2004).

Dr. Gentry is available for speaking engagements and workshops. Interested readers may contact him via e-mail at LiveAngerFree@aol.com.

Dedication

I dedicate this book to my two basset hounds, Max and Dixie, both of whom have absolutely no need for anger management.

Author's Acknowledgments

I would like to thank a number of "teammates" who made writing this book both possible and enjoyable. First, I am indebted — once again — to my agent, Denise Marcil, and her delightful associate, Maura Kye, for all their efforts on my behalf. I was well represented!

The folks at John Wiley & Sons, Inc. — in particular, Lindsay Lefevere, Elizabeth Kuball, and Rebecca Stidham — were fantastic. I deeply appreciate their professionalism, expertise, encouragement, and, most of all, patience during both the acquisition and editorial phases of the project. The energy and passion associated with the *For Dummies* series is, indeed, infectious.

And, as always, I want to thank my loving family — Catherine, Rebecca, and Chris — for yet another show of support for my life's work. They never disappoint.

Basically, we are all dummies when it comes to anger management — a field that remains a work in progress. I learn more every day about ways to harness this complicated and, at times, troublesome emotion, and being able to share this education with my readers is a pleasure. If this book changes the life of a single person for the better, then I am satisfied that the hard work that went into it was worthwhile.

Publisher's Acknowledgments

We're proud of this book; please send us your comments through our Dummies online registration form located at www.dummies.com/register/.

Some of the people who helped bring this book to market include the following:

Acquisitions, Editorial, and Media Development

Project Editor: Elizabeth Kuball

Acquisitions Editor: Lindsay Lefevere

Editorial Program Coordinator: Hanna K. Scott

Technical Editor: Rebecca Stidham, LCSW

Editorial Manager: Michelle Hacker

Consumer Editorial Supervisor and Reprint Editor: Carmen Krikorian

Editorial Assistants: Erin Calligan, David Lutton

Cover Photo: Alejandro Balaguer/Getty Images

Cartoons: Rich Tennant (www.the5thwave.com)

Composition Services

Project Coordinator: Adrienne Martinez

Layout and Graphics: Stephanie D. Jumper, Barry Offringa, Lynsey Osborn, Laura Pence, Julie Trippetti

Proofreaders: David Faust, Christine Pingleton, Techbooks

Indexer: Techbooks

Publishing and Editorial for Consumer Dummies

    Diane Graves Steele, Vice President and Publisher, Consumer Dummies

    Joyce Pepple, Acquisitions Director, Consumer Dummies

    Kristin A. Cocks, Product Development Director, Consumer Dummies

    Michael Spring, Vice President and Publisher, Travel

    Kelly Regan, Editorial Director, Travel

Publishing for Technology Dummies

    Andy Cummings, Vice President and Publisher, Dummies Technology/General User

Composition Services

    Gerry Fahey, Vice President of Production Services

    Debbie Stailey, Director of Composition Services

Contents at a Glance

Table of Contents

Introduction

nger is part of life — no less than memory, happiness, and compassion. No one chooses to be angry. Anger is a reaction that's built into your nervous system. In fact, anger is one of the first emotions mothers recognize in their newborn infants. So, it's never too early to start anger management.

Anger says more about you — your temperament, how you view the world, how balanced your life is, and how easily you forgive others — than it does about other people. You don't have to be a victim of your own anger — you can choose how you respond when the world doesn't treat you the way you want it to. You have just as much choice about how you express your anger as you do about what color shirt you wear, what you eat for breakfast, or what time you go jogging this afternoon. You also have a choice about how much of yesterday's anger you carry into the future and how much anger you are likely to experience tomorrow. If I didn't believe that, I would have been doing something very different with my professional life for the past 40 years!

No one is exempt from problematic anger. Anger is a very democratic emotion — it causes problems for men and women, kids and the elderly, rich and poor, educated and uneducated, people of all colors and ethnic backgrounds, believers and nonbelievers. Tens of millions of human beings needlessly suffer from what I call *toxic anger* — anger that literally poisons your life — each and every day of their lives.

Anger is not something that can — or should be — cured. But you have to *manage* it well — at home, at work, and in your most intimate relationships — if you want to benefit from it. *Anger Management For Dummies* tells you how to manage your anger by focusing on the positive — how to get a good night's sleep, how to change your perspective on life, why confession is better for you than venting, how to transform conflicts into challenges, and much more. Anger management has moved far beyond the simplistic (albeit well-intentioned) advice of years past to count to ten or take a couple of deep breaths every time you get angry — and that's good news!

About This Book

How do you know when you have too much anger? Do you determine that for yourself, or do you let other people make that call? If you're not physically aggressive — physically hurting other people or poking holes in walls — does that mean you're not angry? Does it really help to vent, to get things off your chest, or are you better off keeping your mouth shut in order to keep the peace? Can angry people really change or do they have to go through life suffering because that's just the way they are? And what should you do if you're on the wrong end of someone else's anger? These are all important questions that *Anger Management For Dummies* answers for you.

When I wrote *Anger Management For Dummies,* I had four basic goals in mind:

- ✔ **I wanted to show you that anger is more than a four-letter word — it's an extremely complex emotion that has meaning well beyond the crude and hurtful words we use to express it.** Understanding all that your anger says about you is the essence of anger management.

- ✔ **I wanted to illustrate all the various ways that anger can — and does — adversely affect your life when it occurs too frequently and is too intense.**

- ✔ **I wanted to explain that anger management occurs in three distinct time frames — yesterday, today, and tomorrow.** The strategies I propose to manage anger will, of course, differ depending on whether you're trying to let go of some old anger, deal with the anger you face today, or prevent (yes, I said prevent!) anger that you're otherwise destined to experience tomorrow.

- ✔ **I wanted to show you that managing anger is something that is entirely within your power — and not something you have to seek professional help for — if you're willing to make the necessary lifestyle changes outlined in this book.** It doesn't matter how old you are or how long anger has been a part of your life — it's never too late to manage your anger.

Anger Management For Dummies is not one of those 12-step books where you have to read (and follow the advice) of Step 1 before you can proceed to Step 2, and so on. It's a resource book containing all the information I have at my disposal after four decades of combined clinical practice and scientific research on anger management. You don't have to start with Chapter 1 and read straight through to the end of the book. You can look at the Table of Contents, find something that interests you, and start there. You may want to focus on the area in which you're having the most trouble controlling your temper — at work, for example. Or you may want to head straight for a chapter on managing stress (one of the most common causes of anger). I'm not even going to suggest that you read the whole book — that's up to you. Be like my bassett hounds and go where your nose (or in this case, your eyes!) lead you. Trust me, you'll get where you need to be.

Conventions Used in This Book

I did not want *Anger Management For Dummies* to be yet another book written by psychologists for psychologists. This book is intended to show ordinary people how to lead an anger-free life, so I've eliminated all the professional jargon, and used terms and concepts — as one of my mentors in graduate school used to say — that "my grandmother can understand."

I've also tried to make reading *Anger Management For Dummies* an enjoyable experience. Just because anger is a serious topic doesn't mean that you need to approach it with a deadly serious attitude. One of the most memorable educational experiences of my life, in fact, was one in which the speaker — the infamous physician Patch Adams — painted all of our noses red before he began his lecture.

Most important, *Anger Management For Dummies* is loaded with stories about human beings, just like you, who have successfully overcome a lifetime of anger. The people you'll read about aren't real — they're composites of many relatives, friends, and clients I've encountered over the years who've taught me the important lessons about anger management. The quotations and two-person dialogues that I include in these stories are based on my recollections of conversations I had.

You don't have to know psychology to understand this book. But I do use a couple conventions that you should be aware of:

- ✔ When I introduce a new term, I put the word in *italics* and define it shortly thereafter (usually in parentheses).
- ✔ When I list an e-mail address or Web address, I use a special font called monofont so you know exactly what to type.

And that's it!

What You're Not to Read

Whoever said half a loaf is better than none had the right idea. You don't have to read every single word, sentence, part, and/or chapter of *Anger Management For Dummies* to get your money's worth. And just because you see something marked with a Remember icon doesn't mean that you're expected to remember everything you read. I won't be giving out any tests at the end!

I include lots of sidebars — the text in gray boxes — which, though not essential to the overall message offered in this book, are things I thought you might find interesting in their own right. You can think of them as "side dishes" to the main course — whether you read them depends on how hungry (for information) you are. But you can safely skip them without missing anything critical to the topic at hand.

You can also safely skip the paragraphs marked with Technical Stuff icons (see "Icons Used in This Book," later in this Introduction, for more information).

Foolish Assumptions

I made a few assumptions about you when I was writing this book:

- ✔ **You may or may not have a problem with anger — but if you don't have a problem with anger yourself, you know or love someone who does.** If you didn't buy this book for yourself, you bought it for your husband, wife, brother, sister, son, daughter, father, mother, friend, or co-worker. Or one of those people bought it for you.

- ✔ **You don't want to know everything there is to know about anger — you just want to know what you need to know to manage anger effectively.** Scientists have studied anger for years, but you won't find a bunch of scientific mumbo-jumbo in these pages. I focus on proven strategies to help you manage your anger, and that's it.

How This Book Is Organized

I organized *Anger Management For Dummies* into 7 parts and 25 chapters. Here's what you can find in each part.

Part 1: The Basics of Anger

In the first three chapters, I acquaint you with some basic facts about anger as a universal emotion, the role that emotions like anger play in your life, and help you decide whether anger is poisoning your health, career, and relationships. Chapter 2 shows you how to quantify your anger and distinguish between what I call *toxic anger* and *nontoxic anger*. I want you to be able to respond to anger (and the circumstances that provoke it) instead of just reacting in some predictable, mindless, knee-jerk fashion that almost always takes you someplace you really don't want to go.

Part II: Managing Your Anger Today

In this part, I help you tackle the challenge of managing anger *in the moment*. Most people get in trouble simply because they don't know what to do when they begin to experience anger. In effect, it's what you don't know (for example, that all emotions are transient) and don't do (for example, let the other person have the last word) that leads to anger mismanagement. Chapter 6 offers you a structured, multistep, *effective* method you can use to keep your cool.

Part III: Preventing Anger Tomorrow

Chapters 7 through 11 show you ways to deal with anger *before it happens*. This is a radical new approach — most anger-management strategies are designed to work after the fact (which is difficult if not impossible — try counting to ten when you're in the middle of a rage!). As far as I'm concerned, preventing anger is the most exciting aspect of anger management. In this part, I also talk about "getting your mind right" in terms of what you expect and will tolerate from the world around you, why it's imperative that you quit disguising your anger and just say what you feel (but with civility!), how to make a private confession of your anger, how to become the type of person who doesn't invite so much anger, and — perhaps most important — how you can use your anger constructively. If you can make anger your ally, you no longer have to worry about avoiding it.

Part IV: Handling Anger from the Past

If you're like me, you often find yourself getting much angrier than the situation you're in warrants. You're left with the question: "What in the world got into me?" Chances are, you just tapped into some old anger that's rolling around in your unconscious (Freud was right!) just waiting for an opportunity to express itself. In Chapter 12, I offer some tips on how not to let today's anger become tomorrow's anger — strategies like saying "Excuse you!" and the ten-minute rant. In Chapter 13, I get into the mechanics of forgiveness as applied to anger management. I'm not looking at forgiveness as a spiritual issue here, but rather as a tool for letting go of anger from the past that has long since outlived its usefulness.

Part V: Lifestyle Changes That Improve More Than Your Anger

Here's what I believe: Healthy people rarely get angry. In this part, I show you that toxic anger is a byproduct of a toxic lifestyle. If you're on the verge of stress burnout, if your daily diet consists mainly of caffeine and alcohol (with some nicotine thrown in for good measure!), if your life is all out of balance (too much work, too little play), if you never get a good night's sleep, if you carry the whole world on your shoulders because you don't believe in some sort of higher power, and if you're depressed as hell, why in the world *wouldn't* you be angry? Change all that and you'll see some major changes in how angry you are.

Part VI: Managing Anger in Key Relationships

Most of us compartmentalize our day-to-day lives into where we spend the most time — at work, at home, and in intimate relationships. These three chapters are designed to address anger-management issues that are situation specific — what works at work doesn't necessarily work at home. The benefit of having one meal a day together as a family, in an effort to reduce family conflict, may not be achievable in the executive boardroom. What is common to all three chapters in this section is a set of strategies that are aimed at turning hostility into harmony.

Part VII: The Part of Tens

If you're looking for quick ideas about how to raise a non-angry child or combat road rage, or you just want some easy-to-remember anger-freeing thoughts, you find them here.

Icons Used in This Book

Icons are those little pictures in the margins throughout this book, and they're there to draw your attention to certain kinds of information:

This icon alerts you to important ideas and concepts that you'll want to remember and that you can use even when you don't have *Anger Management For Dummies* in hand.

Every once in a while, the scientist in me gets a little chatty, and when I do, I mark the paragraph with this icon. You can read these paragraphs if you want, but the information they contain isn't essential to your understanding of the topic at hand.

The Tip icon suggests practical how-to strategies for managing anger.

This icon appears when I think a cautionary note is in order or when you need to seek professional help.

Where to Go from Here

Each part and chapter in this book is meant to stand alone in its discussion of anger management. When I was writing, I skipped around, writing chapters in no particular order — when I finished one, I looked at the Table of Contents to see what interested me next and went with that. Feel free to do likewise — choose a topic that interests you, and dive in.

If you do read *Anger Management For Dummies* in its entirety and you still find that you're struggling with anger, I suggest you seriously consider getting the help of a professional. Anger management is a niche market and you need to find someone who has credentials and expertise in this area. If you're interested in a medical remedy for abnormal anger — one that focuses on prescribed medication — you'll want to find a psychiatrist who specializes in this area. If you're more open to *psychotherapeutic strategies* (where change results from an interpersonal relationship between you and a therapist), look for a licensed clinical psychologist or mental health counselor. Either way, be sure to get the help you need.

Part I
The Basics of Anger

The 5th Wave   By Rich Tennant

"So much of what we know is still theoretical."

In this part . . .

I talk about why anger is a universal emotion and help you distinguish between an emotional *reaction* and an emotional *response*. I show you how to quantify just how angry you are by answering two simple questions: "How often are you angry?" and "How intense is your anger?" With the information I provide in this part, you don't have to be a rocket scientist to figure out if you suffer from toxic anger.

Finally, in this part, you can discover the many ways in which anger can poison your life — robbing you of energy, affecting your health, derailing your career, and harming those you love. You may be surprised about what anger says about your life now and in the future.

Chapter 1

Anger: The Universal Emotion

· ·

In This Chapter

▶ Examining the myths about anger

▶ Understanding what emotions are

▶ Getting help when you need it

· ·

*W*hat do college students, corporate executives, housewives, and preliterate tribesmen in Borneo and New Guinea have in common? They all recognize an angry face when they see it. Anger — along with joy, fear, sadness, and surprise — is a universal emotion. All cultures around the globe have anger in their peoples as an integral part of day-to-day life.

Anger is part of the survival mechanism of human beings. When faced with a threat — not unlike other animals — humans either run away or attack. Anger is the fuel behind that attack. But anger can also have the opposite effect and lead to our untimely demise. As Chapter 3 explains, too much anger can cause heart attacks, precipitate disabling work injuries, and facilitate risky sexual behavior. Anger truly is a double-edged sword.

Dispelling Common Anger Myths

Before you can manage your own anger, you need to be aware of what anger is and isn't. Unfortunately, myths about anger seem to abound. Here are some of the myths I want to dispel right from the get-go:

> ✔ **Males are angrier than females.** If by angrier you mean how often people experience anger, it's simply not true that men are angrier than women. Surveys show that women get mad just as frequently as men — about once or twice a week on average. On the other hand, men tend to report more *intense* anger, while women tend to hang on to anger *longer*.

✔ **Anger is bad.** Anger serves a variety of positive purposes when it comes to coping with stress. It energizes you, improves your communication with other people, promotes your self-esteem, and defends you against fear and insecurity. (Jesus, Gandhi, and Martin Luther King, Jr., were all angry men — but they turned that anger into social reform that made the world a better place.)

✔ **Anger is good.** When it leads to domestic violence, property damage, sexual abuse, drug addiction, ulcers, and self-mutilation, anger is definitely not good.

✔ **Anger is only a problem when you openly express it.** As few as 10 percent of people act out their feelings when they get angry. The other 90 percent either suppress their anger ("I don't want to talk about it!") or repress their anger ("I'm not angry at all — really!"). People who express their anger are the squeaky wheels who get everyone's attention; people who repress or suppress their anger need anger management just as much.

✔ **The older you get, the more irritable you are.** It's the other way around — as people age, they report fewer negative emotions and greater emotional control. People — like wine and cheese — do tend to improve with age.

✔ **Anger is all in the mind.** Nothing could be farther from the truth. Emotions are primarily physical in nature. If anger were only a state of mind, why would someone say, "I feel like I have a big fist in my chest when I get that angry"? Believe me, when you get mad, that emotion is instantly manifested in muscles throughout your entire body, the hairs on the back of your neck, your blood pressure, your blood sugar levels, your heart rate, your respiration rate, your gut, even your finger temperature (it warms up!) — long before you're aware of what's happening.

✔ **Anger is all about getting even.** The most common motive behind anger has been shown to be a desire to assert authority or independence, or to improve one's image — not necessarily to cause harm. Revenge is a secondary motive. A third motive involves letting off steam over accumulated frustrations — again with no apparent intent to harm anyone else.

✔ **Only certain types of people have a problem with anger.** Actually, over the years I've spent helping people with anger management, I've worked with all types of people — truck drivers, college professors, physicians, housewives, grandmothers, lawyers, policemen, career criminals, poor people, millionaires, children, the elderly, people of various colors, nationalities, and religions. Anger is a universal emotion!

✔ **Anger results from human conflict.** Sometimes yes, sometimes no. One of the leading experts on anger has found that people can get angry by being exposed to foul odors, aches and pains, and hot temperatures — none of which involve (or can be blamed on) the actions of others.

Understanding the Role of Emotions in Your Life

Emotion is a compound word. The *e* stands for "energy" and the *motion* means exactly what it says — "movement." Emotions *move* you to act in ways that defend you from threat, lead to social attachments and procreation, cause you to engage in pleasurable pursuits, lead to reattachment after some type of meaningful loss, and lead you to explore your environment. Without emotion, life would be at a standstill.

Psychiatrists have a term for people who lack appear to lack emotions — including anger: It's *alexithymia*. Alexithymics tend to:

- ✔ Have difficulty identifying different types of feelings
- ✔ Appear stiff and wooden in relating to others
- ✔ Lack emotional awareness
- ✔ Lack enjoyment
- ✔ Have trouble distinguishing between emotions and bodily feelings
- ✔ Appear overly logical when it comes to decision making

Putting the focus where it needs to be

For most of my early academic career, like many other psychologists, I was caught up in the debate about whether anger was best kept in or let out. The emphasis of my research at the time was on how people express their anger and its impact on health. I was one of the anger-out proponents (and proud of it!), who was firmly convinced that venting anger was the right way to go — better to protest aloud than suffer high blood pressure or so I thought.

In hindsight, I now see that my colleagues and I were wrong in our appraisal of what the focus of anger management should be. What I have since discovered — more from practice than science — is that the real culprit when it comes to anger is *how much* of it a person experiences. The logic here is simple: If you rarely get

angry; if, when you do, it's not too intense; and if it's over in a minute, it really doesn't matter whether you keep it in or let it out. You don't have enough of it to cause you, or anyone else, a problem.

Similarly, if you're repeatedly angry throughout the day, your anger is extremely intense, and you stay that way for the rest of the day or longer, it doesn't matter whether you're an anger-in or anger-out type — either way you have a problem. If you keep that much anger in, you'll pay a price — in the form of depression, heart attack, resentment, and so on. If you let that much anger out, you'll pay a different price — in the form of legal fees, divorce, job loss, and so on. The mode of expression simply determines the type of consequences you pay.

Habituation: It can be a bitch

The worst thing about bad things — including a bad temper — is that you get used to them, and that makes it difficult for you to change. Overweight people know they need to lose weight, but they continue eating too much (and exercising too little) nevertheless. Smokers know that they're killing themselves with every drag on those cigarettes, but very few quit. The same goes for alcoholics and drug addicts and people who are addicted to gambling. People even get accustomed to poverty and illiteracy. Call it complaisance, inertia, a lack of will power, or not wanting to leave your comfort zone — it all amounts to the same thing: a built-in resistance to change.

I believe in being honest with my angry clients, so I tell them from the outset that it's far easier to stay the same than it is to change. So, if you're looking for the easy way out, stay like you are and live with the consequences. Not changing requires absolutely no energy, motivation, or commitment on your part — but change does. If you think you're up to it, this book is for you — and the rewards will be amazing. As a friend of mine who struggled for years with a bad temper said, "Since I took control of my anger, I have a peaceful mind. I don't have to go to bed every night wondering what I have to do to get even with someone." What a wonderful testimony to the power of anger management.

   ✔ Lack sympathy for others

   ✔ Appear perplexed by other people's emotions

   ✔ Be unmoved by art, literature, and music

   ✔ Have few, if any, emotional memories (for example, memories of childhood)

You want to have emotions but you want to be in control of those emotions. You want to let anger move you to write a letter to the editor in your local newspaper about some social injustice. You want your anger to move you to stand up for yourself when your talents are being exploited in the workplace. Anger that says to your spouse, "Hey, something is not working here" is good for a marriage. But if your anger only moves you to hurt others — or yourself — then you definitely have a problem. Think of anger as a tool that can help you throughout life if you know how to use it — and think of *Anger Management For Dummies* as a reference on how best to use that tool.

Getting the Help You Need

Everybody needs support — nobody can go through life completely alone. When you're embarking on a major change in your life, the help of other people is especially important. And believe me, managing your anger is a major life change.

Support comes in many forms. To manage your anger effectively, you need all the following kinds of support:

- ✔ **Emotional support:** You need people who are behind you 100 percent, people who know about your problems with anger and are cheering you on as you figure out how to manage it.

- ✔ **Informational support:** You can have the best of intentions, but if you don't have the information you need about anger and how to manage it, you won't get far. Lucky for you, you hold in your hands all the information you need to get a handle on your anger.

- ✔ **Tangible support:** Sometimes you need some hands-on support. An angry mother who is on the verge of losing her temper and abusing her child can sure use a neighbor who can step in and become a surrogate parent while mom goes somewhere and cools off.

- ✔ **Appraisal support:** You need people who are willing to give you honest feedback about your anger, as well as how much improvement you've made — no matter how small.

Here's how you can garner all the support you need in order to succeed at anger management:

- ✔ **Keep in mind that most people want to be supportive — they're just waiting on you to give them an opportunity.** Take the initiative and ask your closest friends and family members for their support. Support that goes unrecognized or unused does you no good. Most people have far more support than they take advantage of. This is no time to think, "I don't want to be a burden on anyone." Believe me, you're more of a burden when you're angry than when you're not!

- ✔ **Be willing to give support to your friends and family in turn.** Support must be reciprocal. In order to receive it, you must give it.

- ✔ **Keep in mind that no one person can satisfy all your support needs.** One person may be able to offer emotional support, while another may help out in a more tangible way.

Don't be too surprised if, at first, you have trouble getting support for your efforts at anger management. *Remember:* You've probably hurt a lot of people with your anger over the years — and they may have some lingering resentment, fear, and uncertainty. That's natural. But if you're truly committed to managing your anger, chances are they'll eventually rally to your cause.

You'll Know When You're There

Often, people who have been successful at anger management have a hard time appreciating just how far they've come in their emotional life. I've made great strides in managing my own anger over the past several years — something my wife and kids appreciate very much! — but I really didn't understand how healthy I was until I recently had a moment of full-blown rage at a social event. I found myself so angry I couldn't speak for fear of what awful things would come out of my mouth and, as if that wasn't enough, I experienced mild chest pain that took an hour or so to go away.

Believe me, it took all the skills I outline in this book to calm down and regain some semblance of emotional equilibrium. I had forgotten what that level of anger felt like and it scared me. But after it subsided and I thought about it, I realized that the reason it got my attention and felt so awful was because this was the first time in years that I'd experienced what, earlier in my life was, regrettably, an all-too-usual part of my day.

One way you know you're succeeding in managing your anger is when you begin to realize that things that used to set you off no longer do. Another way you know you've changed is when people who know you well begin to give you unsolicited positive feedback about your improved temperament. And you know you've succeeded when that angry "fist" you feel in your chest day after day is no longer there — replaced by an abiding sense of inner peace.

In many respects, the work of anger management is never done — you're always a work in progress. Every day is an opportunity to exercise your anger-management muscles.

Chapter 2

When Is Anger a Problem?

*H*ow do you know when you have an anger problem? Some people would say that any time you get angry, that's a problem. Others would disagree, arguing that anger is never a problem as long as it communicates that something is wrong in your life.

Stan came to see me because his wife (and her therapist) thought he wasn't emotional enough. She wanted him to be more in touch with his feelings so they could experience a deeper level of intimacy in their marriage. Well, she got her wish. In no time, Stan was talking about all sorts of emotions he'd kept under wraps for years. Then, one day, his wife asked if she could join us. Stan agreed, so in she came. Right off the bat, she let me know in no uncertain terms how dissatisfied (read: angry) she was about how Stan's therapy was going. "All he does now is tell me how irritated he is with me and I'm sick of it," she explained. "But I thought you wanted him to be more emotional," I replied. "I did, but I didn't want to hear about his *anger* — just the positive emotions. He can keep his anger to himself. That's *his* problem," she added.

Ellie rarely shows any expression of anger — she's too nice a person. She has never cussed anyone out or struck anyone in a moment of rage. On the other hand, she is often disgusted with herself, distressed about her life in general, and disillusioned by what is going on at her current job. Ellie definitely has a problem with anger, but you'd have to be a detective to know it — her anger is disguised.

In this chapter, I take all the mystery out of trying to decide who does and does not have too much anger. You can easily quantify your experience with anger so you can tell if you have a problem that needs managing. All you have to do is answer a couple of simple questions, do a little math, and — voila! — you have your answer.

I wish it were simple

As the reader, I know you'd like a simple answer to the question "Why am I so angry, and what's the single most effective thing I can do about it?" You're hoping that one chapter in this book will provide that answer. But, alas, that's not the way it works.

Anger is a complex human emotion. By reading this book, you can come to understand where your anger is coming from — that is, which and how many of those factors that are unique to you are at work here. It may be three things: youth, poor communication, and substance abuse, for example. Or it may be half a dozen — poor coping skills, a life that is sorely out of balance, a cynical outlook, too few sources of support, the fact that you're a guy, and a high-stress job. The important thing at this point is to find the right recipe for anger management and to use the information and resources in this book to bring your emotional life to a better place.

Evaluating How Angry You Are

Everyone gets angry. After all, anger is one of those universal emotions — along with sadness, joy, and fear — that people throughout the world recognize when they see or hear it. But you and I may not experience anger to the same degree — and that's really the crux of what this book is about. What you need to determine is exactly how angry you are.

To do this, you first have to agree on what anger is and what it isn't. Anger is often defined as:

- The emotion you reserve for your enemies
- The emotion that most often accompanies or precedes aggressive behavior
- The emotion that triggers the *fight* component of your nervous system's fight-or-flight response
- The emotion that is the opposite of fear
- The emotion that expresses itself in revenge
- The emotion that signals that you feel personally threatened
- The emotion that's associated with blame
- The emotion that's negative in tone
- The emotion that can be deadly when it comes to your health
- The emotion that gets your blood boiling

✔ The emotion that you're most afraid of

✔ The emotion that expresses the combative side of your personality

✔ The emotion that everyone else around you is most afraid of

✔ The emotion that always does more harm than good

Anger, on the other hand, is *not* the same as:

✔ **Hostility:** An attitude of ill will synonymous with cynicism, mistrust, and paranoia

✔ **Aggression or violence:** Various types of behavior that are always intended to inflict harm on others

I also have to distinguish between the *experience* of anger and the *expression* of anger. In this chapter, you only need to focus on evaluating the degree to which you experience anger — how often you have this feeling and how strong it is. In other chapters throughout this book, you focus more on how you express it — what you do with your anger.

How often do you get angry?

Start by answering the following question.

How often during a typical week in the past month did you get irritated, mad, or angry?

A. Not at all

B. Once or twice a week

C. Three to five times a week

D. One or two times a day

E. Three times a day

F. Four or five times a day

G. Six to ten times a day

H. More than ten times a day

Be honest. And don't just think of the times you flew into a rage — think of all the times you felt even the *least* bit angry.

If you answered A, B, or C, your anger is within a healthy, normal range. If you answered D, E, F, G, or H, your anger is probably excessive (you're angrier than 75 percent of most people I have surveyed).

Annoyances count

In one study where 50 college students were asked to keep a weekly diary of how often they got annoyed or angry, they recorded 1,536 instances of emotion. The average student reported getting angry seven times a week, roughly once a day. However, the average student also reported feeling annoyed 24 times a week or approximately 3 times a day. In other words, their report of anger was four times greater when they included milder forms of emotions like annoyance.

Most people tend to underestimate the extent to which they feel things. This is partially due to memory — only the more dramatic episodes of anger come to mind. Also, anger is one of those emotions everyone wants to forget as quickly as possible. Make sure that you're being honest with yourself about how often you feel angry.

How intense is your anger?

Now you need to evaluate the *strength* of your anger. Think about how you feel most of the time when you get angry and answer this question honestly:

On average, how intense is your anger when you get mad? (Circle one)

     1   2   3   4   5   6   7   8   9   10

Mild   Extreme

If your intensity rating is 6 or below, your anger is within a healthy, normal range. If your intensity rating is 7 or above, you likely have a problem with anger.

Of course, your anger may be more intense in some situations than others. But, by and large, feelings tend to be consistent from one episode of emotion to the next. We humans, after all, are creatures of habit!

Figuring Out Whether Your Anger Is Toxic

I coined the term *toxic anger* to convey the fact that certain subtypes of anger can be poisonous, even lethal (see Chapter 3 for an in-depth discussion of toxic anger). Other forms of anger are benign (nontoxic) and really cannot hurt you in any appreciable way. The trick is to know which is which.

First, go to the "How often do you get angry?" section, earlier in this chapter, where you indicate how frequently you find yourself getting angry during a typical week. If you selected A, B, or C — "Not at all" up to "Three to five times a week" — your anger can be considered intermittent or *episodic* in nature. If you checked any of the other answers — "One or two times a day" through "More than ten times a day" — your anger is *chronic.* Generally speaking, episodic anger isn't a problem, but chronic anger is.

Now, go to the "How intense is your anger?" section, where you rate the intensity of your anger. If your intensity rating was between 1 and 3, I call that *irritability.* If your rating was between 4 and 6, I call that *anger.* And, if you rated yourself between 7 and 10, I call that *rage. Rage is always a problem.*

When two or more people admit to being angry, obviously they aren't talking about having the exact same emotional experience. Anger is just a word — a fairly meaningless concept — until you break it down into something that can be quantified.

Here's where things get interesting. The final step in evaluating whether you have a problem with anger is to combine your anger scores in a way that generates six possible subcategories of anger. These are illustrated in Table 2-1.

Table 2-1	Various Types of Anger Experience		
	Intensity		
Frequency	*1–3*	*4–6*	*7–10*
Less than once a day	Episodic irritation	Episodic anger	Episodic rage
At least once a day	Chronic irritation	Chronic anger	Chronic rage

Which category did you fall into? Does it make the problem more real when you put these types of labels on it? I find that most people are comfortable with terms like *irritated* and *angry,* but they don't like the label *rage* at all. There's something equally unsettling about the label *chronic.* And when you put the two together, people really jump out of their seats! In the following sections, I help you see beyond the labels.

Episodic irritation

In a community sample, I found that roughly 25 percent of 284 people surveyed fell into this category. That is, one out of every four people are like Cathy, a woman in her 60s, who seldom finds herself experiencing even mild anger. Everyone regards her as upbeat, cheerful, easygoing, and pleasant to be around. No problem here. If you fall into this category, your anger is not toxic.

Episodic anger

Slightly more than a third (36 percent) of those sampled acknowledged the fact that they got angry a couple of times a week. However, like Peter, their anger never amounted to anything. Sure, Peter gets mad on occasion — like when his secretary spoils his mood by starting the day off with some negative remark — but he doesn't dwell on it and it passes fairly quickly. If you fall into this category, your anger is not toxic.

Episodic rage

This is our first glimpse at what I call toxic anger. Approximately 15 percent of the sample readily admitted to getting this angry on occasion, although not daily. I like to refer to these individuals as *sleeping lions* or *occasional hotheads* — they're fine until they get aroused, and then watch out!

Chronic irritation

You may think that chronic irritation is a problem, but it's really not all that toxic. People may see you as moody or bitchy, but they still tolerate you most of the time. Interestingly, only about 2 percent of people fall in this category — thank goodness.

Chronic anger

This is the second category of toxic anger. It included 11 percent of those surveyed, people like Nathan, a retired salesman who finds himself getting angry repeatedly every day about one thing or another. "I get mad when my wife takes too long shopping, when things break around the house, when gas prices go up — just about anything that doesn't suit me," he says. "But don't get me wrong — I don't go off the deep end and rant and rave." Like many people, Nathan thinks he doesn't have a problem with anger because it never rises to the level of uncontrollable rage — but he's wrong. It's just not healthy to be angry as frequently as he is.

Chronic rage

This is our worst-case example of toxic anger. I'm sorry to say that 12 percent of those responding fell into this subgroup. If you find yourself in this group, your anger is *volatile* (as in volcano!) and there's absolutely no question that anger is poisoning just about every aspect of your life. This type of anger is dangerous and serves no useful purpose.

Students versus teachers

If you want to know why there are so many problems in public schools these days, consider this. I surveyed high school teachers and students alike and found that only 5 percent of the teachers admitted to experiencing rage as contrasted with 30 percent of the students. That's a lot of rage floating around the school environment every day — and the teachers are clearly outmatched.

The term *anger management* is really a misnomer. The vast majority of people referred for this type of therapy are experiencing rage, not anger. If I could get them to just get angry when something provokes them, that would be progress.

Calculating the Risks of Toxic Anger

You can calculate how at risk you are for toxic anger. Review the following sections and see how many of these factors fit you.

Are you male?

Men and women don't differ in how *often* they get angry, but men do tend to experience anger more *intensely* than women at all ages. Thus, men are more likely to experience rage as opposed to irritability or anger.

Are you under 40 years of age?

There really are some benefits to growing older. As Table 2-2 illustrates, the frequency and intensity of anger both tend to decrease with age — people actually do mellow over time. Anger is a much bigger problem during the adolescent and young adult years (ages 13 to 39) and begins to decline steadily thereafter for most people. It's not that unusual for children and adolescents to throw temper tantrums, but if you're still doing that at age 60, you definitely have a problem.

Table 2-2	Age-Related Changes in Anger	
Age	*Average Frequency*	*Average Intensity*
13–19	Daily	6 (very angry)
20–29	Daily	6 (very angry)
30–39	3–5 times/week	5 (moderately angry)
40–49	1–2 times/week	5 (moderately angry)
50–59	1–2 times/week	4 (mildly angry)
60+	1–2 times/week	3 (irritated, annoyed)

Are you temperamental?

Temperament defines inherited, inborn traits that basically describe the tone or quality of your emotional reactions. The two traits that set people up for toxic anger are *impulsivity* (an inability to delay gratification or tolerate frustration when your needs are not immediately satisfied) and *excitability* (how easily your emotions are triggered). More good news: Both of these traits decrease with age.

Do you have too many opportunities to get mad?

Common sense tells you that the more provocation you have in life, the more opportunity you have to be angry. Take, for example, policemen who spend their days trying to get citizens to obey the law and who put up with a lot of abuse in the process. What about schoolteachers who have to put up with defiant, unmotivated children all day? Even pharmacists — I see more angry people waiting for prescriptions in the local drugstore than almost anywhere else I go ("What do you mean my doctor didn't call in my medication?" and "I can't believe drugs are so expensive — do you people think I'm made of money?"). The same goes for family and intimate relationships — some are more burdened with problems than others.

Are you looking at life the wrong way?

Anger is in the eye of the beholder. It's not the things that happen to you that make you angry as much as it is the way you respond to those things. Here are four ways of looking at the world that tend to facilitate anger:

✔ **With cynicism:** Do you wake up every morning expecting (and preparing yourself for) the worst? Do you anticipate that good things are *not* in store for you today? Do you mistrust your fellow man — even your loved ones? Are you constantly on guard in case other people somehow take advantage of you? If this sounds familiar, you're ready to react in anger at a moment's notice.

✔ **As though everything is a catastrophe:** Would you agree that there are no little stresses in life? A friend was ten minutes late meeting you for lunch — everything is a big damned deal! What others might regard as a minor irritant, you see as a major life crisis. If so, the intensity of your emotions — panic, rage — reflect just how overwhelmed you feel most of the time.

✔ **With compulsiveness:** Do you ascribe to the philosophy that "everything in life is either black or white" and "it's my way or the highway?" Do you demand perfection in yourself and everyone around you? Are you all work and no play? Do you eat, sleep, and breathe one thing: control? Are you always exhausted and never able to relax? No wonder you get angry so easily.

✔ **With self-absorption:** Is your life really "all about me"? Are you the center of your own little universe? Are the rest of us just here to serve your needs? If we do that well, fortune smiles on us, right? But if we don't tell you what you want to hear, don't make you feel "special," or — dare I say it — talk about ourselves, there's hell to pay. If this sounds familiar, anger is not far away.

Do you have an aggressive personality?

If so, you'll experience more anger than if you don't. How can you tell if you have an aggressive personality? You have an aggressive personality if the following are true:

✔ You're competitive.

✔ You like to dominate others.

✔ You're impatient.

✔ You're intense.

✔ You're demanding.

✔ You're confrontational.

✔ You're forceful in pursuing goals.

If you're not sure about this one, ask someone who knows you well what he thinks — but don't get angry if he tells you the truth!

Of course you're angry — you're on top

I was asked to consult with a corporation whose CEO was having difficulty getting his top executives to curtail their anger in day-to-day discussions. With considerable exasperation, he acknowledged that he, in fact, had on more than one occasion served as a referee between two angry vice-presidents who were engaged in a physical confrontation in the men's room. His question to me: "I pay these guys a good salary and they have all the freedom in the world, so why are they acting like this?" It didn't take me long to find the answer. Actually, it was quite simple. All of them were extremely aggressive personalities who had clawed their way to the top of the organization through a combination of what I like to call achievement-driven and combative behavior. And anger was the fuel — the ammunition, if you will — that got them to where they were and kept them there.

Are you taking the wrong kinds of drugs?

Drugs — even legal drugs — alter brain chemistry and can lead to anger. Here's a list of some drugs to watch out for:

- Alcohol
- Caffeine
- Nicotine
- Tranquilizers (such as Valium)
- Cocaine
- Chemical inhalants
- Phencyclidine (PCP)
- Hypnotics
- Sedatives

Do you stay irritable?

By irritable, I don't mean irritated. Irritable is synonymous with a general feeling of being:

- Grouchy
- Sensitive

- ✔ Touchy
- ✔ Cross
- ✔ On edge
- ✔ Unsettled
- ✔ Uneasy
- ✔ Tense
- ✔ Ill
- ✔ Crabby
- ✔ Agitated
- ✔ Aggravated

Irritability is a nonspecific state of physical and mental discomfort that is often the byproduct of life itself — hot weather, insufficient finances, hangover, being sick, chronic pain due to arthritis or migraine headaches, boredom, secondhand smoke, memories of past hurts and grievances, being overweight, and so on. The point I'm making here is that a highly irritable person is a person waiting to be angry.

Are you suffering from depression?

Mood and emotion go hand in hand. If you're in a positive, *euphoric* mood, you're apt to feel positive emotions like joy and excitement. If you're in a negative, *dysphoric* mood, the opposite, of course, is true — you're more disposed to emotions such as sadness and anger. So, it doesn't take a rocket scientist to understand why depression and anger are so closely linked. If you're suffering from what psychiatrists call *agitated depression*, you'll experience anger often and express it in outrageous ways. If you have what's called *retarded depression*, you'll retreat into a world of angry silence. Either way, anger is a big part of your sickness.

Do you communicate poorly?

Do you have a hard time saying what's on your mind, but have no trouble whatsoever lashing out emotionally? Do you often find yourself saying things like "Get off my back, dammit!" or "I've had it with you people — you make me sick!" when what you really should be saying is, "I'm about to lose my job, I'm scared to death about our future, and I don't know where to turn"? Anger communicates all right, but not too effectively.

Do you lack problem-solving skills?

Are you the type of person who wastes a lot of time and energy getting mad instead of fixing all the things that are wrong with your life? If so, you're a member of a very large club. Quite frankly, I've never understood how anger gets the bills paid, repairs a flat tire, or gets a person out of a toxic relationship. Do you? Wouldn't it be better to save the anger or at least use it constructively to figure out a budget, change the tire, and tell your jerk of a partner to shape up or ship out?

Are you too stressed?

Life is, by its very nature, stressful — but it's fair to say that some folks have more stress than others. Actually, it's the little irritants of life (psychologists refer to these as *hassles*) that upset us the most; most people handle the big stresses (*critical life events,* in psychobabble) pretty well. And then there are different types of stress, some more linked to anger than others. Stresses that persist over time *(chronic),* that build up over time *(cumulative),* that are beyond your control and thus tend to overwhelm you *(catastrophic)* are the real killers. Sound familiar?

Are you too judgmental?

Anger, like other emotions, is a judgment. When you get angry, you're judging other people ("You treated me badly") and situations ("This just doesn't suit"). Anger is a statement — *your* statement — about right and wrong. The more you judge the world, the more likely you'll be angry — about something.

Are you too much into blame?

Are you quick to assign blame to someone or something every time you suffer misfortune? Do you earnestly believe that there are no accidents in life — that everything is the result of someone else's intentional desire to frustrate, mislead, or inflict harm on someone else? Are you forever reading some sinister motive into what others say and do that ends up hurting someone's feelings? Are you a proponent of the idea that we're all suffering at the hand of some kind of conspiracy? Then no wonder you're always mad — and preoccupied with thoughts about how to even the score.

Blame = anger = pain

For over 40 years now, I have worked with patients who suffer chronic, often disabling pain resulting mostly from work injuries. I can attest to the fact that they are an extremely angry group of folks. Fifty-two percent of those who completed my five-week outpatient rehab program, for example, admitted to experiencing either episodic or chronic rage. Why is this relevant? Because studies have shown that work-injured patients who blame someone for their injury are less likely to remain employed, more likely to feel they received no benefit from medical treatment, more likely to suffer from psychological distress, more likely to anticipate greater pain and disability in the future, and less optimistic about further improvement. Those who had a no-fault view of their injury fared much better.

Are you constantly exhausted?

Are you like Pete, the 32-year-old factory worker who referred himself for anger management because he thought anger was endangering his marriage? Pete didn't have a clue as to why he was so irritable all the time and quick to attack his wife over any little thing. Among other things, I asked him if he liked the kind of work he did and he said, "It's okay except for the fact that we're working seven days a week, ten hours a day." And how long had that schedule been in effect? Five months. The poor guy wasn't just tired — he was exhausted! And that, of course, made every other thing in his life a strain. What was the message behind Pete's anger? Simple: "I'm dead. I can't take any more. I need a break!"

Do you have an inadequate support system?

I can only imagine that your life is a struggle — mine is. And in that struggle, we all need help — help in the form of a kind word now and then, some tangible assistance (like a ride to the doctor or a loan until payday), some sense of belonging to a world larger than ourselves, or someone to reassure us at critical times in our lives that we're simply okay and that this too shall pass.

But what if you don't have that support? What if you're struggling all alone, out there on a limb by yourself? Wouldn't you be angry — angry that you don't have something (a resource) that other people do, angry that you have to reach out for help because no one is reaching out to you, angry at God for allowing your life to come to this end? Sure, you would — and you are.

What'd you say?

At the end of every first session I have with a new client — especially those who've come for help with anger management — I say, "Tell me what you do for fun." I invariably get one of the following four answers:

✔ "Huh?"

✔ "What did you say?"

✔ "I'm paying $85 an hour for this."

✔ "Nothing!"

And, therein lies their problem.

Is your life seriously out of balance?

Is your life all yin and no yang? Are there too many downs and not enough ups? Do you seem to habitually give more than you take? Are you all work and no play? Is there no room in your life for pleasure, frivolity, or those moments when you simply enjoy the ridiculous side of life? Do you spend far more time with clients and customers than you do with friends and loved ones? Well then, your life is obviously way out of balance. And until you correct that imbalance, you're a sitting duck for anger.

Chapter 3

Is Anger Poisoning Your Life?

*A*nger Kills. The title of a book by my colleague, Dr. Redford Williams, and his wife, Virginia, turned out to be prophetic for Dwayne, who died an untimely death at age 41. Dwayne injured his back at work 11 years earlier and had been unemployed and in constant pain ever since. He was also a very angry man — angry about being hurt, angry that his doctors couldn't fix his back, angry about being mistreated by his employer, angry at family and friends who he felt weren't sympathetic enough, even angry at God for allowing this whole unfortunate circumstance to occur so early in his life.

Dwayne isolated himself from the world. He stayed home most of the time, refused to return telephone calls from friends, and ruminated about how badly his life had turned out. All you had to do was ask him something about his former life (for example, "Do you still see any of your old friends from work?"), and Dwayne's rage was immediately visible. He suddenly had this contorted look on his face, tears came into his eyes, and his tone of voice elevated almost to a shout as he responded, "Hell no!"

Dwayne had his first heart attack at age 36. He was walking down the street when he saw one of his "enemies" from his old job, and he instantly fell down clutching his chest. He was taken by ambulance to the local hospital, where he told his family physician that he had gotten intensely angry when he saw that person and then felt a sharp pain in his chest. The doctor didn't believe him.

Dwayne continued his angry ways and had a second heart attack at age 41. Surrounded in the hospital by his cardiologist, psychologist, minister, brother, and wife, Dwayne was given an ultimatum: "Let go of all this anger or you're going to die. Your heart can't take it anymore." Once again, his face took on that all-too-familiar look, his eyes teared up, and he forecast his own death by saying, "Never. I'll never stop being angry. I'll die first."

Three weeks later, while shouting angrily into the telephone, Dwayne had his third and final heart attack. Moments later, his wife found him dead on the floor, the phone still in his hand.

In this chapter, I show you the many ways in which anger can be toxic. I also discuss the secondhand effects of toxic anger — they're as dangerous to your health as secondhand smoke. If you find yourself feeling like a battery that is losing its charge, if you can't seem to lose weight or stop smoking, if you have headaches all the time, if you're taking blood-pressure medication, if you're concerned about the health of your loved ones, or if your career seems like a train wreck, you'll find this chapter especially enlightening.

Robbing Your Energy

Anger and fatigue go hand in hand. Emotions spend energy. The body requires energy to mobilize itself into an attack posture — heart pounding, blood pressure up, muscles tense from head to toe. By its very nature, anger excites you. Your adrenaline flows. And afterward comes the recovery, where you feel physically drained — exhausted.

Now, imagine that you suffer from chronic anger. You go through this vicious cycle of excitation and exhaustion several times every day. Consider how much of your energy is being robbed by this intrusive emotion! It makes me tired just thinking about it.

If you want the proof, in one study, 67 percent of not-very-angry people woke up feeling fresh and rested each morning. Among their counterparts, the angry people, only 33 percent woke up feeling fresh and rested. When asked if they ever feel like a battery that's losing its charge, 56 percent of the not-very-angry people said yes, compared to 78 percent of the angry people.

Steve sat and quietly watched the older man angrily bite the pharmacist's head off because he would have to wait a while to have his prescription filled. "You people don't know what you're doing," "You're inefficient," and "I don't have time to be sitting here because you can't do your job right" were just a few of his heated comments. As the older man sat down next to him, Steve volunteered, "You feel terrible don't you? Drained. Worn out by all that emotion. I know. I've been there, my friend. But, you know, it's not worth it — it really isn't." Later, he told his wife, "Guess who I ran into today? My old, angry self!"

Vital exhaustion: Vital to avoid

Dutch medical researchers have coined the term *vital exhaustion* to describe a pattern of symptoms — excessive fatigue, increased irritability, and feelings of demoralization — that often precede a heart attack. They found that vital exhaustion and chronic anger separately increase a person's chances of sudden cardiac death by 42 percent. But *together* they increase it even more — a whopping 69 percent. This held true even when they considered other risk factors such as high blood pressure, smoking, diabetes, and cholesterol.

Making You Ill

The link between emotion and physical health can be both direct and indirect. Anger, for example, has an instantaneous effect on your blood pressure — but that effect is short lived and generally doesn't cause any immediate harm. Anger also elevates blood pressure through its link to smoking and obesity — and, *that* effect is permanent.

In the following sections, I fill you in on the damage anger may be doing to your health.

How anger indirectly affects your health

The best example of how anger can indirectly make you sick has to do with your risk for having a heart attack. People who smoke cigarettes, are overweight, have high blood pressure and high cholesterol, or drink alcohol (or some combination of these) are at greater risk for some type of coronary episode — chest pain, heart attack, stroke associated with a history of heart disease. Anger contributes to all these risk factors.

Your risk, of course, is determined not by any one of these factors, but by how many you have operating in your life at any point. Jot down your answers to the following questions:

- ✔ Have you smoked cigarettes in the last 30 days?
- ✔ Do you have two or more alcoholic drinks at one sitting?
- ✔ Has a doctor ever told you that you have high blood pressure?
- ✔ Are you currently being treated for high blood pressure?
- ✔ Has a doctor ever told you that you have high cholesterol?
- ✔ Are you currently being treated for high cholesterol?

> ✔ Do you consider yourself overweight?
>
> ✔ Do you consider yourself obese?

It may surprise you to know that your answer to all these questions may reflect how much anger there is in your life. In the following sections, I explain.

Smoking

Your risk for being a cigarette smoker, believe it or not, is 65 percent higher if you typically experience intense anger (rage) than if you typically experience mild anger (irritation).

Using nicotine reduces the likelihood that you'll react aggressively when you're provoked to anger. That's the good news. The bad news is that smoking is linked to heart disease (and cancer!). Angry smokers are far less likely to succeed in their attempts to quit smoking than non-angry smokers. In one published study, the risk of dropping out of treatment early or continuing to smoke after treatment was 12 times greater for angry smokers. Finally, anger is the second leading cause of relapse among ex-smokers — less than stress/anxiety but greater than depression.

Being hooked on cigarettes may also mean that you're hooked on anger.

Drinking

Alcohol is a risk factor for heart disease, and alcohol consumption is higher in people who experience intense anger. Among people with only mild anger, only 22 percent have two or more alcoholic drinks at a time, whereas 44 percent of their intensely angry counterparts drink that much.

Alcohol is a numbing agent when it comes to emotions. People drink to forget not only their troubles but also what they're feeling at the moment — sadness, anxiety, shame, guilt, and anger. The more you drink, the less connected you are to those feelings. Most people don't drink to make themselves feel good — they drink to feel less bad.

Alice was well into middle age before she finally admitted she had a drinking problem and got the help she needed to get sober. For years, Alice blamed her excessive use of alcohol on her domineering mother and her equally angry, overbearing husband — both of whom provided her with a convenient excuse to continue drinking. What she failed to realize all along was that the real driving force behind her drinking was her own aggressive personality — and abiding anger — which she suppressed by staying intoxicated. Alcohol allowed Alice to be nice to the very people with whom she was the most angry. Ironically, all of this came to light only after she began accompanying her husband to anger-management therapy — something he was now willing to do since she had gotten sober. A further irony was the fact that, as her husband began to control his temper, she began to lose hers.

If you plan to continue to drink alcohol but you're concerned about anger, consider the following:

- **Contrary to popular belief, alcohol initially acts as a stimulant, leading to increased arousal and excitation in the person who is drinking.** This increased state of arousal may set the stage for an angry reaction to some otherwise innocuous event or circumstance.

- **Alcohol — even in small quantities — can cause you to misperceive the motives and actions of others.** What might otherwise be viewed as unintended or accidental is now seen as intended to inflict harm.

- **Alcohol has a disinhibitory effect on emotions and behavior.** It lowers the nervous system's threshold for emotional experiences, allowing you to feel things you otherwise would not if you were sober. It also transforms behavior and makes you feel you have the "right" to act opposite to your normal self — the quiet person becomes loud, the submissive person becomes dominant, the sweet person becomes angry.

- **Alcohol affects mood in the aftermath of drinking.** That is, if you're a heavy drinker, you can expect to feel more depressed after you sober up than if you use less alcohol.

- **If you are what's called an *angry drinker* — you get angry when you drink — you can expect to have a more intense hangover afterward.** Angry drinkers are much more apt to experience headaches, stomach discomfort, diarrhea, tremors, and nervousness when they sober up. This is particularly true for men, but then again men are more likely to fit the angry-drinker profile.

Two drinks a day is considered moderate drinking. Anything more than this is excessive.

Obesity

Do you head for the refrigerator or the nearest fast-food restaurant when something pisses you off? If you do, you're not alone! Food is, unfortunately, the solution that millions of people choose to satisfy their anger. Obesity is yet another risk factor for heart disease.

Amy, a nice married woman in her mid-40s, is a self-acknowledged emotional eater. She currently weighs 100 pounds more than she did when she got married 20 years ago. She constantly finds herself stifling her feelings — even positive ones — because of her husband's discomfort with any open expression of emotion. Hiding emotion under a façade of niceness is unnatural for Amy, who was raised in a family where everyone sat around the dinner table and shared their thoughts and feelings with each other. She lives in emotional isolation day after day, self-medicating with food as a means of assuaging her pent-up anger. "I hold in my anger as long as I can — usually for three to six months — but then I blow up and let it all out at once," she says. But then the cycle begins all over again. Bottom line: "I can't imagine how many hundreds of pounds I have put on and taken off because of all this anger, but it's a lot."

Poor health habits

Researchers at the University of Texas Health Science Center at Houston have concluded that overweight kids, especially girls, have poor health habits "including anger expression" that contribute to a lifetime of obesity. Whereas non-obese adolescents show greater control over their anger as they grow up, overweight teens lag behind. They are able to acknowledge their angry feelings, but they can't express those feelings in an appropriate way. For these kids, anger management is just as important as diet and exercise.

People like Amy use food both to comfort themselves when they're upset with the world and also as a distraction — in her case, mostly from the anger she feels toward her husband. In an attempt to hide her anger, Amy is literally transformed into a larger-than-life person whose health is now at risk. If you're like Amy, check out Chapters 5 and 8 in this book, which address the perils of suppressed anger.

High blood pressure

People who have high blood pressure have a much higher risk for heart disease. And people who are habitually angry have a much higher risk for high blood pressure — in fact, three times the risk! (Only 15 percent of not-very-angry people have high blood pressure, whereas 44 percent of their highly anger counterparts have high blood pressure.)

The way you respond to anger also affects your blood pressure. If you keep it in, your odds of having hypertension are 21 percent. If you let it out, your odds are only 11 percent. Of course, how you let it out can make a difference too (Chapter 11 talks about how to do this constructively).

High cholesterol

Anger doesn't cause you to have high cholesterol, which places you at risk for heart disease. That basically comes from your family history. But there is no question that anger aggravates the problem. When I asked people to tell us about how intense their anger was typically and whether or not they had high cholesterol, only 15 percent of people with low anger had high cholesterol, compared to 22 percent of the highly angry group.

Plus, medical studies have consistently shown that high levels of anger among Type A personalities — not their sense of time urgency or overcommitment to work — are related to elevated levels of total cholesterol and LDL ("bad") cholesterol.

When your physician tells you that you need to lose weight and start exercising to lower your cholesterol levels, you should follow his advice. But you should also consider the potential benefit of anger management in achieving the same result.

How anger directly affects your health

Emotions are not only distracting, but they can interfere with reason and cause you to make decisions or take actions that end up being hazardous to your health. In the following sections, I cover three of the primary behaviors that can directly result from uncontrolled anger.

Unsafe sex

Most people are well aware of the hazards associated with unprotected sexual intercourse, having sex with multiple partners, or having sex while under the influence of drugs. You know that all these behaviors raise your odds of becoming HIV-infected and possibly dying of AIDS (not to mention contracting other sexually transmitted diseases [STDs]).

High-risk sex, it turns out, is often accompanied by anger. When women, for example, are presented with an opportunity for unsafe sex — and they are not angry at the time — they typically abstain or take reasonable precautions such as using a condom. They weigh the consequences and act accordingly. But if they are mad — for example, at a parent who has forbidden them to continue a relationship with their boyfriend — all that reason flies out the window. It's the old "I'll show you I can do anything I want with whomever I want — *so there!*" mentality.

On-the-job injuries

You'll likely spend most of your adult life working. So if you're injured, it's most likely to occur on the job — and that's true no matter what you do for a living. So, what does that have to do with anger? As it turns out, a whole lot.

Here's what we know about on-the-job injuries:

- Up to a third of people who were injured on the job admit that they were experiencing some level of anger prior to the injury.
- The angrier they were at the time, the more likely they were to be injured.
- If they were extremely irritated, they were five times more likely to be injured than if they weren't irritated at all.

Are you absent without leave?

I asked a large group of employees about their anger and about various health issues, including one question about absenteeism: In the past three months, I asked, have you missed work because of illness?

Interestingly, those who suffered from chronic anger — one or more episodes of anger every day — were five-and-a-half times more likely to have answered yes to that question than employees who got angry less often. Similarly, those who reported intense anger (rage) were three times more likely to miss work because of illness than those who were only irritated.

Findings like this lead me to believe that many employed people go AWOL when they get fed up with work — and, illness provides them with a legitimate excuse.

✔ If they were extremely angry, they were seven times more likely to be injured than if they weren't angry.

✔ If they were in a rage, they were 12 times more likely to be injured than if you weren't in a rage.

✔ Anger is more likely to lead to injury in men.

✔ Anger increases the odds of your injuring another employee and inflicting injury on yourself.

✔ Anger and alcohol use prior to injury are highly linked, and both independently increase a person's odds of being injured on the job.

Road rage

Psychologist Jerry Deffenbacher at Colorado State University has two important messages for all of us: Anger is hazardous to driving and if you're a self-professed high-anger driver, do yourself a favor and get some help.

The AAA Foundation for Traffic Safety estimates — conservatively — that, between 1990 and 1996, road rage caused 218 traffic fatalities and over 12,000 injuries. Even more alarming is their estimate that this problem is increasing yearly by somewhere between 5 and 10 percent. Bottom line: You may literally be putting your life in someone else's hands every time you get behind the wheel.

Road rage isn't about the road (I discuss this more in Chapter 24) — it's about rage. According to Dr. Deffenbacher, high-anger drivers have the following characteristics:

✔ They're highly judgmental of other people's driving.

✔ They have contempt for how others drive.

- They have more vengeful thoughts about other drivers.
- They take more risks while driving — speeding, switching lanes, tailgating, running yellow lights.
- They experience anger on a daily basis (what, in Chapter 2, I call chronic anger).
- They're more likely to get in the car already angry.
- They tend to express their anger outwardly — yelling, honking, finger pointing, tailgating.
- They have less control of their emotions in general.
- They tend to react impulsively when frustrated.

Most of the things in life we call accidents really aren't accidents. And some people are really just accidents waiting to happen. Be honest about yourself about your own road rage — you could not only be saving your life, but also the lives of everyone else on the road with you.

Reviewing the anger-health checklist

Take a look at the following checklist of medical disorders and diseases in which anger can play an active, direct role — either causing the illness or aggravating it. See how many of these apply to you or other angry people you know and love:

- Alcoholism
- Anorexia
- Arthritis
- Asthma
- Bulimia
- Cancer
- Colic
- Chronic fatigue syndrome
- Chronic itching
- Common colds
- Depression
- Eczema
- Epilepsy

Do you really need a doctor?

Imagine that you're in a job that you hate, you're overdue for a raise, the boss keeps piling more work on you all the time, your co-workers are jerks, you can't remember the last time someone told you that you were doing a good job, you feel absolutely stuck — and you're pissed about all of it!

Now, also imagine that it's 6:45 in the morning and you just got out of bed and are about to get ready for work. You didn't sleep well again last night, you're tired, your throat is scratchy, and your head is beginning to throb.

All of a sudden, a thought pops into your head: "I can't go to work today. I'm sick. I'm going to call the doctor and see if he can find out what's causing me to feel so bad. I think I just need some time to myself to rest and get well." So, you call the office to let them know you're out sick and aren't sure when you'll be back in. You instantly feel better!

Here's what I think. I don't think you're sick at all — certainly not enough to see a doctor. Instead, I think you're sick and tired of going to work. You're full of anger and resentment and your body is telling you "I've had it. I've had enough. No more. I need a break."

You need a doctor, all right, just not the kind you think. Your physician can examine you, run blood tests, and even do x-rays, but chances are she won't find out what's wrong with you. She may appease you by saying, "I'm not sure what's causing your symptoms — you may just have a mild case of whatever's going around." She'll probably tell you to just take aspirin every couple of hours, get some rest, and maybe stay home from work for a day or two, and that should do it. But she's wrong because "what's going around" is your constant state of irritation while you're at work eight to ten hours a day. And aspirin and rest won't fix that! What you need is the other kind of doctor — the kind that specializes in anger management.

✔ Fibromyalgia

✔ Genitourinary problems (problems associated with reproductive organs)

✔ Glaucoma

✔ Headaches

✔ Heart disease

✔ High blood pressure

✔ Hives

✔ Insomnia

✔ Low-back pain

✔ Neurodermatitis (inflammations of the skin)

✔ Obesity

- Obsessive-compulsive disorder
- Phobias
- Pruritis (anal itching)
- Psoriasis
- Schizophrenia
- Spastic colitis
- Stroke
- Stuttering or stammering
- Substance abuse
- Teeth grinding
- Temporomandibular joint (TMJ) disorder
- Ulcers

Sabotaging Your Career

Not only can anger rob you of energy and end up making you sick, it can also drastically affect your career — and not in the way you want.

I was driving my family home from vacation and found myself listening to a syndicated talk show that offered career advice. Normally, I'm not interested in that sort of thing, but it was late, everyone else in the car was asleep, and I had a hundred miles to go — besides it was the only thing on.

A 35-year-old unemployed man called in telling the host that he needed advice on how to get a good job. The host asked him about his educational background — he was a college grad — and inquired about his last job. He described what sounded like a pretty good job as a town administrator in a small community.

"How long did that job last?" the host asked.

"About 18 months and then I quit," said the fellow.

"Why did you quit?" the host asked.

"They wouldn't give me the big raise I felt I deserved so I got mad and resigned," was the answer.

"And, what did you do before that?" the host asked.

"Same thing — city administrator for another small community."

"How long were you at that job?" the host inquired.

"I think about two years, but again they wouldn't meet all my demands so I got mad and quit."

The conversation continued until the caller had described six good jobs since he graduated from college, all of which he had left in anger.

Finally, the host said, "I get the picture but I think you're wrong about what your problem is. Your problem isn't how to get a good job. You've had six. Your problem is your inability to control your temper whenever your employer either can't or won't give you exactly what you want."

The man was furious, shouting, "You don't know what you're talking about. I'm not the problem. They are. You're not giving me any help here." Then he hung up. Obviously, what had started out as a highly promising career was now stalled and heading down the toilet — fast.

In the following sections, I cover some other ways in which anger can sabotage your career.

Getting off track early

In today's world, more than ever before, if you hope to succeed at work, you need an education. Without an education, your choices are extremely limited and you'll be lucky if you get what amounts to back-breaking, low-paying, here-today-gone-tomorrow jobs.

What does this have to do with anger? Well, it turns out that men and women who were ill tempered as children and adolescents drop out of school before they graduate from high school a lot more often than even-tempered youngsters. They enter the job market already at a distinct disadvantage and they never catch up.

Heading in the wrong direction

Most people want to have a better life than their parents and grandparents had. You want to make more money, have more creature comforts, drive a bigger car, live in a bigger house, wear more expensive clothes, eat in better restaurants, take more elaborate vacations — and those are the incentives that may spur you to work longer, harder, and smarter year after year.

But not everyone is following that dream. Some people are experiencing just the opposite — by the time they reach midlife, they're actually worse off in terms of job security, job status, and income than their parents. Why? The answer is anger. It turns out that easily angered people have more jobs over a lifetime, get fired or quit more often, are forced to take whatever jobs are available (instead of logically pursuing a career), and have a much more erratic employment history as compared to those who are slow to anger.

To add insult to injury, many ill-tempered adults seek out jobs that tolerate their angry outbursts as long as the job gets done. In effect, they've found a niche for their anger. (Unfortunately, most of these jobs are physically dangerous and low paying.)

Asking the wrong question

To paraphrase President John F. Kennedy, "Ask not what your employer can do for you, but rather what you can do for your employer." Angry employees typically are more in tune with their *own* needs, expectations, needs, wants, goals, and so on, than those of the company for which they work. If your boss comes to you late in the day and asks whether you can stay a little longer to finish up a rush order, you get mad and bark, "Absolutely not! I have plans already. I've done all I'm going to do today" before walking off in a huff. If you think you're entitled to a promotion but someone else gets it, you sulk and proceed to do as little as possible for your employer from that day forward.

You're always asking the same question over and over: "Why aren't they treating me fairly?"

The question you *should* be asking is: "Why do I get so angry whenever I don't get what I want when I want it?" Anger is like a mirror — your own personal mirror. Look into it and see what comes back at you. Maybe you're spoiled or you're a bit grandiose in what you expect of yourself and others at work. Maybe they're not the problem — maybe you are.

Look around at the other people you work with. Are they as angry at work as you are? If not, and if they're doing the same work, you should ask yourself why. Why are you angry and they're not?

Deciding if and when you want to be reemployed

Every once in a while, I run across a piece of research dealing with anger that really grabs my attention — like the one by Dr. James Pennebaker at the University of Texas that linked emotional confession (see Chapter 9) to an employee's likelihood of finding a new job. The strategy Pennebaker used to assist a small group of recently laid off workers was amazingly simple. He had these 25 men spend 30 minutes a day for a week writing down their deepest thoughts and feelings about being laid off. The main emotion they experienced: outrage.

Although the men expressed instant relief after writing each day, the real benefit came from the fact that they were three to five times more likely to be reemployed several months later than a comparable group of employees who only received the usual types of employer assistance — help in updating their résumés. Dr. Pennebaker surmised that helping these men come to terms with the anger they felt over losing their jobs enabled them to be less defensive and hostile when they were interviewed for other positions. In effect, they became more desirable candidates.

Engaging in counterproductive work behavior

Have you ever engaged in any of the following behaviors while at work lately?

- ✔ Come to work late without permission
- ✔ Made fun of someone at work
- ✔ Found yourself daydreaming rather than doing your job
- ✔ Behaved rudely to a client or co-worker
- ✔ Refused to assist a colleague at work
- ✔ Blamed someone else for a mistake you made
- ✔ Tried to look busy while doing nothing
- ✔ Taken a longer break than you were entitled to
- ✔ Avoided returning a phone call to someone at work
- ✔ Intentionally wasted supplies
- ✔ Stolen something that belongs to a co-worker
- ✔ Hit or pushed someone
- ✔ Made an obscene gesture to a co-worker

If you answered yes to any of these questions, you've engaged in what's called counterproductive work behavior. *Counterproductive work behavior* is any act at work that is clearly intended to hurt the organization you work for or other employees. And which employees are most likely to engage in such behavior? The angry ones, of course.

Now, ask yourself this question: If I act this way at work, am I likely to have a successful career — get a raise, get a promotion, get a pat on the back from the boss? Probably not.

Counterproductive work behavior is subtle and not always easy to observe. For that reason alone, it's likely to persist in an organization. The cost of such behavior to industry is staggering — approximately $200 billion a year.

Ruining Your Marriage

Angry people are difficult to live with, and anger is powerful enough to kill any positive feelings that a married couple has for each other. The idea that "love conquers all" is a myth.

Take Bob, for example, a young man who was married three times before he reached his 30th birthday. Bob's explanation was that he simply was unlucky in his choice of mates — "I seem to find one bitch after another." The truth of the matter, though, was that Bob was a chronic rager, who easily became frustrated and violent when he and his wife faced any type of stress or conflict — problems adhering to a budget, how to discipline the kids, how to satisfy both sets of parents. This problem was not a new one — Bob's temper tantrums had begun when he was a small child and had gradually escalated over the years.

Is Bob unusual? Unfortunately, no. Studies show that the divorce rate for men and women who were ill tempered as children is twice that of even-tempered kids. Why divorce? For two reasons:

- ✔ Their mates have the good sense to finally put an end to the abusive anger they suffer in the marriage.

- ✔ Anger adversely affects how effectively we do our jobs as spouses and parents and, thus, reduces the family's income.

Making the healthy choice

Every day you're faced with choices. Some of those choices are simple, like which socks to wear, whether to have bacon with your eggs, and whether to drink another cup of coffee. Other choices are tough choices. Do you let one of your employees go? Do you confront your teenager about the drugs you found in his dresser drawer? Do you hold your temper — even though you have good reason to lose it? Obviously, some of your options are healthy; others are not.

A man was sent to me for court-ordered anger management after he assaulted his ex-wife. He wasn't all that motivated — he honestly felt that he hadn't done anything wrong, certainly nothing that should be regarded as a crime. His reasoning was: "Basically, I hate conflict. I avoid it wherever possible, always have. I don't tell people — like my ex-wife — when I'm angry, because I don't want to hurt their feelings or make them uncomfortable. So, it builds up. I was actually trying to avoid a confrontation with her — trying to leave rather than argue — but she stood in the door and blocked my exit. So, I pushed her out of the way, and she called the police."

I asked him, "If you had to choose between hurting your ex-wife's — or your current fiancée's — feelings or assaulting one of them physically, which would you do?"

He tried to avoid the answer, instead saying that he kept his emotions to himself in order not to hurt other people's feelings. I pressed him for an answer: "I understand that, but I'm asking you to choose between possibly hurting someone's feelings versus hurting her physically."

Once again, he attempted to avoid the choice. But after I pressed him a third time, he finally said, "Well, of course, I guess I'd rather hurt her feelings."

"Good," I replied " because the last time you made the unhealthy choice and that's why you're here."

If you choose to hold in your anger to the point where you finally explode in rage, the consequences of that rage are the result of the choice you made. If you want to have fewer negative consequences, then you've got to find how to make healthier choices. And, that's what this book is all about — choosing solutions that "detoxify" your anger.

Affecting the Health of Those You Care About

If you're not all that concerned about the fact that your anger is poisoning *your* life, at least be concerned about what it's doing to those you live with and love. Living with a habitually angry — sometimes rageful — person is no different from living with someone who is a heavy smoker. Spouses of heavy smokers breathe in all that smoke and, as a result, have a 25 percent greater risk for both heart disease and lung cancer, even though they never smoked themselves. Well, the same is true of anger — all that anger that you're spewing out over the years can rob your family of energy, make them ill, and ruin their careers as well.

My father's choices

Growing up, our family wasn't poor, but we were just one step above it. Too many kids, too little money. My father was at heart a good man, hardworking, intelligent, and resourceful. But he had two strikes against him: He was an alcoholic and he had an awful temper.

My parents always argued about money. My mother was always on my father's back to earn more so that they could keep up with the bills and do some nice things for us five children once in a while. My father's answer most often was to simply get drunk and then turn violent.

Then one day he got a break. His employer offered him a white-collar sales job with higher pay. We were all excited, especially my mother. But things didn't go well from the outset. Dad just wasn't comfortable wearing a shirt and tie, working with his head rather than his hands, and keeping his cool with difficult customers. His boss eventually took the new position away from him and demoted him back to his old job in the warehouse.

And there we were — back to being nearly poor. My mother was furious with my dad. I don't think she ever forgave him for losing that white-collar job, and I'm sure that had something to do with their eventual divorce a few years later.

Strangely enough, though, my father seemed relieved and happier with himself. He was back in his element — where he could get angry with his co-workers whenever he felt like it, stop off at the tavern on the way home, and end up fighting with his wife all night. I guess you could say that sabotaging this once-in-a-lifetime opportunity for advancement was a good choice for my father, but it sure wasn't for the family. Years later, my father died angry and broke — just as he had lived his whole life.

Sometimes the repercussions of being the spouse or child of an angry person are obvious — bruises, broken bones, scars, trips to the emergency room. Most often, however, they're more subtle and less visible — but no less devastating or emotionally crippling.

Rhonda's father was, as she put it, "difficult, always difficult," which turned out to mean he was a chronic rager. Growing up, Rhonda and her sister were used to him yelling, throwing things, and being constantly disgusted by everything they did. Unlike her sister, who would fight back even as a child, Rhonda's way of surviving her father's angry abuse was to escape by becoming invisible — that is, she found how to behave in ways that escaped notice, something she still does at age 56. The other legacies of Rhonda's early childhood — common to all victims of angry parenting — included

- ✔ Low self-esteem
- ✔ A lack of identity
- ✔ Suppressed emotions (most especially anger!)
- ✔ A feeling of estrangement and discomfort when in the company of others

✔ An insatiable need to please people

✔ Critical self-judgment

✔ An inability to experience intimacy in adult relationships

✔ A defensive orientation toward life ("I'm sorry — it must be my fault!")

✔ A lack of assertiveness

✔ A tendency to underachieve in her choice of occupation

✔ Frequent bouts of depression

Rhonda did one other thing common to children of angry parents. She married a man just like her father, a man she felt subordinate to, a man she was afraid of, a man who made her want to continue being invisible. So, all the symptoms and behaviors of her unhappy childhood continued throughout her adult years. Her father's anger affected Rhonda on every level — just as your anger affects those you love on every level.

Part II
Managing Your Anger Today

The 5th Wave   By Rich Tennant

"A lot of the anger I expressed in the past was inappropriate and I want to apologize. I'm in anger therapy now, but I've only just begun, so make it snappy."

In this part . . .

I tell you how emotions, like anger, are supposed to be transient — they come and go — and why you need to take immediate, decisive action as soon as you start to lose your temper in order to prevent anger from taking hold of your mind and body. In this part, you see why it's not always wise to have the last (angry) word and you find out how to ratchet down the volume of your own anger.

Anger management is really all about mind over matter. It's about giving yourself adequate time to respond to your feelings, asking the right questions about your anger, choosing how to respond when you get mad, and deciding if you're willing to pay the consequences for outrageous behavior. Bottom line: Just because you have the right to be angry doesn't mean you have to exercise that right!

Chapter 4

Taking Immediate Action

· ·

· ·

The first thing you should do when you feel anger coming on is to take immediate action. As the saying goes, "He who hesitates is lost" — lost as in losing your temper. Sometimes it's as easy as counting to ten, sometimes not.

Ninety percent of people, unfortunately, don't act as soon as they start feeling angry — and, all too often, they quickly progress from a petty-annoyance stage to full-blown rage. This chapter shows you how to keep that from happening. The idea that emotions need to just run their course is a myth — and a dangerous one at that. The sooner you take control of your anger, the better off you are (and that goes doubly for those around you who may end up on the receiving end of your wrath).

Drawing the Line — the Sooner the Better

Anger, by its very nature, is meant to be short lived. It comes and it goes like a wave hitting the beach. For most people, anger is over within five to ten minutes. But for some people, it lingers and grows in intensity, accelerating under its own steam.

To understand this process a bit better, consider a conversation I had recently with an angry client:

> **Gentry:** You mentioned an incident you had with your girlfriend this past weekend. Tell me about it.
>
> **Client:** It was nothing really. We had made some plans for the weekend and all of a sudden she changed them without letting me know. So, I got annoyed.
>
> **Gentry:** On a scale of 1 to 10, how annoyed were you when you first heard that she had changed the plan?
>
> **Client:** A 4, I guess.
>
> **Gentry:** Okay. Actually, a 4 indicates that you weren't annoyed — you were angry or mad. What I call *mad* is between 4 and 6. A rating of 1 through 3 would signify annoyance. Did you tell your girlfriend that you were mad?
>
> **Client:** No. I just kept it to myself, like always.
>
> **Gentry:** Then what happened?
>
> **Client:** We went out to eat, but we had to wait a long time for the food to come. And I kept getting madder.
>
> **Gentry:** What number was your anger then?
>
> **Client:** It was up to about a 6 or 7, I guess.
>
> **Gentry:** Well, there's a difference. A rating of 6 means you were really mad — a score of 7 would suggest you were in a state of mild rage, but rage nevertheless.
>
> **Client:** I guess it was a 6.
>
> **Gentry:** So, at that point, you were just a tick away from rage. Did you do anything about your anger at that point?
>
> **Client:** Not really — just got quiet and headed off to a ballgame with my girlfriend. And that's when we got into this big fight in the car. I'm not sure what set me off, but I got so angry I punched the vent in my car and damaged it.
>
> **Gentry:** And how angry were you at that point?
>
> **Client:** Oh, I was definitely a 9 or 10!

Had my client asserted himself when he first became upset — telling his girlfriend how unfair he thought it was for her to frequently alter their plans without consulting him — I seriously doubt the incident in question would have occurred. But he *didn't* and *it* did!

Settling for Just Being Annoyed

Annoyance is the mildest form of anger. It lies at the opposite end of the spectrum from rage. Typically, you don't have to worry about managing annoyance.

Annoyance is more commonplace than anger. Roughly half of the people I surveyed told me that, at best, they got annoyed during the course of a week. Because annoyance is less intense than anger, people get over being annoyed quicker than they do being angry. Also, annoyance is more likely to go away on its own.

In short, being annoyed is usually not a problem — if that's where it ends.

How do you settle for just being annoyed? The next time someone pushes your buttons, try the following:

- ✔ **Don't think of the incident or situation as more serious than it is.** Keep things in perspective. If someone cuts you off in traffic, that's annoying, but it's not the end of the world.

- ✔ **Don't take it personally.** That same guy who cut you off doesn't know you — he's probably oblivious to you, and even if he's acting out his own little road-rage drama, it's not about you in particular.

- ✔ **Don't blame the other person.** When you start blaming someone else, it's easy to let your annoyance escalate. Just let it go.

- ✔ **Don't think about revenge.** Revenge is often the next step after you start assigning blame. Spend your energy on more useful things than revenge.

- ✔ **Keep striving for a non-angry way of coping with the situation.** So you're annoyed at that other driver. How can you deal with the situation without getting angry? Maybe you turn on your favorite music or turn the radio dial to NPR (it's pretty hard to be angry when you're listening to Bob Edwards or Terry Gross).

- ✔ **Refuse to see yourself as a helpless victim.** Take some type of action to adjust to or correct the annoying situation. It really doesn't matter what you do as long as you do something — other than just be angry.

- ✔ **Don't let a negative mood — like depression — magnify your emotion.** Anger only intensifies depression. Tell yourself: I'm not going to let this annoying situation add to what is already a down mood. Ask yourself: What would I do if I weren't depressed? And then do that.

Way beyond annoyed

A client of mine and I were reviewing an incident where he lost his temper. As soon as I started to ask questions about what actually provoked his anger, he literally sprang up from the couch, his face taking on a menacing look. He looked like a panther ready to strike. I asked him how he was feeling and he said, "I'm annoyed just talking about it." I asked him to rate the intensity of his emotion on a 10-point scale and he said he was at a 5½ or 6.

"Well, I have news for you," I said. "You're way beyond being annoyed. A rating of 5 or 6 means you're very angry, bordering on rage." Then I knew why he had been referred to anger management. What he labeled as *annoyed,* most people call *anger.* And, what he called *anger,* they call *rage.* This man never just got annoyed.

Understanding Why Your Fuse Is So Short

Some people have a short fuse, meaning that their anger accelerates so quickly that they don't have much of an opportunity to take control of it before it gets out of hand. The length of your fuse is determined by a number of factors, such as:

- **Your temperament:** You came into the world wired differently from your siblings or your parents or your best friend. And they came into the world wired differently from you. Some people are impulsive (acting quickly and without much thought), while others are more deliberate (taking their time to think things through). You may be more excitable or reactive, which means that you'll be physically aroused more than someone who is easygoing or laid back. These differences are evident even before birth and continue from cradle to grave. Impulsive and excitable people have much shorter fuses than their laid-back counterparts.

- **Your role models:** Often, the apple doesn't fall far from the tree. In other words, you pick up how to react to stress during childhood — from your parents and others who raised you. If they're quick tempered, most likely you will be, too.

- **Your personality:** Do you have a combative personality? Are you impatient, impulsive, confrontational, demanding, and domineering in the way you deal with life? If the answer is yes, you're apt to have a short fuse — because you're always poised to move against the world at a moment's notice. (See Chapter 20 for more about how this plays itself out in the workplace.)

Why not tranquilizers?

Ironically, the drugs that physicians prescribe to calm you down may, inadvertently, make it easier for you to lose your temper. For example, the use of diazepam (Valium) tends to allay anxiety, but at the same time can cause people to lose control and act out aggressively. This begs the question: Should tranquilizers be used in anger management? I would argue not. Antidepressant drugs, on the other hand, appear to be both safe and effective in toning down a person's potential for anger. (You can find more on this in Chapter 19.)

✔ **Your use of chemicals such as caffeine, nicotine, and alcohol:** Chemicals that affect your brain affect your emotions. That includes drugs such as caffeine, nicotine, alcohol, cocaine, and tranquilizers, to name but a few. If you regularly use any of these substances, you're more likely to have a shorter fuse.

✔ **Your mood:** There's no question about it: If you suffer from certain types of mood disorders (such as agitated depression or bipolar disorder), it won't take much to make you angry. I'm not sure what percentage of my anger-management clients suffer from an undiagnosed, untreated mood disorder, but I know it's pretty high.

✔ **Your stress level:** There's normal stress and then there's abnormal, excessive, over-the-top stress. The farther away from normal stress you get, the shorter your fuse. Abrupt outbursts of anger are often your nervous system's way of saying, "Stop! I can't take any more stress. It's killing me! Back off."

✔ **How much sleep you're getting:** Without adequate sleep (seven to nine hours per night), life becomes a real strain. Everything seems to take more effort. Your nerves are frayed. You're less effective at everything you do. And, it doesn't take much to set off your temper. (See Chapter 17 for more on sleep and anger.)

✔ **Whether you have a defensive outlook:** If you have a cynical, hostile view of the world — expecting things not to go your way and thinking of everyone around you as potential enemies — you're always on the verge of lashing out in anger. Any little spark can (and will) set you off.

Lengthening Your Fuse

So how can you lengthen your fuse? Well, you can't easily change your temperament and you certainly can't undo your childhood, but you can cut back on caffeine, drink alcohol only in moderation, get more sleep, get counseling for depression, employ some stress-management techniques (Chapter 14 shows you how to be a hardy personality), try to have a more optimistic outlook, and ask for things instead of being demanding. Those things you can do. You can also try some other techniques, ones I cover in the following sections.

Walking away — but coming back

You have a built-in fight-or-flight mechanism that guides and directs your behavior whenever you're faced with some type of threat — regardless of whether the threat is a physical one or a threat to your self-esteem. This explains why you probably respond to provocation either with some type of angry reaction (fight) or simply run the other way and try to avoid the problem altogether (flight).

The problem is that neither of these extreme options helps you manage anger. If you decide to stand and fight, you need to remain angry long enough to overcome the threat — and the intensity of your anger may become accelerated in the process. On the other hand, if you retreat from the threat, you end up taking your angry feelings with you. You can outrun the threat, but not your own emotions.

The good news? There is a third, viable option — another way to take immediate action. You can disengage (walk away) initially, but return later, after you've calmed down sufficiently to discuss how to resolve the conflict. This is the most mature way to handle anger-provoking problems, but also the one most people are least likely to choose.

The choice of how you respond to provocation in large part depends on how angry you get initially. Table 4-1 shows how a group of ninth-grade high-school students responded when asked the question: What would you do if another student got angry with you for no apparent reason? As students got angrier, the chances that they would walk away and later return to discuss their anger decreased dramatically. Yet another good reason to settle for just being annoyed (mildly angry) when things don't go your way.

Table 4-1	How Ninth Graders Respond		
If the Students Are . . .	*Percent Who Would Walk Away*	*Percent Who Would Get Angry Back*	*Percent Who Would Walk Away and Then Come Back to Discuss the Situation*
Not angry	38	18	44
Mildly angry	21	51	28
Moderately angry	29	58	13
Extremely angry	0	87	13

Highly aggressive, combative personalities are poised to move against whatever is provoking them instead of disengaging and walking away, even if it means calming down. It just goes against their instinctive nature!

Letting the other person have the last word

People get *irritated* with *things* — a leaky faucet, a car that won't start — but they get *angry* with *people*. So most anger occurs within the context of a social exchange. Somebody always has the first word — that's the provocation, the thing that gets the ball rolling. The question is: Who stops the ball? Who has the last word?

After you realize that you're angry, you can decide to let the person who had the first word also have the last. And the sooner the better — unless you're willing to risk things getting out of hand.

Consider the following two conversations between a parent and a teenager and see which one you think is best. Here's the first conversation:

> **Parent:** I want you to clean up your room before dinner.
>
> **Adolescent:** I'm doing something now.
>
> **Parent:** (irritated) I said I want this room cleaned up.
>
> **Adolescent:** (angry) Leave me alone.
>
> **Parent:** (angry) Don't talk to me that way. Start cleaning up your room — *now!*
>
> **Adolescent:** (throwing book across the room in a rage) I told you to get out of my room!
>
> **Parent:** (very angry) Don't you *dare* throw that at me. Start cleaning this room right now and I mean it.

And here's the second conversation:

> **Parent:** I want you to clean your room before dinner.
>
> **Adolescent:** (irritated) I'm doing something now.
>
> **Parent:** (irritated) Yes, I can see that, but I want you to clean your room.
>
> **Adolescent:** (angry) Leave me alone.
>
> **Parent:** (irritated but not yet angry) Okay. That'll give you a chance to get started on your room.
>
> **Adolescent:** (angry) I'll do it when I feel like it.

Often, people are so eager to have the last word in disagreements with other people that they totally lose sight of how out of hand things are getting. Anger management is more about process than it is about outcome. If you can improve the process by letting the other person have the last word, by all means do so.

If you insist on having the last word — you just can't help yourself — then by all means make it a nondefensive one. My personal favorite is, "Whatever." If someone gets mad at me and wants to launch into a tirade about what a jerk I am, I don't argue with him (like I used to). I just say, "Whatever" — whatever you say, whatever you think — and walk away. That way, I don't have to play his angry game.

Sometimes It Pays to Feel Guilty

Guilt isn't necessarily good or bad. It depends on whether you feel guilty before you act out your anger or after you act out your anger. If guilt keeps you from harming another person with your anger — verbally or physically — that's a good thing. If you wait to feel guilty until after you've satisfied your thirst for revenge, that's bad.

John gets angry with his wife whenever she hollers, "Look out!" when he's driving the car. A couple of times, her nervousness has almost caused him to have an accident. He feels like yelling at her, "Dammit, don't do that! You're going to get us killed." But, he doesn't. He loves his wife — a partner for over 40 years — and he knows that yelling at her will only hurt her feelings. So, he lets it pass.

John's brother doesn't let *anything* pass. If he gets angry with his wife, she hears about it immediately and in the harshest terms. Sometimes, he just hollers; other times, he expresses his anger physically.

The next time you find yourself irritated (or just plain mad), before you act, consider the consequences of what's in your mind. If you know for sure it's something you're going to want to apologize for later, don't do it. Think of a nonhurtful way of expressing your feelings. In this kind of situation, an ounce of prevention really *is* worth a pound of cure!

Distraction Works

You experience whatever captures your brain's attention. If you get aroused with anger, your brain turns its attention to that and away from other things. That's why anger can be such a disruptive emotion. The stronger the emotion, the more captivated your brain becomes. You can be irritated and continue to at least partially attend to other things — but rage, now, that's a different story.

Morality and religion

I've been in and around religion most of my life. By birthright, I'm a Protestant and at one time or another I've been an Episcopalian, Baptist, Methodist, and Presbyterian. Despite that, I attended a Catholic school for the first nine years and, like all other students, was immersed in catechism. I also have several good friends who are Jewish.

What I've discovered from all this exposure to different religions is that guilt is an inherent component of *all* religions — because religion and morality go hand in hand. Morality shows people right from wrong, what constitutes civil behavior, and where societal boundaries are. Guilt is what we're taught to feel when we cross those boundaries. Some of those boundaries have to do with anger and violence (for example, "Thou shalt not kill"), and these boundaries are no less important today than they were thousands of years ago.

Intense emotional experiences — positive or negative — override your senses. That's how people end up "blinded" by love or in a state of "blind rage." *Blind,* in this context, simply means your brain is not paying attention to anything outside of your own emotion.

The good news, however, is that the brain can be distracted — meaning it can turn its attention elsewhere at any point in time. So, the trick in anger management is to give your brain something else to attend to besides anger.

Changing your situation

In most people, emotions are situational. Something in the here and now irritates you or makes you mad. The emotion itself is tied to the situation in which it originates. As long as you remain in that provocative situation, you're likely to stay angry. If you *leave* the situation, the opposite is true — the emotion begins to fade as soon as you move away from the situation. Moving away from the situation prevents it from getting a grip on you.

Psychologists often advise clients to get some emotional distance from whatever is bothering them. One easy way to do that is to *geographically* separate yourself from the source of your anger.

Andy employed this principle in dealing with his irritating boss. Andy had been referred for anger management after angrily confronting his boss on two different occasions. The fact that he had good reason for doing so didn't matter. He was simply told that the next time he lost it, he would be fired — immediately. With just a few years left before retirement, Andy was not eager for that to happen. Besides, his recurrent anger had also affected his blood pressure and his doctor had warned him of the possibility of some type of coronary event (like a heart attack).

Andy and I talked about some practical ways to for him to keep his cool even in difficult situations — which, unfortunately, occurred on a daily basis on his job. I asked him to pay more attention to his emotions and, as soon as he felt himself begin to get tense in an exchange with his boss, make a quick exit and calm down. Guess what? It worked! Whenever Andy's boss began to confront him, and whenever Andy began to feel his blood start to boil, he would politely say, "Excuse me. Give me a minute. I'll be right back," and then step away. Andy then used some of the techniques I talk about in Chapter 6 to defuse his emotion, returned to his boss (now more in control of his emotions), and said, "Okay, what was it you wanted to say?" That was several years ago and he's still employed.

Stopping the rumination

What is rumination and what does it have to do with anger? Good question. *Rumination* is the human equivalent of a cow chewing on the cud — chewing food already swallowed and then regurgitated. (Gross, I know.) When you continue to rethink, reconsider, relive, and rehash some incident that provoked your anger well beyond the point where it happened, you're ruminating. And rumination invariably intensifies the emotion. At first you may just be irritated, but the more you think and talk about it, the madder you become. You can't let go of the thoughts, so you can't let go of the feelings — you're stuck!

So, how do you get unstuck? Try using the thought-stopping technique. When you become aware that you're entering into the realm of repetitive angry thinking, say aloud to yourself, "Stop!" and shift your attention to something else. Repeat the word as many times as necessary until you have let go of what's irritating you. If you use the technique quickly, before you get too far down that road of chewing too much on your anger, letting go isn't difficult. All you're trying to do here, really, is interrupt that pattern of unproductive thinking that can only make a bad situation worse.

Why employees need breaks

A lot of companies have tightened up on allowing their employees to take work breaks. Apparently, every time you leave your workstation, they feel like they're losing money. For the most part, I believe this is a mistake. Employees need work breaks, if for no other reason than to engage in some much-needed anger management. That's why so many folks take smoke breaks and coffee breaks — these are legitimate, time-honored ways of removing themselves from the stress (and irritation) that surrounds them at work. The fewer the breaks, the hotter the temperature in the office!

If the thought-stopping technique doesn't work, try ruminating about something *other* than your anger. You can engage in some *positive* rumination — otherwise known as daydreaming. Two of my current favorites are walking down a long beach on a cloudless day and sitting in a cozy mountain cabin reading a good book while it snows outside. When I was younger — and more aggressive — I used to like to ruminate about making jump shots from 50 feet and hitting nothing but net. Whatever works for you!

Using imagery to transcend anger

There are many parallels between anger management and pain management — the other area to which I've devoted most of my professional life. Anger and pain can both be intense, chronic experiences — and you can easily find yourself ruminating about both (see the preceding section for more on rumination).

So, what I found out from one of my pain clients has relevance here. Phillip was a man in his 50s who owned and operated an orchard. He enjoyed his life and found real meaning in everything he did — that is, until he was a victim in a car accident, which left him in intractable back and leg pain. Phillip needed to continue doing a lot of physical work in his orchard, but that tended to exacerbate his pain as the day went on. He needed a tool to help him alleviate the pain when it became intolerable so that he could get back to work. The tool we chose was imagery.

Phillip found how to relax and imagine his favorite thing — sitting by a pond fishing, all by himself. It was his version of heaven on earth. At whatever points in the workday, when his pain got to be too much, he would announce aloud to his wife and employees, "I'm going fishing!" They all knew what that meant. Then he would go to the back of the barn, sit down on the ground, close his eyes, and "go fishing" — in other words, imagine himself fishing. Phillip was good at imagery, so it was the next best thing to actually being there. After about ten minutes of this, his pain had lessened to a point where he could once again bear it. He would open his eyes, stand up, and announce to everyone, "I'm back. Let's get to work." Simple, but effective.

You can do the same thing with anger. Here's how:

1. **Find a quiet setting.**

   You can't engage in imagery if you're distracted. Find a quiet place where you can be alone for at least ten minutes. If you're at work, that could be your office — if you close the door and put a DO NOT DISTURB sign on your door. Or you can take your break and find sanctuary elsewhere — an outside bench, sitting in your car in the parking lot, or, as one of my more creative clients, did — sitting in a stall in the bathroom.

2. Rate your preimagery level of anger.

Rate how angry you are at this minute on a scale from 1 (mildly irritated) to 10 (extreme rage).

3. Close your eyes.

Imagery is about visualizing. If you're going to create internal images to use as an antidote to anger, you first have to stop visualizing what's in front of you in the external environment. Closing your eyes is the first step in letting go — and you may find this difficult. It's all about trusting yourself and the world around you.

If you aren't comfortable closing your eyes in the quiet place you've found, chances are you don't feel safe there. Try finding someplace else.

4. Release your hold on reality.

Letting go of the real world so that you can enter into the world of imagery takes more than simply closing your eyes. It also requires a receptive attitude. You have to grant yourself permission to loosen your grip on both the circumstances that provoked your anger and the emotion itself. This is no different than loosening your grip on the steering wheel in order to avoid road rage (see Chapter 24).

5. Imagine something positive.

This is the fun part! You're free here to conjure up any positive image you want. What's your favorite vacation spot, where you're your most relaxed, carefree self? A lot of people say the beach or the mountains. But it could be sitting on the deck in your own backyard. The only requirement is that it be someplace where you're never angry.

6. Be specific in your imagination.

This has to do with the *who, what,* and *where* of the situation you chose. Are you alone or with someone else? Where are you and what are you doing? Lying in a hammock? Sitting on a dock fishing? Working in your herb garden? Imagine what you're wearing. Can you see the colors of your clothes? What kind of day is it — cloudy, windy, warm, rainy, sunny? The more detailed you are about the image, the more into it you are.

7. Stay with the image for at least five minutes.

This exercise is just for use in derailing anger that may otherwise get out of hand. It's not something that you need to do for a long period of time. You'll be surprised at how refreshing five minutes of positive imagery can be and how easy it is to release anger in that short interval.

8. Evaluate your postimagery anger level.

While you're still relaxed and have your eyes closed, rate your anger on a 10-point intensity scale again. Is there a difference now? If so, you've obviously succeeded in your attempt to transcend anger for the moment. If there's no change or you actually find yourself *more* angry than you were earlier, the exercise didn't work. Maybe you just need a few more minutes of positive imagery. Or maybe you'll find the strategies offered in other chapters more helpful. Don't be discouraged, however — no one solution works for everybody.

9. **Linger in the moment.**

   If the exercise did what you wanted it to, why not linger a bit and enjoy the change in your mind and body — the lack of tension, the inner peace. Don't be in too big a hurry to get back to reality!

10. **Open your eyes and move on with your day.**

   As soon as you open your eyes, you'll realize that the world didn't go anywhere — *you* did. You took a short, refreshing trip to some imaginary, anger-free place that you call your own — and, in the process, you left behind the circumstances that provoked your anger in the first place.

You can use this imagery technique in two other ways:

✔ **Instead of imagining yourself in another positive situation, imagine yourself in the same situation that caused your anger, but without any feelings of anger.**

✔ **Imagine yourself in the same (or different) situation, but feeling a negative emotion other than anger (for example, sadness).** Emotions compete with one another. Feeling angry and sad at the same time is difficult (if not impossible). In fact, that's why many people get angry in the first place — it's their way of not feeling sad. For example, imagine feeling sad (rather than angry) about the fact that the person who was just yelling at you doesn't appreciate what a wonderful person you are and how helpful you can be.

How some men handle grief

On more than one occasion, I've worked with men — intelligent, successful men — who become extremely angry after the death of one of their children. Almost without exception, these men resist any effort on my part to tap into feelings of grief. (Who wouldn't be sad after losing a child?) The more I probe, the more defensive and angry they get. The look on their faces tells me, "Believe me, you don't want to go there!" Translated, this means "*I* don't want to go there!"

One man actually threatened me by saying, "I'm warning you: If you ask me one more time how I feel about losing my son, I'm going to hit you. I mean it." Some of these men become angry alcoholics. Some focus their anger on their spouses and end up divorced. Some alienate themselves from their other children (and thus compound their loss). Some take it out at work and end up unemployed. All in an effort not to feel sad.

The Life Savers technique

A simple, inexpensive, handy way to take immediate action when you find yourself getting angry is to suck on a Life Savers — or some other type of hard candy — until it's all gone. It only takes five minutes (I've timed it!), but it short-circuits the natural progression of anger.

So why does it work?

- ✔ **This technique takes advantage of the link between the sucking reflex and achieving a state of calm that is evident in all newborn infants.** Any mother knows that giving an infant something to suck on alleviates the baby's distress. That's why pacifiers are so popular — and difficult for some children to give up as they get older.

- ✔ **The technique involves the ingestion of something sweet — sugar — and sweet sensations are associated at the level of the brain with pleasure, which is the antithesis of anger.** The Life Savers literally sweetens your disposition!

- ✔ **It buys you enough time to formulate a response to your initial anger instead of just *reacting* to it (see Chapter 6).** An angry reaction is immediate, impulsive, thoughtless, predictable, and typically leads to consequences that are later regretted. An angry response, on the other hand, is more deliberate, engages the mind, takes advantage of past experience, is not always predictable (what works in one situation may not work in another), and more often has positive consequences (see Chapter 11 for pointers on how to use anger constructively).

- ✔ **Patiently sucking on a Life Savers runs counter to the combative, Type A behavioral tendencies that characterize many people.** Sucking is a passive response, not an aggressive one. And anger is essential only if you're moving against the world after you're provoked.

- ✔ **By putting something in your mouth to suck on, you can't immediately verbalize your anger in ways that escalate the conflict between you and others or cause you regret later on.** Telling someone "I'm sorry" after you've assaulted her with your angry words and tone of voice is useless and ineffective — it doesn't help you and it certainly doesn't help the other person.

Don't bite the Life Savers. It defeats the purpose of the exercise by shortening the length of time before you act on your anger and, more important, by indulging your aggressive personality. (Aggressive personalities seem to want to constantly "bite" life rather than savor it.)

Chapter 5

Speaking Out in Anger

. . . .

. . . .

*W*hen it comes to emotion, communication is absolutely the key. It's not only *what* you say when you lose your temper; it's also *how* you say it.

Take Lisa for example. Lisa is a newly married 26-year-old, who finds herself constantly raging at her husband, Joe. In some situations, Lisa has even physically assaulted Joe. There's no question that Lisa is frustrated by a number of things about her husband — Joe's friends spend all their time at their house, he doesn't help with even the simplest of household chores, he spends what little money he makes on drugs, and more. When Lisa tries to talk to Joe about all this, he either ignores her or puts her off by saying, "Okay, I'll get to it later." Obviously, that's not the response Lisa is looking for.

When she first entered my anger management program, Lisa expressed her anger toward her husband with expletives like, "You @#$%head!" instead of articulating the *reasons* she was upset. But that's all changed now. She's found how to express her anger in noninflammatory language (for example, "I find that I'm a lot less angry when you're considerate and help me out."), while at the same time turning down the volume — from rage to just plain mad. Most important, she's discovered how to talk rather than hit, which gives her marriage a chance to succeed.

This chapter is all about finding how to effectively communicate anger and how effectively communicating anger, in turn, benefits your health. What you discover in this chapter can save you from a broken heart (literally).

Forget Venting

Have you ever called a friend and said, "I just have to vent"? Venting is airing out stored-up emotion — that's the best-case scenario. At worst, it's like the dictionary definition of *venting,* that says it's an "the discharging of volcanic products." And, believe me, rage is one of those volcanic products.

But doesn't it help to release all that pent-up lava and soot and ash? Is venting a good thing? Well, I'm here to tell you that, contrary to what most people think, *venting anger doesn't work.* Venting doesn't provide the emotional relief you expect, nor does it resolve the real-life problems that trigger your anger in the first place. What is *does* do, unfortunately, is just the opposite: It makes angry people angrier, and aggressive people more aggressive.

Screaming at someone that he's a "@#$%head!" communicates nothing but raw anger. It doesn't tell the person why you're angry. On the other hand, if you tell him he's acting inconsiderately, then he may be forced to examine his own behavior and see what needs correcting. If you use your anger constructively (see Chapter 11), it can be like holding up a mirror in which the other person sees a reflection of himself — his behavior — and it's often a reflection that's unbecoming, if not downright ugly. Many of the people you're angry at would *rather* you vent and call them derogatory names than articulate your anger, forcing them to take a closer look at themselves. In effect, by venting, you may be doing the people you're upset with a big favor — but not the kind that lasts!

Thirty years ago, Dr. Arthur Bohart at California State University conducted a series of experiments to determine the effectiveness of *catharsis* (the psychiatric term for venting) in reducing anger. In one of those studies, he had three groups of distressed subjects do one of three things:

- ✓ Sit quietly in a room thinking about their feelings.
- ✓ Discharge their angry feelings into a tape recorder.
- ✓ Spend 20 minutes talking with a counselor about how they felt.

Dr. Bohart concluded that counseling was the most *effective* way of reducing anger because it involved both the sharing and understanding of one's emotions. He also concluded that being silent (not speaking out) reduced anger *more quickly* than venting — simply getting things off your chest and into a tape recorder.

Bottom line: If you're feeling chronically angry, your best bet is to talk to a counselor about your emotions so you can get to the bottom of them and figure out how to move on. But if you're experiencing an isolated episode of anger, you're better off thinking about them quietly than you are venting to a friend.

TECHNICAL STUFF

What was Freud thinking anyway?

The noted psychiatrist, Sigmund Freud, believed in a "hydraulic" model of human emotion. As he saw it, emotions — including anger — are a natural byproduct of everyday life, but they tend to build up over time just like steam does in a teakettle (or lava does in a volcano). As emotions build up, they create bodily tension that eventually seeks it own discharge. Freud thought that people remained healthy as long as they could freely and openly express their feelings. If you couldn't express emotion in some acceptable, adaptive way as you experienced it, then your health would be adversely affected by the mounting tension within your body.

Freud's term for helping clients discharge their residual anger was *catharsis,* which actually means a dramatic freeing up of deep-seated anger from the past — what I refer to in this book as *yesterday's anger.*

Basically, I think Freud was right — it's just that most people (including lots of anger-management specialists!) misunderstood his concept of catharsis — which was intended to be a therapist-guided, structured reexperiencing of anger that was at the core of our personality — and instead saw it as something akin to plain old venting. They're not the same thing! As far as I'm aware, Freud never had his patients pound mattresses with a tennis racket, beat on inflated lifelike dolls, rip up telephone books, scream to their hearts' content, or engage in mortal combat with bataca bats — all forms of conventional anger-management therapy.

Expressing Your Anger Effectively

If you want to express anger effectively, you would be wise to follow the advice of psychologist George Bach, a pioneer in the field of anger management, who suggested that constructive anger must have what he called *informational impact* and not just be an exercise in hostility. You need to use your anger to educate, inform, and share that part of yourself that is hurt, sad, frustrated, insecure, and feels attacked with the person who tapped into these feelings. That's the message that needs to get out — anger is simply the vehicle. Following are some strategies that you can use instead of venting.

Talking versus hitting

If you can't articulate your anger (clearly express how you're feeling through language), you're destined to act it out through some form of physical aggression. When a guy smashes his fist into a wall or, worse yet, into the face of another person, what exactly does that communicate other than the obvious fact that he's mad as hell? How does that punching benefit him? It doesn't. Does that punch improve his relationship with the person he hits? Nope. Is the angry person calm after he's hauled off and slugged someone (or hit a wall)? Absolutely not. Expressing anger through physical violence has no upside — zip, zero, zilch.

So then is it better to yell and scream out your anger than hit something or someone? If that's the only choice you give yourself at the time, yes. But then again, verbal violence really doesn't get you anywhere either. No one feels better after she's given someone a good tongue-lashing, no matter what she says. And the person on the receiving end of all that yelling and screaming certainly isn't a happy camper either.

So, what's left? *Talking* — using the gift of language to express your emotions (in this case, anger) in a constructive way.

Eddie is just finding how to talk about his anger. Ever since he was a child, he's always kept a tight lid on his anger — withdrawing into himself as soon as he starts to get irritated, until he can't hold in all that anger anymore, and then, predictably, he erupts with volcanic rage. Just recently that rage caused Eddie to physically assault his wife, which has understandably left her shaken and put the future of their marriage in serious doubt. The following conversation illustrates why Eddie needs anger management:

> **Gentry:** You said there was an incident this past week where you lost your temper. Tell me about it.
>
> **Eddie:** Yeah, I got irritated with my wife right before we left the house to go visit some friends. And when we got to our friends' house, I ended up being an ass to everyone the whole time we were there.
>
> **Gentry:** What did you do between the time you left home and the time you arrived at your friends' house?
>
> **Eddie:** Nothing. I didn't say anything to my wife. She tried to get me to talk, but I wouldn't. She finally gave up, and we were both silent until we got there.
>
> **Gentry:** How far a drive is it to your friends' house?
>
> **Eddie:** Over an hour.
>
> **Gentry:** You drove for over an hour without saying a word to your wife?
>
> **Eddie:** Right.
>
> **Gentry:** What were you doing instead?
>
> **Eddie:** I was thinking about how angry I was and all kinds of crazy stuff about my wife.
>
> **Gentry:** And did that make you more angry, or less so?

Eddie: Oh, it definitely made me angrier. By the time we got to their house, I was really upset — tense and ready to explode. I never did relax the whole time we were there and I know it ruined the evening for all of us.

Gentry: What do you imagine would have happened if you had talked to your wife about how you felt during that hour-long drive?

Eddie: It probably would have helped, but I don't know how to do that — I don't know what to say. So, I just stay quiet and it builds and builds. I've always been like that, and I don't know why.

The next time you get so angry you feel like hitting something (or someone), follow these steps:

1. **Come up with a label to identify the intensity of your anger.**

   For example, are you annoyed, irritated, mad, irate, or in a rage? Start by saying, "I feel. . . ." Don't say, "I think. . . ." What you're going for here is your feeling, not your thoughts about how obnoxious the other person was.

2. **Identify the thing that triggered your anger.**

   For example, "Every time I come home, his friends are here. We never have any time to ourselves." Continue your conversation by saying, "I feel _____ *[insert the word you came up with in Step 1]* because. . . ."

3. **Ask yourself what it would take to help you return to a non-angry state.**

   For example, "I would appreciate it if he would ask his friends to leave when I get home from work so we can have some one-on-one time."

When you're able to go through these three steps inside your head, see if you can actually have that conversation with the person you're angry with.

Writing versus speaking

A very nice woman — I'll call her Jane — came to my office complaining of feeling emotionally "burned out." She dreaded getting up in the morning, was unusually tired, found herself crying for no apparent reason on more than one occasion, and felt like there was "a big fist in my chest" all the time. She had decided she was depressed and wanted to know what she could do to feel better.

After talking to her more, I found out that Jane was caught up in a very unhappy situation: She had spent most of her energies over the past several years ministering to one of her grown sons, who suffered from drug addiction, which continued despite all of Jane's well-intentioned efforts. Because she'd been so tied up in her son's problems, she had long since quit devoting any time to her *own* needs or wants — she wanted to travel, meet some new people, do things with her husband. She had, in effect, sacrificed her life for that of her son.

"Your problem is not depression," I told her "Your problem is that you have a ton of anger stuck inside you — anger at the way your life has turned out, anger at your son for not getting well, and most of all anger at yourself for being so stupid to let things get this bad. That's why you feel like you have a fist in your chest — you're wanting to hit something, but you can't." She agreed, adding that she had never been able to talk to anyone about how she felt and instead simply "contained" her feelings behind a façade of niceness.

"Okay," I said, "let's start by having you write down your feelings about your son's drug problem and everything else that's not going right in your life." I gave her 20 minutes to "write from the heart, not the head" and later came back and asked her to read what she wrote — just to herself, not aloud — and circle the emotional terms (for example, *angry, disappointed, upset*). We discussed those words that she circled and then I asked her to throw the sheet of paper into the trash.

Two things were immediately apparent: It was easy for her to write a lot in a short time because the feelings were just beneath the surface, and she tended to circle *issues* more than *feelings*. That's how disconnected she was to the emotional side of her personality.

"This is good," I concluded "Now go home and do this exercise for 20 minutes every day until you come back. That's how we're going to treat your depression."

Turn to Chapter 9 for a detailed, step-by-step guide to making your own private confession about pent-up anger, hostility, and resentment.

Leaving out the four-letter words

Lisa (see the introduction of this chapter) would be far better off and less apt to end up assaulting her husband if she referred to him as an "empty head" — a head that apparently doesn't think about helping around the house or sharing some intimate moments with his wife — rather than a "@#$%head."

Four-letter words are, by definition, incendiary. They add gasoline to the fire and only heighten emotions and increase the probability of some type of physical aggression. They're meant to hurt, not educate. And, they cause the person to whom they're directed to defend himself — either by withdrawing (tuning out what you're saying) or engaging in similar behavior. So now you have two people swearing at each other, which, to quote Bill Shakespeare, amounts to "sound and fury signifying nothing."

Try to distance yourself from anger-laced profanity by starting with the word *I* rather than *you* — "I'm furious" rather than "You're a damn idiot!" Better yet, enlarge your emotional vocabulary to include other words that are synonymous with anger, for example: *irritated, incensed, exasperated, annoyed, displeased, enraged, outraged, disgusted, riled, vexed,* or *piqued.*

Put yourself in the other person's shoes and ask yourself how you would feel if someone called you a "@#$%head" or worse. If he were angry with you, what would you want him to say instead?

Stay focused

When you start speaking out in anger, you may lose sight of the issue, problem, or circumstance that initially provoked you. Your anger heads off on a tangent, jumping from one grievance to another midstream. What starts out as "I asked you to stop at the store for me and you forgot" suddenly evolves into "You never help out around here. You don't listen to me. You don't care about me at all. I don't know why I married you in the first place!"

You'd be surprised at how many of my anger-management clients describe some horrific incident involving anger, but then when I ask them what started the angry exchange they say, "Beats me. All I know is that one minute we were having a civil conversation and the next minute I was yelling and pounding my fist into the wall."

The more intense your anger, the more likely the emotion itself will distract you from the issue at hand. Blind rage (see Chapter 7) is so unfocused that after you calm down, most likely you won't remember anything that you said or did. One way to remain in control of your anger is to stay focused on what it is you're angry about. Keep your eye on the ball, and things are less likely to get out of control.

Keep it short — and breathe

Constructive anger expression should be a give-and-take proposition. You give out your feelings and let others take in their meaning. The best way to lose your audience — and ensure that your message is *not* heard — is to go on and on and on . . . ranting. By all means, speak out in anger, but keep it short. Neurological sciences tell us that human beings can only digest (and remember) so much information at a time. That's why telephone numbers are limited to seven digits — the human brain can only remember seven units of information. Speaking out in anger for five minutes is like asking someone to remember a 50-digit number. It can't be done! So, no wonder kids never remember what their parents tell them when the parents are angry — and you thought they just weren't listening. My advice is to speak out in anger one minute at a time. Then take a breath and let the other person respond. That will also keep the intensity of your anger from accelerating, which is what you want, right? If the person you're angry at reacts defensively, let him have his say — don't interrupt — and then resume expressing how you feel for another minute and take another breath.

It's Not What You Say, It's How You Say It

The louder you speak, the less people hear what you have to say. Your message gets lost in your overheated dialogue. Anger can be an effective means of communication, but if you want to be heard, you have to pay attention to two aspects of your speech:

- **Volume:** The power and fullness of your words. The angrier you are, the louder you sound. You don't have to be a rocket scientist to tell the difference between a person who is irritated versus someone who is in a full-blown rage.

- **Pace:** The speed or velocity with which you speak. As your anger accelerates, you find yourself speaking faster and faster. There is a pressured quality to what you're saying — as if the angry words can't get out fast enough.

Start paying more attention to *how* you speak when you get angry. If you hear yourself getting too loud, talking too rapidly, and/or sounding shrill, adjust your speech accordingly. Think of this as an effort on your part to literally fine-tune how you speak out in anger.

The escalation effect

Professor Aron Wolfe Siegman at the University of Maryland, Baltimore County, found that when people speak out in anger, their speech tends to get louder and faster as they go. Anger arouses your nervous system and, among other things, your heart rate begins to increase. As your heart beats faster, it fuels the intensity of your vocal response. And the louder and more rapid your speech, the angrier you get. You're quickly caught up in a vicious cycle that begins to feed on itself. (I wish I had a dollar for every client who said, "I don't know what happened — I was just telling my wife how irritated I was and the next thing I knew I was ranting and raving and scaring her half to death.")

The good news as far as anger management is concerned is that you can reduce the intensity of your emotion by ratcheting down the your speech. You don't have to necessarily change what you're saying (unless it includes four-letter words!), just how you say it.

Professor Siegman also noted in his experiments that human beings tend to mimic or match the other person's vocal style. The louder you are when you get angry, the louder I am in response. And so it goes. This type of reciprocal exchange also serves to accelerate anger to the point where it's often difficult to control.

This vicious cycle of anger-arousal tone can have dire health consequences over time.

People who engage in this type of outrageous dialogue are far more at risk for developing coronary heart disease. So, not only are you taking the heart (and spirit) out of the person on the receiving end of your angry tirade, but you also may slowly but surely be killing yourself!

Whenever you find yourself on the verge of losing your cool (see Chapter 6), ask yourself this question: Is this worth raising my blood pressure, wearing out my cardiovascular system, and eventually causing a heart attack? If not, it's time for some good old-fashioned anger management.

In my work with angry adolescents, I'm often confronted verbally by a youngster who is obviously in an over-aroused state. I respond (not react!) in a firm, but even-toned fashion. The last thing the kid needs is for me to help exacerbate his rage. Initially, he may accelerate on his own, but I continue to respond to him without any change in the tone of my voice. Most often, the next thing that happens is that he begins to tone his angry rhetoric down — in other words, if I don't match his vocalizations (yelling back), then he matches mine. This is a great way to defuse someone else's anger. So next time you're faced with someone who's getting upset, try to remain calm and defuse the situation.

Chapter 6

Keeping Your Cool

Most people react in anger when they're provoked. You don't think about it — you just react. You react instinctively and your reactions are always the same. You pout; you shout; you ridicule the person who provoked you; you lash out and hit something or someone; or, you just stomp off in a fury. In other words, you lose your cool!

Losing your cool is easy. That's why millions of us do it more than we should. *Keeping* your cool is the challenge. Basically, it comes down to taking control of this thing called anger before it takes control of you. Responding to anger means just that — exerting some mindful control over your emotions rather than letting your anger play itself out in a mindless sort of way.

The approach I outline in this chapter offers a simple, straightforward set of strategies for defusing anger at the very moment you begin to experience it. It's a set of strategies that only takes 90 seconds to accomplish. The key to this approach is to focus on your anger and your reactions to your anger, not the source of your anger (the thing that triggered it). This means turning your attention inward — on yourself — as a means of controlling how intense your anger is and how long it lasts. You can't manage anger if you're always trying to manage the circumstances (people, things) that unleashed it. Letting go of the grievance and asserting some self-control is how you manage today's anger.

Eddie saves his job

One of my clients — I'll call him Eddie — started out skeptical, but soon became a believer. His employer, who made it clear that the next time Eddie lost his temper he would also lose his job, referred him for anger management. Eddie didn't have the time or patience to examine all the reasons he found himself angry so much of the time. Time was short, and the prospect of losing his job was not appealing. He needed a solution and he needed it now!

Saying that Eddie was doubtful about the potential effectiveness of anger management would

be an understatement. But he was willing to give it a chance. A week after I introduced Eddie to the strategies in this chapter, he came in to my office saying enthusiastically, "Man, you saved my job! My boss got in my face at work this morning and my first impulse was to get right back in his. But then I thought about what you said about responding to anger — mine versus his — and I handled things in a whole different way. Not only did I keep my job, but he ended up calming down and then apologizing to me for his anger."

Choose to Respond Rather Than React

Anger therapists who argue that anger is a choice always amuse me. I'm sure they mean well, but they're wrong. The initial feeling of anger is no more the result of conscious choice than other emotions such as joy, sadness, or fear. It just happens!

Anger is your nervous system's intuitive reaction to some perceived threat or danger. The choice has to do with what comes after you feel angry — that is, how you act and whether you continue to feel angry.

Ask yourself the following questions:

- ✔ For the rest of your life, do you want to simply react to your anger in the same old mindless, predictable way you always have?

- ✔ Do you want to always be a victim of your emotions?

- ✔ Do you want to continue to apologize for your angry reactions by telling those you hurt, "I'm sorry, I don't know what came over me. I promise I won't act that way ever again"?

- ✔ Do you want others to begin to judge you by your angry reactions (for example, "Stay away from that guy, he's got a bad temper!")?

I'm betting that your answer to each of these questions is a very clear "No!" More than likely, you're ready for a change. So, before you do anything else, you need to make the decision to *respond* rather than *react* to your anger.

Granted, this strategy is a mental one (as all choices are), but it nevertheless *is* a strategy, and a crucial one at that. To begin to understand the basic differences between reacting and responding to anger, consider Table 6-1.

Table 6-1	Anger Reactions and Responses
When You <u>React</u> to Anger, You Are . . .	**When You <u>Respond</u> to Anger, You Are . . .**
Reflexive	Thoughtful
Impulsive	Deliberate
Predictable	Unpredictable
Out of control	In control

What happens, you ask, if I choose to continue reacting as I always have to my anger? Don't I have a right to react to my anger any way I want to? Of course you do, as long as you're willing to keep paying the same consequences you always have, or worse. You can keep apologizing, trying to undo the harm your anger has done. You can continue down this path to a point where anger ends up poisoning your whole life (see Chapter 3). But then reacting is a conscious choice on your part. You can say loud and proud, "I choose to lose my cool. That's just the way I am. So there!" That's fine. But at least that decision makes you responsible for the outcome of your reactive anger, no matter how negative, and you're no longer a victim of your emotion. And if you are not ready to take that different path now, maybe you will be after you've read this book.

Breaking your lifelong habits of reacting to anger

Reacting to anger may be a habit you've formed over a lifetime, so don't be discouraged if you have trouble when you first try to avoid the reaction and focus on the response. The difficulty you're having may stem from things that have happened in your past that conditioned you to be a reactive person. Or, it may reflect an impulsive temperament that you inherited at birth. Either way, it's a habit that needs to be broken if you're going to get control of your anger.

Sam first began to have explosive anger when he was a teenager, defending himself from bullies in high school. His family moved into a new neighborhood and he was an outsider. "They picked on me and I had to take care of myself. I had to fight for everything I got," he explained. Sam's problem was that he continued this fight for the rest of his life with his wife, children, neighbors, and co-workers.

Linda grew up in an abusive, alcoholic family and found out early on to react in anger as a way of surviving. Unfortunately, at the same time, anger kept her from accomplishing all the things she wanted to in life. "My anger hurt me. It kept me from having things that people I grew up with had, like a college education and a good job," she now laments.

Chris has always had a problem with outbursts of anger. His fuse is short. His anger doesn't build up slowly. It just comes on all of a sudden, as if a switch is thrown. When he was a child, his mother would tell him, "If people push you, you need to walk away." Good advice. But he couldn't do it then, and he still can't do it at age 31.

Think childhood baggage might influence *your* tendency to be a "hot reactor" when it comes to handling anger? It probably does if your parents were

- Unloving
- Not affectionate or tender
- Cold
- Unenthusiastic
- Distant
- Remote
- Aloof
- Reserved
- Stern
- Rigorous
- Uncompromising
- Strict
- Stringent
- Exacting
- Hard
- Unfriendly
- Difficult to deal with

- ✔ Unbearable

- ✔ High strung

- ✔ Highly sensitive

- ✔ Nervous

- ✔ Excitable

- ✔ Easily aroused

- ✔ Easily stirred into action

- ✔ Tense

- ✔ On edge

- ✔ Keyed up

The nice thing about habits is that you can change them at any point in your life. Some of my most successful clients, in fact, have been folks in their 50s and 60s. Who says old dogs can't learn new tricks?

Avoiding the company of other angerholics

Your attempts to stop reacting and make the choice to respond to anger may also be difficult because you're surrounded by people with excessive anger. You know what they say about birds of a feather — they tend to flock together, which means you've probably actively sought the companionship of others with the same temperament. There are three reasons for this:

- ✔ **Your style of reacting to anger leads you into life circumstances where your emotional behavior finds a suitable fit.** For example, most of the corporate executives I work with tend to be very angry people. They pretty much all made it to the top of the organization by using anger to compete with their peers and control their subordinates. To hear them tell it, anger works!

- ✔ **Angry, antisocial people tend to select peers who also engage in outrageous behavior.** Tantrum-prone men and women, for example, are likely to date and marry other men and women who too are easily angered. In effect, you choose what's familiar.

- ✔ **By engaging in intense bouts of anger you're apt to be ostracized by mainstream society; people who, for the most part, handle anger in appropriate and mature ways.** Unfortunately, this means that you're denied an opportunity for corrective feedback that might otherwise come from friends and loved ones, who instead distance themselves from your anger. So, you seek out the company of those who will both tolerate and condone your outbursts.

What you need are some anger allies, the kind of people who can help you form *new* habits of responding effectively to anger. Look for people who:

✔ Show by personal example how to express anger in a healthy way

✔ Will actively listen and support your efforts to bring your anger under control

✔ Are nonjudgmental

✔ Have conquered their own anger demons

✔ Are patient

✔ Are compassionate, appreciating what a burden excessive anger is

✔ Don't assume that what worked for them in bringing their anger under control will necessarily work for you

✔ Are willing to be there for you at a time of emotional crisis

✔ Don't pretend to have all the answers

✔ Are willing to help, but are not willing to be responsible for your anger — that's your job!

You may have to distance yourself from the flock, whether that represents a group of angry peers or angry family members. Walking away from your angry friends takes a good deal of courage and a lot of willpower, but you can do it — and you'll see the positive benefits in your own life very soon!

Assessing Your Anger

The first, and most critical, step in managing anger at the moment you experience it is to assess the intensity of the feeling. I refer to this as the *rate-and-label step*.

To assess your own anger, follow these steps:

1. **Think of a number between 1 and 10 that best describes the intensity of your emotion, with 1 being mild and 10 being severe.**

   A rating of 2, for example, suggests a barely noticeable change in your emotional state, whereas a rating of 8 signifies strong negative feelings. Focus especially on the physical side of anger — how tense, aroused, or agitated you feel.

2. **Convert the number rating into a label that aptly defines just how angry you are at this moment.**

Basically, anger is experienced at three distinct levels. A rating between 1 and 3 suggests that you're annoyed or irritated. A rating between 4 and 6 is typical of folks who are just plain mad. And, finally, if you rated yourself somewhere between 7 and 10, like it or not, you're in a state of rage.

Anger ratings are like golf — the lower the number, the better off you are!

Quantifying anger with numbers gives you useful information:

✔ **Numbers tell you how close you are to losing control.** You're more likely to lose control when you find yourself extremely mad or at the point of rage than you are if you're just irritated.

✔ **Numbers tell you how much of a window of opportunity you have to retain control of your anger.** If you start out with a rating of 4, you obviously have more time to turn things around than if you begin with a 6, where you're only one tick away from rage.

✔ **Numbers provide a baseline from which you can measure progress.** If you start out with feelings of rage and, after employing the strategies I outline in this chapter, you find yourself only just plain mad, that's progress.

Be Patient

Emotions, like anger, are by their very nature transient experiences. Each episode of anger has a beginning point (onset), a middle phase (where it peaks and begins to recede), and an end point (resolution). Emotions also work on the principle of gravity — what goes up must inevitably come down. Anger always resolves itself and will actually do so without any effort on your part. The average adult is over his anger within five to ten minutes. You don't have to react in an attempt to make anger subside. The relief you're seeking from the tension and thoughts that accompany anger will come if you just give it enough time to pass. In fact, time is your ally. The real paradox here is that the more time you allow yourself to be angry, the sooner you'll be free of this emotion.

In order to give yourself enough time, follow these tips:

✔ **Remind yourself that time is on your side.** No one, not the angriest person alive, stays angry very long.

✔ **Remember that patience is a virtue.** No one ever had a heart attack or died an early death as a result of being too patient.

✔ **Repeat to yourself as many times as necessary, "This too shall pass."** Sometimes a little wisdom goes a long way.

✔ **Say to yourself repeatedly, "Less is more."** In managing an episode of anger, it often pays to take a more passive posture.

Too angry? Walk away

A group of 115 eighth graders were surveyed as to how intense their anger was and how they reacted/responded when they got angry. Interestingly, kids who reported the most intense anger and who also tended to react by venting their anger on others took four times longer to calm down than did their counterparts who were just as angry, but who chose to respond to their emotion by walking away and letting their anger subside on its own. The eighth graders who vented, on average, were still angry 1 to 2 hours later, whereas those who walked away got over their anger in less than 30 minutes.

Take a Deep Breath

Anger arouses human beings. Their autonomic nervous system gets excited and floods the body with adrenaline. Blood pressure, heart rate, muscle tension, the hairs on the back of your neck — everything goes up! The angry person is instantly prepared for the attack as a way of defending himself from impending harm. This is, in essence, the physical side of reacting in anger. Responding to anger requires that you begin to reverse this process and calm yourself down. In the following sections, I give you a few options for doing exactly that.

The relaxation response

Everyone has a natural protective mechanism to override the physical tension that accompanies anger. This protective mechanism is the *relaxation response*. To relax in the moment, all you need to do is pause long enough to take a few deep breaths. Breathing away the angry tension you're feeling and replacing it with a feeling of relaxation is as simple as one, two, three:

1. **Take a deep, exaggerated breath in through your nose.**

2. **Hold the breath for a count of one.**

3. **Now, exhale in an exaggerated way through your mouth.**

Repeat the exercise at least ten times (more if you want, depending on the intensity of your anger), being fully conscious of your breathing throughout.

Think the word *release* with each exhale. This is your mind's command to the body to let go of this unwanted tension. Your body will follow the command — it's just the way the mind and body work!

The power of quiet

Quiet is the natural state of the body at rest. Venting your anger verbally only adds more tension, further elevating your heart rate, blood pressure, and so on. Just by being quiet for a few moments, while you continue to formulate your response to anger, you'll begin to calm down. This simple principle underlies the advice of one leading anger expert, who says the first thing the angry person should do is to shut up.

Lighten up

If you want to stay angry (or worse yet get even angrier), then by all means stay serious. Remind yourself that anger is no laughing matter. Don't even think about smiling. And, for goodness sake, do *not* try to find the humor in whatever situation provoked your temper.

However, if you're trying to calm yourself down, you need to lighten up. For example, if you feel compelled to say something to the person at whom you're angry, start by saying, "You know it's funny that. . . ."

Or do what Fred did when another angry person hollered at him to "Go to hell!" Fred thought for a minute and then said, "Good idea. Except that I've already been there. Spent three years there, in fact, and I don't want to go back. It's called Galveston, Texas." Fred was laughing and the other man fell silent. (All kinds of people like Galveston, of course — the point is to think of something that *you* find funny when you're angry, because it's hard to be angry while you're laughing.)

Inoculate yourself

To inoculate yourself against the rising tide of angry tension, you can engage in positive self-talk by repeating (silently or out loud) phrases such as the following:

- ✓ "Easy does it. Don't get so upset."

- ✓ "That person may not be in control, but I am."

- ✓ "That tension in my forehead is normal given how angry I am. If I just relax, it'll go away."

- ✓ "As the saying goes, this too shall pass."

- ✓ "I'm in the eye of the (anger) hurricane. It's safe here."

Ask Yourself Four Crucial Questions

You can't manage something that you don't understand. You have to analyze your feelings in order to respond to them in a healthy and appropriate way. You can do this quickly and easily by asking yourself the following four questions.

Who am I really angry at?

The answer to this question may, at first, seem simple: "The person who just provoked me!" But if you look a little closer, this is often not the case at all. The truth is that you may carry pent-up, unresolved anger from one situation or source to another, without realizing it. Then you end up getting angry at the wrong person and experiencing angry feelings that are stronger than warranted at the time.

Consider the case of an angry youngster who comes to school each day, already angry at her parents and further irritated by having to deal with her peers on the bus. When the teacher tells her to take a seat, the kid reacts by yelling, "Don't tell me what to do, bitch!" Now, is this child really that angry first thing in the morning simply because the teacher invited her to sit down? The reality is, the kid is angry with her parents and the kids on the bus.

So ask yourself: Who am I really angry at?

Is this where I want to be angry?

Unfortunately, you don't usually get to pick the time and place of your anger. More often than not, anger finds you at an inopportune moment.

Nancy found herself angry at a co-worker just as she was about to leave work on Friday afternoon for a long-anticipated fun weekend at the beach with her friends. Clearly, she had a dilemma. Give in to her anger that afternoon and risk continuing to be angry and spoiling her weekend, or put her anger on hold and deal with it when she returns to the office on Monday?

Think about whether this is the right time and place for you to be angry.

Why am I angry?

It is possible that, because anger is often an instinctive, thoughtless reaction, you may actually not know *why* you're angry. You just know that you're angry, but you don't have a clue what the underlying issue is — the thing that sparked your emotion. The most common triggers for anger are

> ✔ **Someone attacking your self-esteem through some type of verbal or physical abuse.**
>
> ✔ **Someone or something preventing you from reaching a desired goal.** This is even more anger provoking if you feel you're entitled to that goal or it's something you're strongly committed to.
>
> ✔ **Someone violating your basic moral principles — fairness, equity, honesty, and responsibility.** Again, the more strongly committed you are to those particular values, the angrier you become.
>
> ✔ **A situation where you feel helpless, unable to correct or fix something that has gone wrong.**

Is the intensity of my anger at this moment consistent with why I'm angry?

Using the earlier example, even if the student is angry at the teacher for telling her to take a seat, does that justify a feeling of rage? Irritation maybe, but rage no. This is where most people get into trouble with their anger — the intensity of their anger is too much for whatever triggers it.

David kissed his wife goodbye and headed out for work one morning. He stopped to get a glass of orange juice from the refrigerator. Seeing that there was none there, he immediately flew up the stairs to the bedroom where his wife was and proceeded to yell at her for ten minutes. When asked whether he thought his rage was justified, he calmly said, "Absolutely, she knows that I like my orange juice in the morning. She should make sure that we don't run out."

You can often find justification for irritation and anger, but there is never a justification for rage.

What Are My Options?

You can choose among an infinite number of responses to your anger. Some of those options are aggressive (yelling at or hitting someone). Others involve retreating from your anger (just walking away). Still others involve some type of assertive response on your part (standing your ground and saying that you're angry but in a nonaggressive manner). The real question is, what's the best way for you to respond in this particular situation? In the following sections, I fill you in.

Always give yourself three ways to go

Give yourself a choice of at least three ways to respond to your anger. If you give yourself only one option (for example, cursing), you really have no choice about what to do next — choice requires at least two possibilities. Plus, no single option (even though it may be your favorite) fits every situation where you find yourself experiencing anger. When you get mad over a disagreement with a friend, for example, you could say, "Fine, I guess we'll just have to agree to disagree" and then walk away; you could snap back aggressively, saying, "You're wrong, dead wrong, and I'm tired of listening to your bitching!"; or you could say, "I think with some more discussion I can convince you that you're mistaken in how you see things, but right now I'm too annoyed to do that. So, if it's all right, I'll get back to you later and we can talk some more."

There is nothing wrong with having an option that involves some type of aggressive response. The problem comes when that is your *only* option!

Consider the consequences of each response

When human beings *react* to their emotions, they never have time to consider the consequences. When they *respond* to these same feelings and circumstances, they do have time.

After you come up with your three options for responding (see the preceding section), and when you're next faced with a situation that makes you angry, take a minute and ask yourself "What is likely to happen if I choose response option #1? What about if I try option #2? And what if I choose option #3?" Each of these options has different consequences, positive and negative, immediately and later on.

Emotions are transient — they come and go. But you have to live with (and often pay for) the consequences of your responses long afterward.

Consider what happens when you lose your cool:

- ✔ Your blood pressure goes up, in some cases dangerously high.
- ✔ You feel like you're going to burst or explode.
- ✔ Your heart pounds.
- ✔ You feel a knot in your stomach.
- ✔ You feel overwhelmed.

✔ You lose your concentration, focusing only on your anger.

✔ You feel depressed and unhappy.

✔ You feel ashamed, embarrassed, and guilty.

✔ You feel nervous and agitated.

✔ Other people have hurt feelings because of your anger.

✔ Other people become defiant.

✔ Other people become indifferent to you.

✔ Other people avoid you.

✔ Other people lose their respect for you.

Now, consider what happens when you keep your cool:

✔ You calm down quicker.

✔ Other people maintain their respect for you.

✔ Other people are more likely to approach you.

✔ You're more likely to come up with constructive solutions to problems.

✔ You minimize future conflict.

✔ You're more likely to understand the other person's point of view.

✔ You and the other person leave the situation feeling good.

✔ You're more empathetic.

✔ You have lower blood pressure.

✔ You feel less agitated.

✔ You leave the situation not holding a grudge.

✔ You're a much more agreeable person.

Motives matter

Given a choice of how to respond to anger, females will most often act in a way that lets the person who made them mad know what they're feeling and what they're thinking, whereas males are much more likely to choose a response that allows them to blow off steam. Unfortunately, the pleasure males feel from the immediate release of angry tension is far outweighed by the long-term negative consequences associated with such outbursts. Anger management is, to a large extent, about delaying the instant gratification of answering anger with anger so that you can experience the eventual satisfaction of being in control of your emotional life.

Don't always exercise your right to be angry

I wish I had a dollar for every time some angry person has said to me, "Dammit, I have a *right* to be angry!" My answer is always the same, "Of course, you do — but that doesn't mean that you also have the right to express anger any way you feel like it."

I believe in freedom of experience, including the freedom to experience emotions. But wisdom sometimes dictates that we hold back on the expression of that experience. To feel without acting is a choice, a difficult choice sometimes, and a mature, courageous choice, but a choice nonetheless.

Go Ahead and Respond

Eventually, you have to decide how you want to respond to your anger. So, think about your options, consider the consequences of each, and think about whether you want to exercise your fundamental right to express anger in this situation. Then go ahead and respond.

Most likely, you'll respond in a way that benefits you more than it hurts you. But if you choose to respond in an aggressive manner (for example, by yelling), so be it. If you've really taken the time to consider the consequences, though, you probably won't waste your energy yelling. (And if you do, you'll see the consequences of your yelling, and next time, you may think even harder before you respond in that way.)

Advantage females

When 518 adolescents were asked how they would react/respond to anger from a peer, the most prevalent response was to answer anger with anger. Forty-two percent of boys chose this reactive means of protecting themselves from the other person's angry behavior, as compared to 32 percent of girls. Contrast this with the finding that only 28 percent of the boys chose to respond in a more mature fashion — by walking away in order to cool down and then returning to discuss the problem they had with the other youngster — whereas more girls (39 percent) chose this response. Females have a clear advantage even at this early age in managing their anger, a trend that appears to continue throughout life.

Now Reward Yourself

If you decided to respond (not react) to today's anger in a different way than you have in the past, feel good about yourself. There is nothing like the feeling of being in charge of your emotions. You need to celebrate the moment by rewarding yourself for making a healthy choice. That's how one-time experiences become lifelong habits.

A long-held tradition of the science of psychology is that human beings learn to behave as a function of consequences. It's really quite simple: If you do something and you get a reward, you repeat the same behavior, looking for the same reward. If you do something and you get no reward or, worse, you're punished for what you did, you won't repeat the behavior. This is the basis of all rat psychology and, as one leading psychologist once said, "People are at least as smart as rats!" Rewarding positive behavior is how habits — patterns of behavior that persist over time and that you do automatically, without any conscious effort on your part — are formed. Repetition by itself is not enough to build a new habit; it must be followed by reward.

So, whenever you use the anger management strategies outlined in this book, be sure to do something to reward yourself. Here are some possibilities:

- ✔ **Reach over and pat yourself on the back and say "Good job!"**

- ✔ **Say to yourself quietly or aloud, "Good for me. Couldn't happen to a nicer guy."**

- ✔ **Sit quietly and reflect on the feeling of accomplishment you feel at this moment.**

- ✔ **Share your triumph over today's anger with someone you care about.**

- ✔ **Treat yourself to something special.** Buy a book or a CD that you've been wanting, stop for a coffee mocha, or buy a lottery ticket (keeping your cool may really pay off!).

- ✔ **Put a dollar bill in a special anger-management jar.** When you accumulate enough money, use it to indulge yourself. Seeing that jar filling up will be a pretty strong reward in and of itself.

- ✔ **Share your triumph over today's anger with a higher power in a moment of thankful prayer.**

- ✔ **Think for a minute about all the negative consequences you *didn't* have to pay this time because you kept your cool.** Experience the joy of what didn't happen!

- ✔ **Repeat with conviction, "I have control of anger; anger does not have control over me."**

It's never too late to figure out how to keep your cool

A client of mine — I'll call him Frank — had a terrible temper his whole life. It ruined his health, caused him to lose most of his friends, but most of all it led to an estranged relationship with his only child. Frank had been so angry during those child-rearing years that he found himself increasingly distant from his son — both geographically and emotionally. Frank said that whenever his son called home and Frank answered, his son would immediately say, "Let me speak to mother." The only things Frank knew about his son (or his grandchildren) he found out secondhand from his wife.

But then Frank did a curious (and courageous) thing at the age of 58: He entered an anger-management program and figured out how to control his temper for the first time ever. Now when his son calls and Frank says "Wait, let me get your mother," his son replies "No, I wanted to talk with you. How are you feeling? What are you doing?" Frank and his son enjoy a relationship that neither one of them thought would ever be possible. By learning to keep his cool, Frank, now 67, gained a son. And he's a very happy man!

Part III
Preventing Anger Tomorrow

The 5th Wave   By Rich Tennant

"This position is good for reaching inner calm, mental clarity, and things that roll behind the refrigerator."

In this part . . .

I tell you how to manage anger before it happens. That's right: You can avoid getting angry tomorrow by the things you do today. In this part, I show you how to create your own recipe for defusing your capacity for anger. If you don't want to be a victim of blind rage, you have to open your eyes to the way life *is* instead of dwelling on how you *want* it to be.

Here you also discover why you need to stop saying you're "fine" when you're not. Hiding anger may be civilized, but it sure isn't healthy. In this part, you find out why you're so dissatisfied with your life and what you can do to remedy that. First, you need to make your own private confession about just how angry you are and why. Then you can quit all that Type A behavior — competition, obsessing about time, and a slavish devotion to work — and enjoy yourself for who, not what, you are. Finally, you can make anger your ally rather than your enemy — this approach is called *using anger constructively,* and it's a whole new way of dealing with your emotion.

Chapter 7

Adopting a New Perspective

Certain points of view invite anger.

Take Walter, for example. He's a man in his early 60s, likeable, intelligent, educated, but always quick to see some evil intent in the actions of others. If he calls someone and leaves a message asking him to call back right away, and if that person doesn't call right back, Walter's initial thought is, "Damn him — he has absolutely no respect for me!"

It would never occur to Walter that the person with whom he's now irritated has other important things to do as well, or that he's stuck somewhere in traffic, or that he's home sick with a cold. Nope. As far as Walter is concerned, there's only one possible explanation for his phone not ringing — a lack of respect — and that's why Walter is angry.

If this were an isolated situation, it wouldn't be a problem. But if you're like Walter, this is the way you view everything that comes your way throughout the day. Every time someone cuts in front of you in traffic, every time you have to wait more than two minutes before a waiter appears at your table in a restaurant, every time your spouse forgets to pick up your dry cleaning, it's just one more example of evil intent — and one more occasion for what you consider legitimate anger.

This chapter is all about the "mental" side of anger. You really can choose how you view the actions of others, and you really can determine how the choices you make affect your emotional life — and in this chapter, I show you how. I explain why I think provocation is terribly overrated. And I also distinguish between hostility and anger and explain why the two are inextricably linked.

Anger Is in the Eye of the Beholder

Humans are the only animals I know of who have a choice about how they view the world. Cats, dogs, squirrels, hamsters, goldfish — they're all creatures of instinct, which means they respond in predictable ways that are prewired into their nervous systems. Instincts are universal — scratch a bassett hound's tummy and he'll instantly begin shaking his hind leg. All bassett hounds do it and no one has a choice in the matter.

The miraculous thing about being human is that you are not ruled by instinct. Not only do you have choices about how you respond to the world around you (for example, when someone mistreats you), but, even before that, you also have a choice about how you perceive that person's actions. Do you think she did that on purpose? Was it an accident, or did he do it deliberately? Is the mistreatment specifically directed at you alone? Do you view this as a catastrophe — a life-altering event? Is this something that you think should not have happened? These questions are all ones your mind considers, albeit unconsciously, before you have a chance to react — or, better yet, *respond* to provocation (see Chapter 6 to better understand the difference between the reacting and responding).

You might say Mike is a born pessimist, but actually that's not true. Human beings aren't *born* with attitudes — those attitudes come from life experience. What *is* true is that Mike is the product of an alcoholic home, where things could be going well one minute and in complete chaos the next. He found out as a child not to expect the good times to last and that he and the rest of his family were always just one beer away from a family crisis. So, for all of his adult life, Mike has expected that most things will eventually turn out badly, given enough time. No matter how loving his wife is or how cooperative his children are, in the back of his mind he harbors this expectation that any minute things will change for the worse — and he's ready to react in anger when that moment comes. Why will he get angry? It's Mike's way of defending himself against chaos, a way of feeling in control — unlike when he was a child hiding under the bed while his alcoholic father ranted and raved well into the night.

Mike is unaware of how his early childhood influenced his view of the world. Like most children of alcoholics, he figures that because he survived those unpleasant years (physically at least), he's okay. He also has no clue why he loses his temper so easily. Mike may as well be a bassett hound!

Understanding why it's called "blind" rage

The more intense your anger, the more it overpowers your central nervous system — in other words, your brain. When you're in a state of rage, you are, for all intents and purposes, deaf, dumb, and blind to everything that's going on around you — something that is *not* true when you're merely irritated or just plain mad (see Chapter 2 for details on how to distinguish these three levels of emotion). Rageful people only hear and feel their own anger and they only see the target of their wrath. Ragers often experience emotional amnesia after they calm down — they can't even tell you exactly what triggered their outrageous behavior in the first place, nor do they remember any of what they said and did during their tirade. Ironically, they're often shocked by the harm they cause, and they can be genuinely remorseful. Problem is, because they're blind to their own dangerous emotions, they have difficulty benefiting from these experiences.

The only way to effectively manage rage is to prevent it from happening in the first place — to act *before* you enter into that state of uncontrollable emotion. That's why it is important to take immediate action when you first realize you're getting angry (see Chapter 4) and to follow my advice about how to keep your cool (see Chapter 6).

The nocturnal rager

I've treated quite a few people who experienced *nocturnal rage* — that is, rage that occurred while they were sound asleep. One man called my office quite upset, asking that I see him right away. Why? Because he had awakened to his wife's screams only to find himself on top of her in the bed with his fist poised to strike her. She was hysterical and he was absolutely mortified. This behavior was unprovoked — they were both asleep at the time — and it was totally foreign to his character. For all his life, he had been a positive, easygoing, non-angry man, who avoided conflict wherever he found it. So, why this rage?

After I talked to him and heard his story, I knew the answer. He had been bottling up all sorts of stresses over the past year — not talking about any of his concerns about losing his job, supporting his family, losing the new house he had just bought, having his son leave home — and the dam had finally burst. I suggested that he start opening up and talking more with his wife, who had always been supportive throughout their long marriage. But he was hesitant to burden her with his problems. He left my office thanking me and believing that this would never happen again.

Three days later, I got a second frantic call — his screaming wife had awakened him again, only this time after he had repeatedly punched her in the head. He was ready to take my advice.

Bottom line: Take the blinders off and start paying attention to all the things that are stressing you out before the dam breaks and releases all that pent-up emotion.

Choosing the lesser of two evils

The first few years after I moved to Virginia, I found myself experiencing a lot of road rage. I had lived in several other states and it seemed to me that Virginia drivers were "a bunch of idiots who were all out to kill me." Talk about being angry! A classic example is when I found myself driving down the highway with no traffic either behind or in front of me, and up ahead was a car on my side of the road ready to pull out. You would think the person would wait until I passed before entering the highway, but no, he pulled out right in front of me, forcing me to quickly swerve into the other lane in order to avoid an accident. I thought to myself, "That SOB did that on purpose!"

One day I finally got tired of being angry all the time while I was driving, so I decided to adopt a different perspective on the driving behavior of Virginians. From that day to the present, I tell myself, "They're not out to get me. They're not purposely trying to force me to hit my brakes and swerve. They're just plain ignorant — they don't know any better." Based on my new perspective, I now always move into the other lane just as soon as I see a car on my side of the highway no matter how close or far away. That way, the other person's ignorance doesn't become my problem.

To me, my new viewpoint is what I would call choosing the lesser of two evils: ignorant versus malevolent. I choose ignorant! It doesn't mean that I approve of the way these folks drive — only that I don't get angry anymore.

Think of a situation that has left you feeling irritated, angry, or in a rage lately. Ask yourself: What did that person do that elicited this emotion? And, more important, why did he act that way? Now, see if you can come up with two other alternative explanations for that person's behavior. Take a piece of paper and write down all three points of view. Consider how you will feel based on each of these possibilities. Then pick the one that will produce the *least* adverse emotional consequences — in other words, the lesser of three evils.

For example, let's say you're irritated at your dentist for running late for your scheduled appointment. Your first assumption is: "This guy is so greedy for money that he's packed his day with too many patients, and now we all have to wait!" Okay, maybe that's the case. But try to come up with two other reasons he could be late. Maybe he had to spend extra time with a patient who was really afraid of dentists. In order to help that patient through the exam, the dentist had to take a little more time. How about another possibility? Maybe the dentist's mother is sick and he had to take a phone call from her doctor about her condition. That could be it, too. Now, which of these scenarios would upset you the least? Maybe it's the sick mother. So now, just for the sake of your own stress level, assume that his mother is sick. Take it another step and try to empathize with him. Wow, it must be hard to have to see patients and keep up such a cheerful façade when he's upset about his mother. Maybe if you're understanding of him, you'll help make his day a little easier. (And if nothing else, you'll have kept your irritation from turning into anger and ruining your day.)

Accepting Life for What It Is, Not What It Should Be

Boy, wouldn't it be nice if everything in your world was the way you thought it should be? You wouldn't get angry, if:

- The red light turned green when you thought it should.
- Your wife paid as much attention to you as you thought she should.
- Your kids respected you the way they should.
- Your employer compensated you the way it should.
- Your retirement fund increased the way you thought it should.
- Government officials did what they should to control the deficit.
- Tires lasted as long as they should.
- Your pants fit the way they should.
- Your children made the kind of grades they should.
- God answered your prayers the way He should.
- You had all the rain or sunshine you thought you should.
- People laughed at your jokes the way they should.

The parent-child dilemma

If you don't want to be angry off and on for about 20 years running, don't have children. Most of the anger I see between family members, especially parents and children, has to do with differences in their perceptions of how things *should* be. For instance, parents think their kids should obey their every command, keep a respectful tone, and in one form or another show their gratitude for all they've done for them. Children — certainly adolescents — on the other hand believe they should be free to do what they want, should be able to talk to their parents any way they feel like, and think parents are only doing what they should be doing for them, so they shouldn't need any thanks. Negotiating around all these *should*s is what makes or breaks a parent-child relationship

The problem we all face, unfortunately, is that things don't always work this way. We're forced to deal with life the way it actually *is,* rather than the way we think it should be.

Begin paying attention to how many times you think or say the word *should* in the course of a day. Each time you hear yourself saying "She should . . . ," stop and ask yourself the following three questions:

- ✔ **Who says she shouldn't act that way?** Where is that written down? Is that a fact or simply your opinion? At what point in life did you start deciding how other people should act?

- ✔ **Why shouldn't she act that way?** Isn't she entitled to the same rights of free speech and expression as you are? Shouldn't she act according to how she sees things? Why does your viewpoint count more than hers?

- ✔ **Is the fact that she's not acting as she should worth your getting angry and perhaps ruining your day?**

I used to get mad when my wife wasn't ready to leave to go to a party when I thought should be — so I paced around the house, getting more agitated by the minute, repeatedly hollering up the stairs, "Are you ready yet? Don't you see what time it is?" and then pouting in the car as we drove to the party. It took me half my life to realize two things: (1) That was a really a stupid way to act and (2) None of that made my wife the least bit more punctual. Now, I still get ready on time, but I go down into the den and cool my heels — and my temper — until she appears and says "Okay, let's go."

Becoming More Tolerant

Anger is the emotion of intolerance. Intolerance means you don't accept another person's viewpoint or behavior. Anger says that you think you're right and the other person is wrong. It can't be any simpler than that.

Anger defends the listener against any change in his way of thinking. Instead of accepting the challenge of an honest difference of opinion, the intolerant person resorts to intimidation, insult, or withdrawal — all fueled by anger — as a way of rigidly holding on to his beliefs.

The more intolerant a person, the more intense his anger.

The next time you find yourself getting angry about something another person says or does, do the following:

- ✔ **Remind yourself that if you're secure in your way of thinking, you have absolutely nothing to defend.** Just because someone else thinks differently from the way you think, doesn't mean you're wrong or that you necessarily have to justify your own beliefs and actions.

- ✔ **Instead of being defensive (that's what intolerance is all about!), go on the offense.** Say to the other person, "Tell me more about that. I'd like to understand how you arrived at that opinion. This is your chance to educate me."

- ✔ **Don't personalize the conversation.** Focus on issues not personalities. Direct your commentary to the matter in dispute (for example, "I disagree that parents should give birth-control pills to their teenage daughters") rather than the *person* on the other end of the debate ("You're stupid for thinking that way!").

- ✔ **Look for points of agreement.** Parents, for example, who are in a discussion about whether to furnish birth-control pills to their daughters can begin by agreeing (out loud) that they are, of course, both concerned about the ultimate safety and well being of their kids.

- ✔ **Avoid the use of expletives.** Swearing and cursing only demeans the other person and stifles any productive exchange of ideas. You're better off saying, "I really don't know what to say when you act like that" than saying, "You're an ass, and you know it!"

- ✔ **By all means, avoid contempt.** Contempt — sighing, rolling your eyes — not only conveys a sense of intolerance, it tells the other party you think he (and his ideas) are utterly worthless. It's just a way of saying, "I'm better than you!"

Seeking diversity in all things

The good news is that, as far as I know, there is no gene for intolerance. It's an attitude that people pick up through life experience. If you grow up in a family that tolerates differing points of view, you tend to be like that yourself. The same is true if you're raised in an intolerant family.

One antidote to intolerance — a black-and-white approach to life — is diversity. Intolerance is one way of trying to simplify what is an ever-changing, complex world. Diversity helps you expand your horizons and see that the "sea of ideas, beliefs, and behavior" is vast and endless. There is, in fact, far more gray than black and white. Truth typically is somewhere between what "I" think and what "you" believe.

Diversity is easier to achieve that you may imagine. Here are some tips on how to become a more worldly — and thus more tolerant — person:

- ✔ **Read about religions different from your own.** You can find *For Dummies* books on the major world religions — and most bookstores are filled with all kinds of religion titles.

- ✔ **Buy newspapers from places other than where you live.** If you're from a small town in the Midwest, subscribe to the *New York Times*. If you live in New York City, have your aunt in upstate New York send you her hometown paper.

- ✔ **Every other time you go into a restaurant, try something new.** This forces you out of your comfort zone.

- ✔ **Be adventurous throughout life.**

- ✔ **When you go to a party, look for the person you don't already know and start up a conversation.** If you only talk to the people you know, you're less likely to discover something new.

- ✔ **Travel as extensively as your pocketbook allows.** And try to go to different regions of the country (or the world). When you're there, spend some time talking to the locals.

- ✔ **Make a point of socializing with people from racial and ethnic backgrounds other than your own.**

- ✔ **Read all editorials in the newspaper every day — not just those you agree with.**

- ✔ **Visit museums and art galleries.**

- ✔ **Hang around with people of different ages.** You'll be amazed at how differently folks much younger and older than you are think.

- ✔ **Attend free lectures by local and out-of-town authorities on various subjects.** Most communities offer lecture series or similar cultural experiences. If you live in a very small town, look to a bigger town nearby and make a point of traveling there to take advantage of these things.

- ✔ **Keep your eyes open and your mouth shut.** Learn now, debate later.

Avoiding the media like the plague

A free press comes with a price. These days, especially with the advent of cable news, the media has transformed itself into a polarizing point-counterpoint expression of extreme viewpoints on virtually any topic you can imagine. Exchanges between "experts" are purposefully intense, loud, argumentative, and at times angry. Instead of expanding your intellect, the media foments uncivil discourse and a climate of intolerance. If you weren't angry *before* you started watching cable news, you will be shortly.

Tired of listening to yourself?

For most of my adult life, I was an outspoken, opinionated person, who — even though I didn't realize it at the time — tried to force my viewpoint about how the world works on anyone who would listen. Well, that all changed when I went through a five-year period of depression during which I was forced to finally listen to what others had to say for once.

After I recovered from the depression, I found that I was tired of always listening to my own voice and I rather liked being an active listener. For the first time in my life, I found that I was, and always had been, surrounded by many intelligent, interesting people, including my wife and children, who were eager to share their own unique takes on life, if allowed. What a delightful surprise!

Although televised media is without doubt more stimulating and entertaining, it also arouses more passion. If you're just interested in knowing what's happening in the world around you — without all the angry rhetoric — you're much better off turning to print media (newspapers, news magazines) or local radio and television.

Jerry who?

Twenty years ago, back before workshops on anger management were popular, I was invited to conduct a seminar at Cape Cod. My daughter accompanied me, and one afternoon while we had some free time she and I found ourselves in a very nice gift shop specializing in teddy bears. As we entered the shop, an elderly woman — who turned out to be the owner — welcomed us and said she would help us as soon as she finished up with other customers. She also asked us where we were from. I told her Virginia, and she asked what city we lived in. "Lynchburg," I replied. "You know, the home of Jerry Falwell." The woman said, "I'm sorry, I don't know who that is."

When she had finished with the other customer, she came over and apologized for not knowing

who Reverend Falwell was. "That's okay," I said "I just thought you might make the connection because he's on television so much." She then went on to tell us a fascinating story about how when she was a young woman, she had suffered from depression and had for years tried to get help from scores of mental health providers — all to no avail. But, then she came upon a behavioral psychologist who asked her to begin keeping track of situations that seemed to bring her mood down. The one that mostly came to mind was when she watched the news on TV. So, he told her to quit watching it, which she did. And, according to her, she had not been depressed for the past 25 years. "Good for you," I told her "I think I'll try that myself!" I believe the same advice holds for anger.

Rarely does the media offer you "good news" — it's slanted toward the negative. If you already have a pessimistic, cynical outlook or you're in a bad mood (see Chapter 19), the last thing you need is more negativity — which is just one more thing that predisposes you to anger.

Figuring Out Where Hostility and Resentment Come From

Hostility is an attitude — a feeling of ill will — that we attach to people and circumstances around us. Like resentment, hostility is a perspective that has a circular relationship with emotions like anger and aggressive behavior. In other words, hostile people more often find themselves angry, and vice versa — anger tends to incite hostile thoughts. And, unlike anger, which comes and goes, hostility can be extremely durable.

So, where do these negative attitudes come from? Two sources really:

- ✔ **From your family:** Like many other things, they are learned early in life.

- ✔ **From your unexpressed, unresolved anger:** Think about a cup that you use to drink coffee out of every day. Now suppose you never wash out that cup. What would happen? Each time you drank coffee, there would be a slight residue left in the cup, which would eventually discolor the insides of the cup and give the coffee poured into it each day a bitter taste. That's exactly what happens when you hide your emotions (see Chapter 8) or when you have an unforgiving nature (see Chapter 13). Hostility becomes that bitter taste that you have for life that discolors how you view and interpret life around you. People generally do not become hostile and resentful over night; it's a slow and insidious process.

Hostility and resentment also come from past experiences that carry over into the present and future. They illustrate, in fact, exactly how yesterday's anger can become today's anger, and today's anger becomes tomorrow's anger.

To avoid being a hostile and resentful person, use the anger-management strategies offered throughout this book and do the following:

- ✔ Acknowledge your anger as soon as you experience it.

- ✔ Use your anger to better understand yourself.

✔ Express your anger without venting (see Chapter 5).

✔ Stop saying you're "fine" when you're not.

✔ Confess your anger on a daily basis.

✔ Think of anger as your ally rather than your enemy.

✔ Find healthy ways — like exercise — to let off steam.

✔ Think of anger as a legitimate emotion just like love and joy.

✔ Start saying "Excuse you!" to people who treat you badly.

✔ Let yourself off the hook by forgiving others.

✔ Live in the present, not the past.

✔ Turn your resentments over to a higher power.

✔ Forgo reciprocity — there's no such thing as getting even.

✔ Establish healthy boundaries between yourself and those you love the most.

✔ Come back and discuss the reasons for your anger after you walk away.

✔ Be more charismatic.

✔ Practice stress inoculation.

✔ Balance out your life with positive experiences to offset the negative ones.

Who's more hostile — men or women?

Current research by psychologist Wolfgang Linden and his colleagues at the University of British Columbia challenge the long-held notion that women tend to suppress anger more than men, which can lead to an increase in resentment. On the contrary, Linden found that women tended to use different anger coping techniques — for example, seeking social support from other women with whom they discuss their feelings — than their male counterparts, who relied more on overt aggression (attack the source) as a means of expressing their anger. This suggests that women are more likely to resolve their anger in a timely fashion and not experience the residual effects of chronic hostility.

When in Doubt, Be Assertive

If you lack assertiveness and never stand up for yourself, you're probably full of resentment — and understandably so. Why? Because you're a virtual storehouse of accumulated frustration and anger. You never let your emotions — especially negative ones — see the light of day, so you never let go of them.

I'm reminded of the joke about the four old men who had played golf together for more than three decades. They were always the first group off the tee on Saturday morning and the first to return to the clubhouse. One morning, a fellow golfer approached one of the men as they came in from play, asking how they played that day. "It was rough" was the reply. Someone added, "You know Harry that plays with us. He had a heart attack on the fourth hole." "Oh my God," said the other man "what did you do?" "There was nothing we could do," the man said, "but hit the ball and drag Harry all the way to the end." Maybe the Harry you're dragging around is your own old, unexpressed anger that has now crystallized into that all-enduring attitude — hostility.

Want to let your Harry rest in peace? Consider asserting yourself in the following ways:

- ✔ If you're not satisfied with the service you get in a restaurant, say something to the waiter or, better yet, the manager.

- ✔ Practice politely saying "no" when people (for example, aggressive sales clerks) invade your personal space.

- ✔ If someone asks you to do something (or, worse yet, demands that you do it), ask why before you act.

- ✔ Get used to returning defective merchandise to stores without feeling embarrassed or apologetic.

- ✔ Don't be afraid to argue with salespeople — it's your money after all.

- ✔ If someone pushes her way in line ahead of you, say "Excuse you!" and then nicely ask her to step to the rear.

Chapter 8

Saying What You Feel

. . . .

In This Chapter

▶ Understanding the importance of speaking openly

▶ Appreciating the downside of civility

▶ Asking yourself, "What am I not thinking (and talking) about?

▶ Releasing healthy anger

. . . .

I was listening to talk radio this morning and a man called in to share his thoughts about burning the U.S. flag. He sounded like a mature guy, and he was speaking in a civil tone. At one point, he said, "If people want to burn the flag, that's fine." But then he corrected himself and said, "No, that's not fine. It irritates me, but I guess I mean that there's nothing I can do to stop them. But, no, it's not fine." It sounded like — in that moment — the man had found his true voice.

How often do you find yourself being politically correct about emotion, saying things are fine when they're really not? If you often hide your real feelings, what effect do you think that has on you? Do you find yourself feeling disappointed, disillusioned, and disinterested with the world around you? What do you believe would happen if you were more open and honest about the things that make you angry?

In this chapter, I guide you through answering those questions and show you how to open the door for some healthy expression. This chapter helps you say what you feel rather than what other people may want to hear — and the more you can do that, the better you'll be able to manage your anger.

Why Hiding Your Emotions Isn't Healthy

Emotions are, by their very nature, meant to be brief, transient experiences. Typically, they come and go throughout the day — moving you in various directions, as evidenced by changes in your behavior. Anger, for example, triggers a fight-or-flight response that is prewired into your nervous system. Not acting on an emotion like anger is unnatural and, in some instances, can be unhealthy. Emotions reflect changes in physiology — elevations in blood pressure, heart rate, blood sugar, and muscle tension — that are usually harmless because they're short lived (that is, if you express them). Emotions that are not expressed remain trapped within your body, causing a sustained state of physiological tension — and that can be deadly.

No such thing as unexpressed anger

Suggesting that anger is either expressed or unexpressed is actually untrue. All anger is expressed — the question is how. You probably think that you're expressing your anger when you do so in a way that other people can see, hear, or feel. Otherwise, you figure, you're not expressing it. But the reality is that *all* anger is expressed — some of it in ways that aren't observable right away. For example, you may not *look* or *sound* angry, but your anger may be expressing itself in your cardiovascular system (through high blood pressure or migraine headaches), your gastrointestinal system (through irritable bowel syndrome [IBS] or a spastic colon), or your musculoskeletal system (through TMJ or tension headaches).

The non-injury injury

Over the years, I've been impressed with how many of my clients suffering from back pain actually never had an injury to their backs. I remember one man — a really nice guy — who came in complaining of unremitting pain in his lower back that he said began when he put his foot on a shovel to dig a hole in sand, something he did countless times over the years. That was the injury that caused him unbearable pain, resulted in extensive medical treatment, and caused him to be unemployed.

Upon further investigation, it turned out that this man had quit this same employer some years before because he was dissatisfied (angry) about low pay, lack of benefits, and mistreatment by his foreman. He had taken a much better job in another state and was quite happy at work until his new employer unexpectedly declared bankruptcy. He was then forced to return to his old job — same low pay, lack of benefits, and foreman — all the while feeling both defeated and dejected. His way of coping was to "grin and bear it," absorb whatever mistreatment came his way, and never — I mean *never* — let himself get angry.

Then, one day — like any other day — his back suddenly went out. The result: He could get paid without returning to work and also avoid dealing with his boss. I agreed the man had been injured — but it was his *spirit* that was injured, not his back. After he went through my pain rehabilitation program, where he got insight into the inner dynamics of his back pain, he found new employment and his back eventually quit hurting.

Or anger may express itself in negative attitudes — pessimism, cynicism, hopelessness, bitterness, and stubbornness — or some form of avoidance behavior (giving people the silent treatment), oppositional behavior ("I don't *think* so!"), or passive-aggressive behavior ("I'm sorry — did you want something?"). Anger may also sour your mood and leave you feeling down or depressed. You suddenly lose the enthusiasm you had previously. (For additional examples, take a look at the anger-health checklist in Chapter 3.)

Dissatisfaction can be lethal

Being chronically — morning, noon, and night — dissatisfied can be dangerous to your health. Dr. Ernest Harburg and his colleagues at the University of Michigan did a study asking people how satisfied they were with their jobs. They specifically asked the people how satisfied they were:

- ✔ That their job offered an opportunity to earn a higher salary

- ✔ That they had an opportunity to work with people who were friendly and helpful

- ✔ With their ability to acquire new skills in their line of work

- ✔ With job security (were they not likely to get laid off or fired)

- ✔ That they were allowed to do those things they were best at on their jobs

- ✔ That they had an opportunity to get ahead at work (be promoted)

He also asked questions to determine whether they tended to habitually express or suppress their anger. Interestingly, what I found when I analyzed these data was that those employees who were highly dissatisfied at work but who suppressed their anger had, by far, the highest blood-pressure levels on average — as compared to those who were highly satisfied with their work or dissatisfied workers who expressed their anger in some way. And the increase in blood pressure resulting from this combination of chronic dissatisfaction and suppressed anger was enough to place them at risk for potentially lethal heart attacks and strokes.

The same, it turned out, was true when they asked similar questions to determine how satisfied these people were with their home/family situation. Again, those who were the most dissatisfied but least expressive about their anger had the highest blood pressure.

Focusing on your own part — and letting other people focus on theirs

His company's human resource manager referred Carl for anger management. A man in his late 50s, who had worked at the same job for almost 20 years, Carl was now being disciplined for several recent rather uncharacteristic outbursts of anger, directed at his immediate supervisor. Carl had been given an ultimatum: Learn to keep your cool or you're fired! To make matters worse, recent stresses at work had suddenly caused Carl to have problems with his blood pressure and cholesterol levels, even though he had successfully managed both with medication for years. The problem, as Carl saw it, was that his boss was young, inexperienced, and incompetent — in his words, "an idiot who doesn't have a clue about how we do things around here."

Clearly, Carl was dissatisfied — not with his own work, but rather with how his new boss did his. He had tried for the longest time to let things ride and keep his dissatisfaction to himself, but lately he had boiled over with anger. Given his age, Carl couldn't afford to lose his job and benefits and he most assuredly didn't want to "stroke out" because of his job, but he was at a loss as to what he could do to resolve his anger.

I suggested that he make a compromise — that he be content to be satisfied with how he did *his* job and let his boss answer to those above him for his own mistakes. "Do your part as well as ever, sign off on it, and if your boss screws things up after that, that's his problem," I said. "Just be responsible for yourself, not for the whole world."

It worked. I'm not sure how his boss is doing, but Carl's blood pressure and cholesterol levels are once again stable, he hasn't had any more outbursts, and his human resources manager is delighted with how things turned out. And he's still working!

Being Civil Doesn't Always Mean Being Nice

Being civil simply means being a good citizen — someone who operates within the social rules of a society. It means acting toward others in ways that show mutual respect. It means not being rude, insensitive, thoughtless, and purposely antagonistic. On the other hand, it doesn't mean that you're always nice, tolerant, or accepting of whatever mistreatment comes your way. It doesn't require that you be passive, someone's doormat, or the proverbial pushover. And, it doesn't mean that you don't ever experience or express reasonable levels of anger.

Civil people get irritated and angry, but they express it in constructive ways (see Chapter 11 for examples). They respond to their angry feelings instead of reacting in some mindless, shoot-from-the-hip kind of way (see Chapter 6). And they speak out in ways that inform and educate those within hearing distance about the issues that underlie their anger (see Chapter 5).

Stop saying "I'm fine" when you're not

You may have found how to avoid taking responsibility for your anger by always saying "I'm fine!" even in circumstances where that's far from the truth. This response is an example of what politicians call a *non-response response.* It's a polite way of saying, "I'm not going to tell you how I feel. Maybe I don't trust whether you'll accept my feelings. Maybe you'll get mad because I'm mad. Or maybe I don't trust my feelings myself — should I really feel that irritated?" You'd be surprised how many of my therapy clients, when I ask them how they are, say, "Fine." My immediate thought is, "Well, if you're fine, why are you sitting on my couch?"

The next time someone asks you how you feel about something, choose an emotional label that fits the situation — for example, happy, sad, mad, glad. Being honest about how you're doing helps reduce your tension and can help keep you from getting angrier.

Stop apologizing for what others do

When someone bumps into you out in public, don't say, "Excuse me." *You* haven't done anything wrong — *he* has. *You're* not the inconsiderate person here — *he* is. So, why should you apologize? Apologizing is what people do when they take ownership for some misdeed. Unless you're the one who rammed into someone, you shouldn't apologize. What you should do instead is say, "Excuse you!" It's a civil way of giving the person feedback about his boorish behavior. (I'm not suggesting that everyone who bumps into you does it intentionally — you still want to give people the benefit of the doubt — but don't apologize unless you were the one who slammed into him.)

If "Excuse you!" feels a bit rude, it's okay to say "Pardon you" — it still puts the responsibility where it belongs.

If you're going to be Type A, be charismatic

Type A's who are also charismatic — enthusiastic, inspiring, animated, and emotionally expressive — appear less at risk for coronary heart disease than Type A's who lack this quality. How do you know if someone is charismatic? They're the ones who can't keep still when the music starts, who laugh outrageously when they hear something funny, whose emotions show on their face, and who aren't shy around strangers. They release a lot of tension by expressing their feelings openly and accurately with no real regard for what others might say or think. It's the quiet, stoic, nonexpressive Type A's — the ones who keep their hostility close to the vest — whose health is in danger.

Apologizing for someone else's behavior is often seen by them as a way of condoning what they're doing. If someone bumps into you, what is it that you're exuding — the fact that you had the audacity to be in their way? Is that how you really feel and is that the message you want to send?

Express your anger without worrying that you're being a bitch

Despite the advances women have made worldwide — political, economic, social — some remnants of the old world order, in which there were different standards of what constitutes acceptable emotional behavior among men and women, remain. Even today, women who show signs of anger and who express themselves in some assertive way are likely to be labeled a "bitch" for doing so. No such reference is made to men who do exactly the same thing. Many women are sensitive to this double standard and are hesitant to be completely honest about their feelings unless those feelings are positive ones. (The reverse is true when it comes to feelings such as grief, fear, and depression. Men who openly acknowledge such feelings tend to be viewed — by themselves and others — as weak and effeminate.)

If being a bitch means you admit it when you're irritated or even angry, if it means setting limits on the bad behavior of others, if it means saying "Well, excuse you!" when it's deserved, then my advice is to be a bitch. Be a *proud* bitch, be an *articulate* (no profanity please) bitch, be a *passionate* bitch, be a *self-assured* bitch, be a *charismatic* bitch, and be a *hold-your-head-up-high-and-look-your-adversary-in-the-eye* bitch. And then let that be the other person's problem.

Stop Having Issues and Start Having Feelings

One of the trendy catchphrases used these days to describe people who are in some type of conflict is, "She's got issues." *Issues* are those problematic situations that trigger emotions like fear, sadness, and anger. The problem I see, though, is that many people are so focused on their issues that they lose sight of what it is they're actually *feeling*.

The following conversation with one of my anger-management clients illustrates how difficult it can be to get a person to stop having issues and start having feelings:

> **Gentry:** How have things been at work this week?
>
> **Client:** The same. My supervisor is still not including me in things that go on in the office, like a luncheon that was given for one of our staff members who's leaving. Everybody else, it seems, knew about it but me.
>
> **Gentry:** And how did that make you feel?
>
> **Client:** I didn't think it was fair.
>
> **Gentry:** That's what you thought. I want to know how you *felt* about it.
>
> **Client:** (Pause) I'm not sure what you want. It's just another example of how I'm excluded around the office.
>
> **Gentry:** I get the part about being excluded. What I want you to tell me is how you *felt* when you realized, once again, that you had been left out.
>
> **Client:** (Exasperated) I told you — I thought it was unfair! I don't know what else you want me to say.
>
> **Gentry:** Try this: When you found that you had been excluded from the luncheon, did you feel happy, sad, mad, or glad? Choose one.
>
> **Client:** You keep asking me how I feel about things. I don't know. None of those fit. I just thought it was unfair. (Looks perplexed.)

His employer had referred this man to me because he was seen as being uncooperative with co-workers and insolent toward his boss, both of which he denied. "I don't know why they want me to come to anger management, because I'm not angry," he said. The problem, as I saw it, was that he *was* angry (a natural response to being excluded). But instead of being able to say how he felt, he acted out his anger through what his superior saw as oppositional behavior. I believed him when he said he wasn't angry — I don't think he realized he was.

Practice what I call *feeling-cause language.* Start with how you feel ("I am irritated . . .") and then identify the issue that provoked the feeling (". . . because I always seem to be excluded from whatever is going on in the office"). My research has found that feeling-cause statements serve to reduce hostile behavior in others and engender empathy — a concern for your welfare — in the person with whom you have an issue. Would the client I mention earlier have continued to be excluded by his supervisor if he had simply told him how he felt and why he felt that way, instead of communicating his feelings the way he did? Possibly, but you never know.

Having a good cry is not the answer

A study of 177 female college undergraduates found that crying was a symptom of suppressed anger, which in turn was associated with a higher risk for depression and anxiety. Younger women tended to cry more often than older women. Having a "good cry" may, in fact, not be as good for your health as mental health professionals once thought.

Walking Away and Still Having Your Say

If you give people a choice of how to respond to someone else's anger (or their own anger at someone else's behavior), they'll typically either stand and fight back or run away. The old fight-or-flight response is built into your nervous system. Unfortunately, neither of these choices results in an effective resolution of whatever it is that underlies the emotional response.

My friend Ernest Harburg at the University of Michigan classifies both of these extreme responses under the heading of *resentful* anger coping, which he contrasts with what he calls *reflective* coping (for example, talking to someone about your anger after you've cooled down). The same distinction, I believe, holds true when you get mad at someone else. You can express your anger immediately in some hostile, aggressive manner or you can simply walk (or stomp!) off without a word. *Or* you can choose a middle-of-the-road response — walk off until you cool down and then return later to the source of your anger and verbalize exactly why you feel the way you do.

Harburg found that people who tended more often to use the reflective anger coping style had lower blood pressure than those whose primary way of dealing with anger was resentful. He also noted that the tendency to utilize reflective anger coping was greater among women and middle-class respondents (those who had more education, higher family incomes, and higher job status). They appeared to be more immune from the unhealthy effects of other people's anger.

Try the following self-role-playing exercise:

1. **Think of some recent situation where you felt you were treated unfairly or unjustly but didn't say how you felt at the time.**

2. **Write out the situation on a piece of paper in as much detail as possible.**

3. **Read what you've written down.**

4. **Write down how you felt about the situation — not what you thought or what you did, but how you *felt* (your emotions).**

   It's okay to list more than one emotion — for example, "I was angry and hurt."

5. **Write down the cause of your feelings ("She made an unkind remark about my weight").**

6. **Write down what you want to say to the person with whom you were angry.**

   Be sure to use feeling-cause language, starting with feeling and then the cause (see "Stop Having Issues and Start Having Feelings" earlier in this chapter). Avoid using inflammatory language (swear words).

7. **Now, ask yourself how you feel — better, relieved?**

8. **Reinforce what you've done here with a positive self-statement — "Good for me! Couldn't happen to a nicer guy!"**

Make this a weekly exercise until you get better at expressing your feelings on a day-to-day basis.

Emotional maturity: You're not born with it

You don't start out life knowing how to manage your emotions well. You have to discover how to manage your emotions as you journey through life — a journey toward emotional maturity.

In a study of eighth-grade school students, I found that only one-quarter of the boys and less than a third of the girls chose the mature way of dealing with anger from another student — walk away and come back later to discuss the problem. The vast majority of people that age, who by anybody's definition are immature, was to fight back — that is, answer anger with anger. Simply put, they don't know any better!

What was even worse, however, was the fact that reflective anger expression seemed to *decrease* as children moved through their middle school years — grades 6 through 8 — and into high school. That's right — they appeared to be getting more emotionally *immature* as they got older, clearly moving in the wrong direction. What we're still trying to figure out is how this affects the way these individuals will handle anger when they reach adulthood.

Remember: If you want to be seen by others as a mature person, you have to handle your emotions — including anger — in something other than a childlike manner. Tantrums may be a normal occurrence for 2-year-olds, but not for those who have supposedly reached adulthood.

Chapter 9

Confessing Your Anger

· ·

· ·

I was teaching an anger seminar at a local college. One evening, I asked students to begin class by quietly writing down how they were feeling. They were told to focus specifically on negative feelings, but the feelings could be about anything or anyone in their day-to-day lives — classes, grades, relationships, family, finances. . . . Some students began writing immediately, while others protested, "I don't have any negative feelings. I'm good! I don't have anything to write about." I encouraged them to proceed anyway.

After a few minutes, the students were writing furiously, filling up page after page with emotion. At the end of 20 minutes, I told them to stop and asked them how they felt. One young woman who was reluctant to do the exercise in the first place spoke up and said, "I feel terrible — like I'm going to explode! I don't know where all these feelings came from — about my anger at my mother and my roommate. I was fine and now I feel awful." Other students reported similar experiences. Some were tearful as they spoke. Many felt relieved, as though they had unburdened themselves. Mostly they were amazed at how powerful this simple exercise was in tapping into their hidden emotional life.

In this chapter, I walk you through an exercise called *emotional journaling*. It's a technique that will allow you to confess — to yourself — what is in your heart but not necessarily on your mind. Journaling puts you in touch with emotions — like anger — that you have intentionally tucked away because they make you feel uncomfortable and you don't want to deal with them. Problem is, these emotions build up over time and eventually come back to haunt you. By not dealing with today's irritations, you carry them forward into tomorrow. You end up doing the very thing you've been trying so hard not to do — you get mad.

Tell me what you're not thinking

A patient of mine — I'll call him Tom — suffered from depression. One of Tom's biggest problems was that he was unable to sleep. He found himself night after night wide awake for hours in bed or, worse yet, sitting and staring aimlessly at the television set at 3:00 in the morning.

Repeatedly, I asked Tom, "What was going through your mind while you were trying to get to sleep?" His answer was always the same, "Nothing — I wasn't thinking about anything."

Then one day I decided to put a different question to him: "Tell me what you *weren't* thinking about as you were lying there awake." Tom sat there for a moment and then suddenly burst into tears, confessing how sad he was about his best friend's untimely death several months earlier, how much he missed his father who

recently died of cancer, how worried he was about losing his job because of a major reorganization within his company, his feeling of emptiness now that his daughter had left for college, and more.

Like any good therapist (or priest, rabbi, friend, spouse, or teacher), I sat quietly and heard his confession. That was the therapeutic breakthrough! Tom's homework assignment from that session on was to spend 15 minutes each evening before he went to bed writing out all his negative feelings for that day. Tom quickly discovered that the real therapy is not waiting to make a weekly confession to a professional, but rather confessing to *himself* — about his emotional vulnerability. In no time at all, he was sleeping like a baby and his depression slowly began to lift.

Confession: It's Good for What Ails You

Behavioral medicine (the science that connects mind and body) advises that excessive inhibition of emotions, especially strong emotions like anger, is unhealthy. That's right — holding back on emotions can actually make you sick. It makes sense if you think about it. Holding back on emotions is unnatural for humans. As babies, we begin life by crying whenever we're uncomfortable — hungry, thirsty, lonely, or in pain. But then life gets a hold of us and teaches us to do just the opposite — to keep our feelings to ourselves and, in effect, cry inside. Our bodies want to let go, but our minds tell us to hold back.

So, we end up in a state of emotional paralysis, which plays itself out in a variety of emotional and physical ailments. Some of those ailments include

- High blood pressure
- Insomnia
- Headaches
- Bruxism (grinding your teeth)
- TMJ (pain in the jaw joint)

10,000 Israelis can't be wrong

A fascinating study of 10,000 Israeli male civil-service employees looked at a total of 90 medical, social, and psychological factors that might explain the development of hypertension. Four of the factors that made a real difference in a person's odds of having high blood pressure were:

✔ Brooding over being hurt by a co-worker

✔ Brooding over being hurt by a supervisor

✔ Restraining from retaliating when being hurt by a supervisor

✔ Keeping conflicts with one's spouse to oneself

Restraining and repressing emotions were found to have the same effect on blood pressure as cigarette smoking and obesity do.

✔ Back spasms

✔ Impaired immune function

✔ Depression

✔ Panic attacks

Will confessing your negative feelings on a regular basis result in a decrease in your need for medical services or in how often you end up being absent from work because of illness? Current science suggests that the answer is yes.

Who Can Benefit from Confessing

If you're still somewhat unsure whether you really need this confession exercise in order to control your anger in the days, months, and years ahead, the following sections fill you in on the types of people who need to (and will benefit from) keeping an anger journal. If you see yourself in any of these categories, you can benefit from the experience.

Men in general

There tend to be two distinct types of men:

✔ Those who all too readily express their emotions as they experience them

✔ Those who deny their feelings and act cool

The latter group far outnumbers the former, interestingly even when it involves getting angry. For every man who loses his cool in public, there are nine more who keep their feelings under control — to the point where they don't even realize that they're angry. A colleague of mine who studies the effect of emotions such as anger, depression, and anxiety on heart disease, made this very point in titling one of his papers, "Men deny and women cry. . . ."

African-American men

Contrary to accounts in the mainstream media, African-American men are much more likely to keep their anger bottled up inside than are African-American women or white men and women. In one public-health survey of over 1,000 residents of an urban Midwest city, African-American men were almost twice as likely to deny feeling angry or keep such feelings to themselves than white men of comparable age.

Women who cry a lot

Women who engage in more emotional crying are more likely to suppress angry feelings than those who don't cry. Crying because you're slicing onions or have an allergy doesn't count!

People who are prone to guilt

Guilt is a real barrier to emotional expression. For example, one study I was involved in many years ago found that women who felt guilty about expressing anger toward their parents had higher blood pressure than women who weren't sorry about their outrageous behavior. Many women, I suspect, discover early in life that it's easier to bottle up anger than it is to get rid of guilt.

People who are too empathetic

Normally *empathy* (being in sync with another person's emotions) is a good thing. But when you have too much empathy, it can cause you to be hide your true emotions so that you don't hurt someone else's feelings.

People who are hostile

Hostility is an attitude that all too often leads to anger. The combination of hostility and anger-suppression tendencies can be lethal when it comes to things like blood pressure and all the health problems that go along with that.

People who lack charisma

If you're charismatic, you have that personal magnetism that allows you to easily attract and influence others. You don't need to keep an anger journal because everyone already knows how you feel about things — good or bad. Actually, that's a big part of your appeal!

But for the less charismatic, emotions are not as easily expressed. Here are some indicators of lacking charisma:

- ✔ A subdued laugh
- ✔ A neutral facial expression (you'll make a better poker player!)
- ✔ A desire to remain unnoticed in a crowd

Introverts

An *introvert* is a private person, someone who tends to be shy and timid. His emotions are not available for public scrutiny. He tends to be serious and cautious about life, and he plays by the rules imposed by society — usually without complaint. Introverts are the proverbial nice guys and gals who tend to say things are fine when they're really not. Introverts are self-contained personalities, so emotional journaling should come easy to them.

People who have suffered a lot of trauma

The more that human beings suffer unusual, intense, traumatic experiences — such as child abuse, rape, death of a child, loss of a spouse — the more likely they are to spend a lot of energy defending themselves from future hurts. One way to do this is to ignore your feelings about what goes on in your day-to-day life, going about your business, smiling, and reassuring everyone that you are "okay" no matter what. Journaling is a process by which you can heal from within by both acknowledging and grieving over the damage the trauma caused in your life.

One breakdown is enough

Someone I know well had a nervous breakdown at age 45. Basically, he appeared to be fine one day and then suddenly, without warning, became a deeply depressed man the next. It took him five years of therapy and medication to get back to normal. Once a week year after year, he drove to a nearby city to make his confession about all the difficulties in his life — raised in an alcoholic, violent family; seriously ill as a child; living in public housing during his adolescent years; scores of personal rejections; loss of loved ones; and on and on — to a psychiatrist who listened without judgment to his rage, despair, hopelessness, fear, and abiding sadness.

It took a while, but he purged himself of all that stuff, and he's been unbelievably happy and healthy for the past decade. Somewhere in the middle of all that therapy — after he got some insight into the perils of storing up bad feelings — he vowed to himself that for the remainder of his life he would laugh more, love more, cry more, fuss more, and use words like *hurt, sad,* and *scared* more when people asked him how he was doing. So far, he's kept his vow.

People who are chronically ill

People who live with chronic, progressive, and disabling illness — such as multiple sclerosis, arthritis, fibromyalgia, diabetes, asthma — experience a whole host of negative emotions in their never-ending struggle to remain alive. Bottling up emotions like anger and sadness only serves to heighten their struggle to maintain some quality of life.

Young people

As people grow older, they tend to be more open with their feelings. Maybe it's because at their age they believe they have less to lose by being honest about how they feel about life. Or maybe somewhere along life's way they achieved a measure of wisdom about how to deal with emotions in a healthy way. Either way, they have a distinct advantage over their younger counterparts.

Understanding the Difference between a Diary and a Journal

Keeping an anger journal is not the same as keeping a diary. Anger diaries can be useful in monitoring anger throughout the day. They allow you to keep track of how many times you experience anger, how intense the feelings are each time, and how long your anger lasts — information that helps you measure just how angry you are (see Chapter 2 for more). But that's all an anger diary does.

An anger *journal* does much more. Keeping an anger journal requires that you actually put your feelings into words, not numbers, and that you describe the context in which your feelings arose. An anger diary might typically read: "Got angry at 11:30 a.m.; rated as a 5 on 10-point scale; lasted about 20 minutes." An anger journal, on the other hand, might read: "I really got angry at lunchtime when my friend, Amy, once again failed to show up. I can't believe she's that irresponsible! I would never treat her that way. She obviously has no respect for me whatsoever. I don't understand why I let people treat me that way."

As you can see, anger journals are more revealing. They tell you something about yourself more than just the fact that you got angry. In this example, the writer can begin to appreciate the fact that her anger isn't the result of her irresponsible friend (the world is full of those!), but rather her willingness to let other people treat her badly without standing up for herself. Her real confession here is that: "I don't respect myself enough to command respect from others."

Some people keep anger diaries to see if their anger experience is changing over time — the diaries provide an opportunity to look back and answer the question, "Am I becoming a less angry person?" Journals, on the other hand, are only useful at the time you write them — you write, you read, you learn, and then you discard them. With journaling, each day is a new day!

Telling Your Story Your Way

Making your confession, in this case about anger and other unpleasant emotions, is about telling a story — *your* story. How you construct that story, however, makes the difference between whether or not this exercise is a therapeutic one. Just like there are rules for Catholics who make their confession to their priest, there are rules about making this type of confession. In the following sections, I cover some of the more important rules that you should abide by when working on your anger journal.

Make yourself the audience

In confessing the emotions that made up your day, you are both the speaker and the audience. In effect, you're entering into a private conversation that is for your eyes only. You won't share your confession with anyone and your confession will end when you complete the exercise. So, there is no need to construct a story to impress, educate, or make someone else feel better.

I can't emphasize this enough: Your anger journal is meant to be a dialogue between you and yourself, not between you and someone else. In my office practice, for example, when I ask patients to journal, I make it clear from the outset that I won't read what they write, nor do I want them to read their journals to me after they finish. The exercise is for their benefit, not mine! All I ask when they finish is that they tell me how they feel and to summarize what, if anything, they discovered about themselves in that few minutes.

Use the first person

Writing in the first person (using *I*) may be the most difficult aspect of making your confession. Most people are so accustomed to defining and understanding their emotional experiences in terms of *other* people's actions that they feel things in the third person. To illustrate this, think about how you and others you know talk about anger:

"My **mother** made me so angry."

"My **boss** got me so pissed off!"

"If **they** didn't push my buttons, I wouldn't get so mad."

If you think about your emotions like this and you write this way in your journal, everything you glean will be about those other people and not about yourself. Writing in the first person makes you responsible for your emotions:

"**I** got so angry at my mother."

"**I** got pissed off at my boss."

"**I** get angry when they push my buttons."

If you write in the third person about your emotions, you'll feel more like a victim — a victim of the other person's behavior. And, victims end up feeling *more* angry when they finish writing, not less. Feeling more upset is exactly the opposite of what you want to accomplish with this exercise.

Don't worry about grammar

You don't have to be an English major to keep an anger journal. What is important here is putting your true feelings into words that not only gives you some immediate relief from the physical tension required to hold on to unexpressed emotion, but also educates you about your own emotional self.

Grammar, spelling, and punctuation are completely irrelevant. (So you have a few dangling participles or split infinitives? Who cares!) My advice instead is to:

- Write spontaneously.
- Write carelessly.
- Write with abandonment.
- Write continuously.
- Write without a clear sense of purpose.
- Write with your heart, not your head.
- Write with passion, not perspective (perspective will come later).
- Write for no one but yourself.
- Write as if this is the last conversation you will ever have on earth.
- Write just for the hell of it!.
- Write first, read later.

Focus on the negative

There is no medicinal effect to confessing positive emotions. Storing up feelings of joy and satisfaction will not make you sick, whereas storing up emotions such as anger and sadness will. So, the focus of an anger journal must be on anger and other negative feelings. What you're trying to do here is to purge those feelings that can poison your life as time goes by (more about this in Chapter 3). Think of it this way: Holding on to positive feelings leads to contentment; holding on to negative emotions ends up in resentment. The aim of the anger journal is to avoid the latter.

You may confuse feelings with thoughts and actions such that, if asked about how you feel, you'll answer, "Well, I thought he was stupid!" or "I just got up and left after I realized that she forgot about our lunch meeting." Emotions are simply statements about how happy, mad, sad, or glad you are, not why you feel that way or what you're going to do about those feelings.

You may not be fluent when it comes to emotional terminology. In fact, even if you aced your SAT vocabulary words, your *emotional* vocabulary may be limited to a few general terms like *upset, bothered,* and *nervous.* Here is a list of words people often use to describe the emotion of anger. If you are at a loss for words to describe your feelings, you may want to choose some from this list.

- ✔ Annoyed
- ✔ Disappointed
- ✔ Disgusted
- ✔ Displeased
- ✔ Dissatisfied
- ✔ Enraged
- ✔ Fuming
- ✔ Furious
- ✔ Incensed
- ✔ Indignant
- ✔ Irate
- ✔ Irritated
- ✔ Mad
- ✔ Outraged
- ✔ Pissed
- ✔ Vexed

Establish causal connections

In carrying out this exercise, try to identify the causes of your negative feelings. In other words, as you write in your journal, you need to ask yourself exactly *why* you felt angry, sad, or hurt. Although simply acknowledging uncomfortable emotions through journal writing can purge these feelings (and the tension that accompanies them) from your mind and body, that alone will not provide the insight and understanding of why anger plays such a prominent role in your emotional life. The insight — which is how you eventually gain greater control over your anger — comes from giving meaning to these feelings.

Here are some excerpts from an anger journal kept by Carol, a 22-year-old single mom, who was trying to understand why she stayed irritated so much of the time:

> "I got really annoyed **because** the kids wouldn't stop running through the house when I told them not to."

> "**Why** do I always have to get mad before anyone **understands** that I need some help getting everything done around here?"

"I think I'll go crazy if one more person tells me that there's no **reason** for me to get so upset — I've got plenty of reasons!"

"I **realize** I need help; I just don't know where to turn."

The boldface words help Carol engage in some much needed self-reflection, which will eventually lead to self-correction. In this case, what Carol is confessing to herself is that she can't deal with life's challenges without support. If she gets the message and acts on it, her situation will become much less stressful and she'll have a lot less reason to constantly be on the verge of becoming angry. If she doesn't hear her own confession, however, her emotional life will remain unchanged.

Write until time is up

Give yourself sufficient time to do the exercise in a meaningful way. I recommend 15 to 20 minutes. Make it easy on yourself by setting a kitchen timer (or some other type of timekeeping device) and writing until you hear the bell, which is your cue to stop what you're doing immediately. Stop writing even if you're in midsentence or haven't completed your thought.

Grammar and sentence construction are not important. What is important is that you write until time is up.

If you do run out of things to write about before the end of the allotted time (not likely when you get started!), go back and read what you've already written and find something that you can expand on. Trust me: With a little prompting, you'll quickly tap back into those emotions that are just waiting for a chance to be expressed.

Don't let emotions get in the way

Most likely you'll feel relieved, content, and far less tense when you finish with your anger journal for the day. That, after all, is the goal of the exercise. But sometimes — typically when you first start journaling — you may also experience negative emotions such as sadness, apprehension, and nervousness. These feelings may be quite strong and can even be overwhelming at the moment. Look back at the example I gave in the introduction to this chapter about the reactions of my students — some were in tears, others felt like they would explode. Keep in mind that these feelings are natural — after all, you're confronting uncomfortable emotions that you've kept hidden away throughout the day — and they usually go away quickly.

If you become upset while you're writing in your journal, don't let the feelings stop you from completing your work. You can write and cry at the same time, right?

If the negative feelings you encounter after journaling are too strong for you to handle or if the feelings persist and interfere with your day-to-day life, consider stopping the exercise and talk to a therapist. Counseling provides a safe, structured, and supportive environment in which you can make your confession. And if you need to talk to someone, it doesn't mean that you're crazy — everyone needs some outside help from time to time.

Suspend judgment

Human beings are, by definition, judgmental creatures. You make literally thousands of judgments each and every day of your life about one thing or another: What should you wear today? What should you have for breakfast? Which freeway should you to take to work? Where should you have lunch? Which emotions should you express and which ones should you keep to yourself?

Unfortunately, anger is one of those emotions that people tend to judge harshly. You may think of anger as one of the "bad" feelings, and you may assume that no one around you wants to hear about your anger. You probably think it's all right to tell another person you feel wonderful, happy, or blessed if they ask how you are, but I'm betting you won't be as honest or candid if the answer is instead "bitchy, pissed off, and mad as hell!"

You're telling yourself that the world around you doesn't really want hear the bad news about your emotional life — they only want the good news. If there is no good news, then the best course of action is to keep quiet or lie — "I'm fine." And, maybe you're right. But judgments like this cause you to store up negative feelings like irritation, sadness, and hopelessness — feelings that need to be confessed later on.

Don't be judgmental when writing in your journal. Be open, honest, and forthright. As the famed sportscaster Howard Cosell used to say, "I tell it like it is." Adopt the same motto for your anger journal.

As far as the rest of your world is concerned, you're writing in your journal with anonymity. What you write is for your eyes only. No one else is going to see what you write, so they can't judge it — and you shouldn't either. This may be harder for you to do than you think. You may be so used to critiquing your emotions as — or before — you experience them in order to be politically correct that letting the feelings flow freely may be difficult at first. That's okay. In fact, that is also part of the goal — helping you become a less emotionally constricted person.

Stick to pen and pencil

You're probably asking yourself, "Can't I make my confession on the computer? That's how I communicate with the rest of the world." Well, of course, you can. But I encourage you instead to stick to some old-fashioned technology for this exercise — pen and pencil. The reasoning behind this is simply that writing by hand is a much more intimate mode of expression. There's something much more personal about hand-written messages than those that are typed or e-mailed. I remember getting a typed memo once from a friend telling me off in a very angry way. I found the whole thing so funny that I threw it away without ever fully appreciating what his grievance was. I would have much preferred a penned ("Dear Doyle . . .") note advising me that he would think of me from that day forth as a "no good son-of-a-bitch!"

If writing is not your thing and you tend to be more fluent (and comfortable) with the spoken word, then you may want to find a tape recorder and use that. But don't change anything else — talk for your ears only, speak in the first person, continue the conversation for 15 to 20 minutes, suspend judgment, and so forth.

Keeping a safe distance

Not too long ago, I was invited to apply for a major administrative position in a large university. I was delighted. I sent all my materials (which everyone agreed were impressive) and was soon notified that they wanted me and my wife to come for a visit. We gladly accepted and ended up spending three enlightening but grueling 16-hour days meeting with countless people, touring the campus, finding out all about the history of the school, and looking at real estate. We left exhausted but optimistic that an offer would be forthcoming.

When I didn't hear anything from the university after ten days (they had said a decision would be made in five or six days), I e-mailed the head of the search committee and asked how things were proceeding. I was shocked by what came next. He immediately replied via e-mail that I would be receiving a letter in the next day or two indicating that in the end I was judged as "unacceptable" for the position in question. And that was it!

When I tried to talk to him about what had happened (because everyone — including him — had been so positive throughout my time there), he made it clear — again via e-mail — that he wasn't at liberty to talk about it any further. I subsequently found out what had transpired behind the scenes and that I was just the latest of many acceptable candidates who had been turned away. I think I was more bothered — angry, in fact — about how I was told about the decision than the decision itself. They certainly have a right to choose or not choose anyone they like. But to do it that impersonally — wow! All I can think is that they were trying to distance themselves from their own sense of shame in the Machiavellian way they had comported themselves.

Find a quite place

You need to find a quite place to write in your anger journal, a place where you can be alone (and uninterrupted) with your thoughts and feelings. Journaling is not a community activity. If you can't allow yourself any personal time until everyone else's needs are taken care of and all the chores are done, then make writing in your journal the last thing you do — after everyone else has been safely put to bed. Another good time (though sometimes a bit tricky to engineer) is right after you come home from a day at work but before you jump headfirst into the demands and challenges of the evening (or as some put it — the second half of your workday). In fact, if you purge the unwanted emotions of the day, you'll most assuredly enjoy better relationships with your loved ones.

If you have the kind of job where you find yourself more and more fed up as the day progresses, you may want to use your lunch break to journal. It may make the rest of the workday go a little smoother and avoid any blowups along the way.

You probably don't want to do this over a cup of coffee at Starbucks (that's not a good place to access strong emotions and start crying). If there's a place of worship (like a church or synagogue) nearby (ah, sanctuary!), that would be perfect. Even a quiet corner in a library, or a park bench would do the trick.

Chapter 10

Becoming a Type B

. . . .

In This Chapter

▶ Listing your Type B tendencies

▶ Becoming someone unique

▶ Doing what doesn't come naturally

▶ Finding the right environment for you

. . . .

*O*dds are, you've come across Type A people in your everyday life:

✔ The friend who never lets you finish a sentence, always hurrying you along with "yeah, right"

✔ The boss who gets increasingly impatient when it looks like a deadline is not going to be met

✔ The person who finishes eating long before everyone else

✔ The neighbor who works all the time, never spending time with his family, but who also makes a lot more money than you do

✔ The colleague whose eyes are constantly scanning the room while you're trying to talk to him

✔ The guy who can't join any organization without promptly running for an elective office

✔ The co-worker who prefers to work alone because she feels like she can get the job done quicker and more efficiently if she's not part of a team

✔ People who always appear a bit too serious about life, who have an "edge" about them, and who seem to be *moving against* everyone and everything that comes their way

These are Type A personalities, and their pattern of behavior implies both an aggressive approach to life and a heightened potential for anger. If you express Type A behavior, you probably won't win very many friends and admirers. The problem is, if you *don't* express your Type A behavior, the stress can shorten your life.

If you're a Type A, you may be thinking that you're in a lose-lose situation. But fear not: In this chapter, I offer you a way to move *beyond* being a Type A. Your goal is to become a Type B — a personality type in which anger is much less likely to occur in the first place. And I assure you, you really *can* change — you just need the tools that this chapter provides.

Moving Beyond Type A

I know, you're probably thinking, "Change my Type A ways? That can't be easy. I've been this way most of my life!" My response to that is: It may be easier than you imagine — and it absolutely is possible to change. The only question that matters is: Are you willing to work a little at this, in order to experience peace of mind and a big change of heart? If so, read on!

Focusing on who you are rather than what you do

Type A behavior is in large part an adaptation to a culture that seems more concerned about performance (what you do) than anything else that might define you as a unique human being.

Typically, what's the first question a stranger asks you when you meet at a party? "So what do you do?" People ask questions like this as a way of measuring a person's social and economic status compared to their own (he's more powerful; I'm wealthier; and so on). Another reason people ask this type of question is because the answer allows them to more quickly judge the other person without really getting to know them. It's sort of like the SAT score which, unfortunately, decides who gets into which college and who ultimately receives a scholarship.

The "So, what do you do?" question allows for quick judgments, but it's not exactly an accurate way of finding out who someone is. Think of this question as being similar to a high-school senior's SAT score: It's a lousy predictor of how well a student will perform, yet colleges weed out applicants based on that number. It's the same here: Telling someone that you're a neurosurgeon only tells him that you're well educated and make a lot of money. It doesn't necessarily follow, though, that you're a decent human being, that you're generous, that you're kind, that you're a good mother, that you're a loving wife, that you're a faithful daughter, that you're a good neighbor, that you're curious or have a good sense of humor. In fact, you may be none of these even though you're a talented surgeon.

You can tell a lot about whether people are Type A or Type B by the kinds of conversations they have. Here's my recollection of what transpired between myself (*after* I changed my own Type A ways and became a Type B) and a former colleague when we crossed paths at a medical convention.

Me: It's good to see you. It's been a while. How have you been?

Colleague: Fine. I'm busy as ever — work, work, work. What have you been up to?

Me: Well, you know I'm in private practice now and I'm enjoying that. Catherine and the kids are all well. Everybody's healthy. We like where we live — peaceful, great scenery. We're all pretty happy.

Colleague: Great. Did I tell you that I got a big five-year research grant? It's a really big deal!

Me: No, I didn't know that. Congratulations! And how is your family?

Colleague: They're fine. Yeah, this grant means I can pretty much call the shots at work now. We're going to be cranking out papers like you wouldn't believe.

Me: I'm glad for you. But, how are you — your health good? Enjoying life, that sort of thing?

Colleague: Couldn't be better. Just a lot going on, lots to get done. Oh, and did I tell you that I have a book coming out?

Me: Wow. That's great — let me know when it's published and I'll get a copy. Be sure and give my regards to Nancy, will you?

Colleague: Absolutely. Well, I need to press on. Sorry I can't stay and catch up some more, but I've got a whole bunch of meetings to go to today, make a presentation, that kind of thing. Rush, rush, rush! Good seeing you, though.

Does this sound familiar? The irony here is that Type A people are terribly self-absorbed — preoccupied with what they're doing, what they have, what they need to do right now — so they dominate the conversation with self-referencing statements such as "I'm busy as ever," "I got a five-year research grant," "I can pretty much call the shots," "I have a book coming out," and "I need to press on" without actually telling us much about themselves at all.

If you want to move beyond Type A, you can start by sharing with the world more about who you *are* than what you *do*. In the following sections, I cover three simple exercises you can do to work toward that goal.

Reframe the question

TIP

The next time someone starts a conversation with you by asking, "So, what exactly is it that you do?", answer by asking the following question in response: "Are you asking me what I get *paid* to do or what I'm doing with my *life?*"

Don't be surprised if this strategy results in a bit of an awkward moment for the other person. If she responds, "By all means, tell me what you're doing with your life!," then great — you're off to an engaging Type B conversation. If she comes back with, "I guess I was asking what you get paid to do — your work," tell her what you do for a living, and then do one of the following:

✔ Say, "Now that you know what I do for a living, would you like to know more?" In effect, you're giving the person a second chance.

✔ Exit from the conversation as quickly and gracefully as you can and look elsewhere for some pleasant Type B company.

Take the tombstone test

No matter how old you are, you can start thinking right now how you want your tombstone to read. Take a look at all the epitaphs in Table 10-1 and, as honestly as possible, choose the one that you think the people in your life say is accurate about you.

Table 10-1	The Tombstone Test
Type A Epitaph	**Type B Epitaph**
Here lies a person who made a fortune.	Here lies a person who was a friend to everyone.
Here lies a person who was feared but respected by all.	Here lies a person who was intelligent.
Here lies a person who hated to be late for anything.	Here lies a person who could be trusted.
Here lies a person who was a mover-shaker.	Here lies a person who was a real team player.
Here lies a person who wasn't afraid to be angry.	Here lies a person who had an abiding curiosity about life.
Here lies a person who was a great provider.	Here lies a person who loved passionately.
Here lies a person who left this world with his plate full.	Here lies a person who left this world satisfied.

After you've chosen your epitaph, ask yourself if that's how you *want* to be remembered. If the epitaph that others think is most accurate for you happens to be in the Type A column, maybe it's time for a change. For example, if the epitaph that most accurately describes you is, "Here lies a person who made a fortune," you can begin to enrich your life with new friendships — preferably ones that have no relationship to what you do for a living. If your Type A epitaph is, "Here lies a person who was feared, but respected," you can sign up for a course at the community college, dealing with a subject you know absolutely nothing about and then people can respect you for what you know that they don't, rather than respect you simply because they're afraid of you.

Write a life essay

Take out a sheet of paper and write the word *I* on the first line. Then spend 15 minutes writing an essay about your life up to now; include anything and everything you think is relevant and important. Stop at the end of 15 minutes (set a timer, if necessary) and read what you wrote. Try to be as objective as you can — pretend you're reading about someone else's life.

After you've finished reading what you just wrote, answer the following questions:

- ✔ How much of your life essay is about *you* versus other people?

- ✔ How much of your essay has to do with your work?

- ✔ How much of your essay has to do with financial successes or failures?

- ✔ Does it sound like a life story in which the person is satisfied and content?

- ✔ Would you say that this essay is about someone who has a sense of purpose or meaning in life?

- ✔ How much of the essay is about what you have gotten from life versus how much you've given back?

- ✔ If this were, in fact, another person's life story, would you want to trade places with that person?

If your essay has a healthy balance between references to yourself versus references to others; if work and financial success (or failure) are not the sole focus; if your essay portrays a reasonably content person, whose life is full of purpose; if there is balance between *getting* and *giving;* and if you would actually want to live that person's life, you can be fairly sure that you're a Type B!

If you answered otherwise, take a long, hard look at yourself and think of ways that you can change your story. Repeat this exercise once a week for the next six weeks, each time asking yourself those same questions afterward, and see if you're beginning to move beyond Type A. If you work at changing the focus of your life, the focus of your essay should change as well.

Looking at your own competitive streak

Competition is at the heart of the Type A personality. It's not just that Type A folks are competitive — it's that their need (some would say *obsession*) to compete is insatiable. Type A's compete over *everything* — there's absolutely nothing that won't get their competitive juices flowing. And when they're in that competitive mode, they take no prisoners.

I remember listening some years ago to a Type A training tape, used by former colleagues of mine at Duke University Medical Center. The man being interviewed was asked, "Would you let your child win a game you were play-ing just to make him feel good or boost his ego?" His immediate reply was, "Hell no. If he wants to win, he has to beat me. That's what life is all about." Now, that's a Type A! Better to crush the kid's spirit than to lose the game.

Type B's compete, too — they're just are more selective about it. They don't compete unfairly. And they often compete with different goals in mind.

The following is a list of ways in which you can modify your competitive nature and engage in *healthy* competition:

- ✓ **Try playing a round of golf without keeping score.** Here's something you may not know: Type A golfers not only keep their own score, they keep the other players' scores as well — so the other players don't cheat. And if the other players make a mistake, you can bet the Type A will tell them about it.

- ✓ **Let your children win at family games at least half the time.** Let them win even more often if you want them to love you 40 years from now.

- ✓ **If you feel like you have to compete with your spouse over ideas and decisions, be sure to let your spouse win half the time.** If you do, you'll stay together longer!

- ✓ **Never ask co-workers how much they get paid, how well their stocks are doing, or how much "face time" they have with the boss.** Just do your job, make your own investments, and you'll be fine.

- ✓ **If you're going somewhere, don't try to see how fast you can get there.** Go the speed limit and enjoy the ride. *Remember:* Life is not meant to be a race.

- ✓ **Practice meditation.** If you've never meditated, or you don't really know where to start, pick up *Meditation For Dummies,* 2nd Edition, by Stephan Bodian (Wiley). It comes with a CD of guided meditations that you can use to get started.

- ✓ **Walk on a track with someone who walks slower than you do and go at that person's speed.** Walking — without competing against your partner — does wonders for your heart.

✔ **Alternate between competitive activities and noncompetitive activities.** For example, one Saturday afternoon, play tennis with your friend (and allow yourself to keep score), and the next Saturday, visit a museum.

✔ **The next time you have sex with your partner, instead of trying to see how quickly you can reach that moment of climax, see how long you can stay in that moment of intimacy (closeness).** And don't ask your partner, "How was it?" That question translates to, "How was I? How did I perform?" Intimacy shouldn't be about keeping score.

✔ **The next time a group you belong to holds an election, raise your hand and nominate someone else.** You don't have to be the head of every committee — you can trust other people to take charge and follow their lead for a change.

Come up with other creative ways you can reduce your competitive nature. If you're less competitive, you won't be as likely to get angry, and that's definitely a good thing.

Conversing without numbers

Type A's love to quantify life as a way of measuring how successful they are in their incessant competition with everything and everyone in the universe. They're quick to tell you how much money they make a year (and they'll try to find out how much you're making), how much they made or lost in buying and selling various properties (homes, stocks, land, cars — you name it), how well they're doing at sports (what number they are on the tennis ladder at the local country club or what their golf handicap is), how many surgeries they performed last year, how many publications they have, the size and revenue figures for the companies they work for, and so on.

It's all number-speak and the crazy thing is that Type A's don't even hear themselves doing it. Here's a typical example:

Max: Glad we could get together for lunch — it's been a while.

Type A: I know. I've just been so darned busy. You know we just added a new *thousand*-square-foot addition to our office building. And we also added *six* new salesmen. How's your business doing?

Max: Okay, we're holding our own — nothing special. The good news is that lately I have more time to relax and catch up on stuff.

Type A: Boy, I could use some of that, but not likely. We're *43 percent* ahead of where we were last year at this time. I think there's a good chance we may exceed *50 percent* before year's end.

Max: So, other than work, what have you been up to? The family and I are spending a lot of time lately up at the lake — you know we have a little place up there. The kids love it.

Type A: Boy, I'd love to be at the lake more. I told you I bought a new boat last year — paid *$60,000* for that sucker and we hardly ever use it. And we almost never use the place we have up there — *five* bedrooms, *four* baths, *two* acres of waterfront property just going to waste. I told my wife we ought to sell it and make a nice profit — with the way the demand is these days, I bet I could get at least *$350,000* easy. What do you think your place is worth?

To begin conversing without numbers, try the following seven-step exercise:

1. **Get a tape recorder.**

2. **Tape a ten-minute casual conversation about some topic of mutual interest with a family member or close friend.**

3. **Go back and listen to the tape and count how many times you refer to numbers.**

4. **Tape a second ten-minute conversation with this same person, only this time make a conscious effort not to engage in number-speak.**

5. **Do a recount of how many times you referred to numbers the second time around.**

6. **Assess whether you improved by comparing the two.**

7. **Repeat this exercise as often as necessary to build a new habit of Type B speech.**

When you begin to see a change in how you talk in this "experimental" setting, start paying more attention to how you converse with others in everyday life. Pay attention to how they speak, too — you'll quickly find out that you're not the only Type A in the world. Again, make an effort to get your message across without all the numbers. It's fine to simply say, "I'm having a fantastic day!" You don't need to add, "I've already made $2,300 and it's only lunchtime."

Taking off your watch

Type A's are obsessed with time as well. "This is taking too much time," "Damn it, it's getting late — I'll never get finished on time," "I wish they would hurry up."

Type A's have an accelerated sense of time. They feel time "slipping away" more and more as the day goes by. This leads to an increased feeling of time anxiety or what the originators of the Type A concept (Dr. Meyer Friedman and Dr. Ray Rosenman) called *hurry sickness.* And, that explains why Type A's get so irritated when circumstances and people slow them down.

The irony, of course, is that this perception that time is passing all too quickly is false. Time passes at the same rate for Type A's as it does for Type B's. The difference is that Type B's are more in sync with time — they have a more accurate perception of how much time has elapsed from one moment to the next.

To test how aware you are of time, have someone you know pick a time anywhere from 5 to 15 minutes — but tell him not to tell you how many minutes he picked. Then ask the person to engage you in a conversation for that length of time. (Oh, by the way, you can't have a watch on while you're taking this test — that's cheating!). When that set amount of time has passed, try telling that person how many minutes you think elapsed. If you're Type A, you'll most likely *over*estimate the actual time. If you're Type B, you're more likely to either be right on the mark or *under*estimate how much time has gone by.

One of the best ways to become a Type B is to quit wearing a watch. If you're a Type A, I'm sure your first thought as you read that was, "My God, I can't do that — how would I know what time it is, how would I stay on my hectic schedule, how would I get all this stuff done?" The answer is that you wouldn't — but, guess what? The world wouldn't end. On the other hand, the quality of your work might improve; in fact, people are much more creative in their thinking and problem solving when they aren't bound by deadlines.

For a Type A, taking off a watch is like asking a lifetime smoker to hand over his pack of cigarettes or an alcoholic to get rid of all the liquor in her house. It's asking a lot. You may be able to go cold turkey, put your watch away, and never look back. (I did that one morning on a plane 35 years ago and I haven't worn a watch since. That was actually the first step in my Type A recovery program.) If you're like most people, however, you'll have to wean yourself off your watch slowly.

Here are some helpful hints on how to wean yourself from your watch:

- ✔ **Think about which part of the day or week would be easier for you to not wear a watch.** Then see if you can take it off for an hour or two during those times.

- ✔ **When you're in your office during the day, put your watch in your pocket or purse and rely on a desk clock to keep track of time.** Only put on your watch when you leave the office.

✔ **Wear an old-fashioned pocket watch.** You still have a way of keeping time but it's not as obvious, staring you in the face all the time.

✔ **Set a timer on your watch to let you know when it's time to move on.** For example, when you're having lunch with a friend, set the time for when you need to wrap up the lunch. Then put the watch out of sight.

✔ **See how many new, interesting, nice-looking people you can meet throughout the course of a day by asking for the time.** It's a great way to start a conversation!

Resisting what society tells you to do

The *A* in Type A might as well stand for *American*. The values that underlie all the major components of Type A behavior — competitiveness, a sense of time urgency, overinvolvement with work — typify the extreme of what America, and other similar Western industrialized countries, is all about. (Interestingly, people in Belgium and the Netherlands as a rule are Type B, and those countries have half the number of deaths due to heart disease as does the United States.)

To become more Type B in how you approach life, you need to counteract the cultural principles and beliefs that promote and maintain Type A behavior. The following illustrates differences in beliefs that guide and motivate Type A's and Type B's. If you're a Type A, try adopting some of these Type B philosophies.

Type A: I must perform to a higher standard than other individuals.

Type B: I should adopt a universal standard for what it reasonably efficient performance in all aspects of daily life and be satisfied when I reach it.

Type A: Success is achieved only through effort — the more intense the effort, the greater the success.

Type B: Success has mostly to do with my ability — people with greater ability will always do better despite their efforts.

Type A: Life is mostly about competing with others for success.

Type B: Cooperation, not competition, is the strategy that will, in the long term, ensure my success in life.

Type A: Each individual in society bears the burden of her own success — now and in the future.

Type B: Social cohesion — being connected to and working with others — lessens the burden each individual carries as they collectively strive toward group success and survival. Life should be about what we do, and not just about what *I* do!

In a big hurry

One of the more interesting studies I was involved in was in collaboration with Dutch colleagues at the University of Nijmegen. We were looking at differences in how Type A and Type B patients behaved while they were hospitalized for heart problems. We found that Type A patients had a much shorter hospital stay than Type B's. Why? Because they were in a hurry to get back out in the world and resume the very lifestyle that had caused their heart problems in the first place. As our most typically Type A patient put it: "I have to make something of my life in the future. Time is short. The first 30 years of my life have been for nothing! I have to enjoy it! I'm in a big hurry to do this."

Acquiring Wisdom

My lifelong friend and mentor, Dr. Berton Kaplan at the University of North Carolina School of Public Health, argues that Type B personalities live longer and have greater satisfaction (as well as less anger) simply because they're wiser when it comes to navigating their way through life's twists and turns. He also offers three simple, but effective, prescriptions for acquiring this wisdom. I fill you in on these strategies in the following sections.

Seeking diversity in relationships

Wisdom is something you acquire from your own life experience, but also from those around you. For example, I became a wise parent long before I had children, having found out from my own two parents how not to raise kids. My children benefited greatly from the mistakes my parents made on me — and there were many!

Wisdom can just as well be acquired from people younger than you. My son taught me how to enjoy my weekends instead of spending the entire time checking things off my Type A list of chores.

In order to acquire wisdom, you should seek new relationships with people different from yourself (the last thing you need is another Type A friend!), because with each new relationship comes a new perspective about what is really important in life, how to cope with adversity, and how to balance the good with the bad (more about this in Chapter 16).

Cultivating the arts

I would venture to say that, at the very least, Type A's are bored with artistic endeavors — music, painting, sculpture, novels — and at worst they hate such things. I say this because cultivating the arts is antithetical to the Type A mentality. Art appreciation, whether sitting through a musical concert or strolling through an art museum, invokes — no, *demands* — quiet, an appreci-ation of past (not future) efforts, a historical perspective on life (not just what's going on today), and a stillness of spirit that you can't find in the merry-go-round of everyday life. Art challenges you to give your mind a much needed respite from external pursuits, to reflect on matters that go beyond the material world, to focus on the beauty of things rather than their utility. It allows you to transcend mind and body into the subjective world of the artist. What a wonderful "waste" of time!

Letting curiosity rein

Type A's lack curiosity. If you're curious, you tend to be curious about things that will allow you to be more productive at your job and more dominant in your social relationships. Healthy curiosity — the kind found in Type B's — knows no bounds. Type B's are curious about life in general. They tend to gravitate toward a wide variety of new experiences that catch their attention. Some of their curiosity is satisfied through reading or talking with someone; in other instances, it comes from hands-on involvement.

To enlarge your sense of curiosity, you might try one or more of the following:

- ✔ Once a month, go to your local bookstore and buy a book on some topic you know absolutely nothing about.

- ✔ Check the newspaper each weekend for interesting "happenings" in your community and then go and find out what they're all about.

- ✔ Join a book club that covers a diversity of topics and has a discussion component.

- ✔ Spend some time now and then with friends who have unique hobbies and skills. Ask them to educate you about how to do these things.

- ✔ Watch educational television. *Careful:* You might actually learn some-thing!

Finding the Right Environmental Fit

The next best thing to actually becoming a Type B is to move yourself into a Type B environment. It turns out that workplaces and companies have distinct personalities just like people do. Type A's, as you might expect, tend most often to seek out places to work that are hard driving, time pressured, frenetic, competitive, and full of deadlines. But what if you found yourself in a Type B work situation — one that was more relaxed and easygoing? That wouldn't suit you, or would it? Well, if you found yourself in a Type B environment, you could expect to:

- ✔ Experience fewer health complaints (for example, headaches, indigestion, backache, depression)

- ✔ Feel much less stressed while at work

- ✔ Be more satisfied with your work and that of your co-workers

- ✔ Have fewer days when you felt you couldn't work up to par because you weren't feeling well

If you're willing to work toward becoming a Type B *and* you seek out a Type B work situation, you can anticipate further health benefits:

- ✔ Fewer stress-related mental health problems

- ✔ Feeling less like you're in "high gear" throughout the workday

- ✔ Having less difficulty relaxing outside of work

- ✔ Feeling less often that your health in some way affects how much work you get done

You may be living in a Type A city and, if so, you might consider moving — yes, I'm serious. Cities differ in terms of their pace of life (for example, how fast people talk, how fast they walk, how many people wear watches, how fast business gets transacted) and these differences translate into how likely you are to die from heart disease. It's not the size of the city you live in that determines the pace of your lifestyle, but rather which region of the country the city is in. The northeast United States (with cities like New York City; Providence, Rhode Island; and Patterson, New Jersey) is the worst for Type A living, while the south (Atlanta, Memphis, Knoxville) and west (San Diego, Salt Lake City, and Fresno) has the most Type B cities.

What does all this have to do with managing anger? Well, it turns out that fast-paced living provides far more opportunities to lose your cool than the slow-paced lifestyle. Think of it as the geographic cure!

Chapter 11

Using Anger Constructively

A nger has gotten a bad rap! Typically, you associate anger with aggressive behavior or some other type of destructive outcome in your life. This is true only because no one has shown you how to use anger constructively. In this chapter, I illustrate the *positive* side of anger — the side that can be harnessed to resolve problems of everyday life, understand the other person's point of view, and minimize future conflict.

Emotions are not inherently good or bad. People have suffered heart attacks because of a joyful event, like being promoted, and they've suffered strokes when surprised by the unexpected news of a loved one's death. Does this mean that you should avoid joy and surprise at all costs? Of course not. And you shouldn't try to avoid anger because of some mistaken belief that it can only cause hurt and harm. It's what you *do* with anger — how you express it — that makes it good or bad.

Making Anger Your Ally

If you choose to use anger constructively, you'll join the ranks of some pretty notable folks — George Washington, Martin Luther King, Jr., Jesus Christ, Gandhi, and Mother Teresa, to name a few. These are just few people who admittedly were angry — about poverty, racial injustice, occupation of their countries by foreign powers — but who channeled their anger into constructive action that changed the world for the better.

Honors schmonors: We *all* get angry

I asked 20 honors students I was teaching at a well-known college to write down what they did when they got angry. The following table summarizes their answers:

Positive Expressions	*Negative Expressions*
Talk about it with a friend	Withdraw from everyone
Go exercise	Get sick to my stomach
Go for a walk and think	Get a migraine headache
	Feel depressed
	Play the anger over and over in my head
	Say things I don't mean
	Be self-critical
	Cry
	Snap at people
	Grind my teeth
	Not speak to anyone
	Ignore the person I'm angry with
	Storm off
	Explode
	Throw things
	Scream
	Stomp my feet
	Lay awake all night
	Complain, complain, complain
	Feel guilty
	Get into fights
	Feel nauseated

Two other personal favorites of mine were "Find a brick wall and kick it 'til I can't feel my feet" and "Bite someone." The ratio of negative-to-positive expressions of anger in this group of academically outstanding kids was a whopping 13-to-1. No wonder we think of anger as a bad thing!

In the following sections, I cover a few reasons why you should consider making anger your ally in constructing a new healthier, happier, and more productive life.

Anger is a built-in resource

We're born with a capacity for anger. Mothers recognize anger in newborns as early as 3 months of age. Anger isn't something that has to be learned or earned, like money or friendship. It's yours to experience as the need arises. Think of it as your birthright.

Ask yourself: Do I want to use this inner resource to reconstruct my life?

Anger is invigorating

The *e* in *emotion* stands for "energy." Anger produces an instantaneous surge of adrenaline, which causes your pupils to dilate, your heart to race, your blood pressure to elevate, and your breathing to accelerate. If you're really angry, even the hairs on the back of your neck stand up! Your liver responds by releasing sugar, and blood shifts from your internal organs to your skeletal muscles, causing a generalized state of tension. You're energized and ready for action. Remember, though, that emotions are short lived — they come and go. So, it's imperative that you strike while the iron is (literally) hot and use the angry energy to your benefit before it evaporates.

Ask yourself: Do I want to quit wasting energy on unproductive anger?

I know I'm alive when . . .

Some years ago, I was conducting a workshop on anger management for mental health professionals. I started off by asking the audience to define anger. Some folks offered the usual, easy definitions: "It's an emotion," "It's a feeling," "It's something that feels bad."

But, then, one young woman came up with the most intriguing definition of all: "Anger is one way I know I'm alive." She went on to say how refreshing emotions are because they disrupt the otherwise humdrum nature of daily life and for brief periods leave us feeling energized, full of vitality, alive.

Anger serves as a catalyst for new behavior

The *motion* part of *emotion* has to do with motivating behavior. If you're like me, there are things you want to change in your life. But you're afraid, right? You're uncertain about what will happen if you let go of the status quo and move your life in some new direction — maybe a new relationship, a new career, a new city, or a new, healthier lifestyle (joining a gym, starting a diet, giving up alcohol). So, you do nothing — that is, until you get mad enough about the way things are that you spring into action.

Ask yourself: How can I renew my life through constructive anger?

Anger communicates

Anger tells the world just how miserable you are — how *un*happy, *un*fulfilled, *un*satisfied, *un*excited, and *un*loved you feel. Anger speaks the *un*speakable! Think about the last time you verbally expressed anger. Do you remember what you said? Was it something like, "Get off *my* back," "You don't care about *me*," "*I'm* tired of living hand to mouth," or "*I* give, give, give, and *I* get nothing in return." I'm sure others heard what you said, but did *you?* Did you listen to your anger — listen to what it's telling you about what's wrong with your life and what you need to do to begin correcting it.

No you're not . . . or are you?

Sometimes you just need a kick in the pants. Charlie was having lunch with a friend and was telling her about the new, exciting venture he was planning to begin shortly to turn around his failing business. "I'm going to start the new business in about two months and I'm counting on you sending me some clients," he said. Her reply, without a moment's hesitation, "No, you're not."

Wow! Charlie was stunned and irritated. "Why do you say that?" he asked. "Because you've been talking about this new business for over a year now, and every time we have lunch it's always going to start sometime in the next few months — but it never does. I think it's a wonderful idea and, sure, I'd send you clients, but

honestly, Charlie, you're never going to do it. It's just talk."

Now Charlie was mad. He paid the check, mumbled some pleasantry, and went back to work. But the more he thought about it, the more he realized his friend was right. A year of talk had not translated into action. Charlie decided right then and there — while he was still angry — that he would begin his new business within the next 30 days, and he did. The rest, as they say, is history. His new venture got off to a rousing start, and over the next ten years he made almost a million dollars working part time — all thanks to his good friend who made him angry that day.

The most helpful emotional dialogue you have is the one you have with yourself.

Ask yourself: What is my anger telling me about me?

Anger protects you from harm

Anger is a vital part of that built-in "fight-or-flight" response that helps you adapt to and survive life's challenges. Anger is the fight component — the part that moves you to take offensive measures to defend yourself against actual or perceived threats.

Do you ever get angry enough to stand up for your rights? Do you ever use anger to set limits on other people's rude or inconsiderate behavior? Do you ever get angry and say to someone, "Hey, that's uncalled for!", "Just stop right there — I'm not going to sit here and subject myself any longer to this abuse," or "You may bully other people in this office, but you're not going to bully me." I hope so, because, otherwise, you may be well on your way to becoming a victim!

Ask yourself: How can I use my anger to defend myself in a positive way?

Anger is an antidote to impotence

Impotence — lacking in power and ability — feels lousy. And I'm not just talking about sexual impotence. I mean being impotent in how you deal with the world around you — your relationships, your job, your finances, your health, your weight, the loss of loved ones, and so on. You feel weak and inadequate, not up to the task at hand.

Then you get angry — and suddenly you're infused with a sense of empowerment, a feeling of strength, confidence, and competence. You're standing straight up to the frustrations and conflicts you've been avoiding. Anger is a can-do emotion: "I can fix this problem," "I can make a difference here," "I can be successful if I try."

Pay attention to your posture the next time you feel down, dejected, and impotent about some important thing in your life. Then notice how your posture changes when you get fired up and begin to take charge of the situation. I promise you'll be amazed at the difference.

Ask yourself: How often do I succumb to impotent anger?

The secretary's got it right

I once knew a man who loved to bully his employees. He had a daily ritual of calling someone into his office without warning, usually right as most people were leaving for the day — I suspect so there were fewer witnesses. He would tell his "victim" to have a seat and then immediately proceed to get red in the face with rage, come charging across the office, with his imposing figure standing over his helpless prey, at which point he would harangue about all sorts of things he was displeased with for what seemed like an eternity. Everyone dreaded the day when their name would be called.

Then one day, while several employees were preparing to leave, one of the secretaries was summoned to his office. Everyone felt bad for her, anticipating what was to come. But, before even five minutes had passed, she returned looking unperturbed. "What happened?" they asked, "Why are you back so soon?"

"Well, it was just like everybody said it would be. As soon as I sat down, he came charging across the room and started yelling at me. So, I stood up and started walking out the door, at which point he said, 'Where do you think you're going?' I simply told him that no one had ever spoken to me like that in my entire life and I didn't know how to respond, so I thought it best to leave until he calmed down. And, here I am."

Two days later, another person in that same office was called in and found himself being confronted by the bully. As soon as he started hollering, "I got mad but then immediately thought about the secretary," the man said. "So, I got up and started to walk out. He asked me where I thought I was going and I gave him the same answer the secretary had. He stopped his ranting and calmly asked me to sit back down because he needed to talk with me about something important. I said, 'Okay, as long as you don't start hollering again.'" The two had a civil discussion after that.

Exploring the Motives behind Your Anger

Before you can use anger constructively, you have to examine the motives behind it. Ask yourself these questions:

- ✔ When I get angry, exactly what is it that I want to achieve?
- ✔ What is the desired outcome?
- ✔ What do I want to happen?
- ✔ What am I after?
- ✔ What would satisfy me?

Researchers who study anger suggest there are just three motives behind anger, and I cover each of these motives in the following sections.

Dr. James Averill at the University of Massachusetts has found that the most frequently cited type of anger is constructive anger (63 percent of those surveyed), followed by vengeful anger (57 percent), and finally anger that is aimed simply at letting off steam (37 percent).

Seeking vengeance

Is anger your way of avenging a wrong that has been done to you? Is the goal to hurt someone or destroy something — to hurt their feelings, to physically attack them, or to break something when you're frustrated? Is your anger designed to intentionally inflict suffering and do you experience pleasure in the harm you do to others? If the answer is yes, your anger is, by its very nature, destructive, not constructive — this kind of anger is called *vengeful anger*.

Here's a real-life example of what I'm talking about: Matt had just about finished putting in the new kitchen cabinets. He was putting up the molding around the cabinet tops when he realized he had cut a piece too short. He flew into a rage and proceeded — much to his wife's horror — to take a crowbar and rip out all the cabinets and throw them one by one into the backyard until his anger was satisfied. He destroyed months of hard work in a matter of a few seconds. After he cooled down, he headed off to the local hardware store to buy materials to rebuild the cabinets. Sadly for Matt, this was but one of many episodes of vengeful anger throughout his life. He says, "I can't tell you how many things I've had to rebuild in my life because of my anger."

Ask yourself: Do I want to go through life like Matt, destroying something every time I get angry? Am I willing to bear the expense of my vengeful anger?

Bringing about a positive change

Constructive anger is used to assert one's authority, to achieve independence, and to get another person to do something that's good for him. If you're a parent, have you ever gotten angry with your child when you were just trying to show her to behave safely (for example, not riding in a car with friends who have been drinking or not staying out until 3 o'clock in the morning)? Probably. At work, have you ever gotten angry with your subordinates and said "Enough fooling around. We've got work to do here, so get busy." Most likely. As a young married person, have you ever expressed irritation with your in-laws because they're always telling you what's best for you ("You need to quit that job." "That's too much house for you." "Don't you think it's time you started a family?") instead of letting you make your own independent decisions? Sure. Well, then you've indulged in constructive anger.

Ask yourself: Am I satisfied that I'm using my anger in a way that benefits me more than it hurts me?

Letting off steam

Have you ever felt like you were just going to explode — and then you did? Anger is one way a lot of people — normal people, not crazy or vengeful people — let off steam. Their anger isn't tied to any specific issue or person; it's sort of generic. It reflects a good bit of pent-up frustration and stress that seeks relief. Think of a pressure cooker and you get the idea. Even though it feels good, this type of anger is not constructive. Rather, it's anger that is "full of sound and fury, signifying nothing," as Will Shakespeare would say.

Ask yourself: Is it enough to just "feel good" after I express my anger or would I rather use anger to benefit my life in some meaningful way?

Using Anger to Understand Yourself

Anger is like a mirror — it doesn't build character, and it doesn't destroy it. It simply reveals character. Anger tells you and the world what kind of person you are, what you expect from life, what you're passionate about, how much alcohol you've had to drink, how stressed you are, and much more.

Close your eyes and imagine the last time you got mad at someone. Get that situation fixed in your mind's eye for a minute or two and assume the role of an objective observer. What did you say or do in that moment of anger? Try to be as specific as possible. Stay with the scene until you feel comfortable that you can honestly answer the question: What did my anger say about me in that situation?

Here are some possible answers:

- ✔ My anger says that I am a selfish person whose needs always come before others.
- ✔ My anger says that I am a moral person who believes in fair play and justice.
- ✔ My anger says that I am impatient — my needs have to be met *now.*
- ✔ My anger says that my life is in chaos — nothing is working right.
- ✔ My anger says that I care enough about you to get upset when you put yourself in harm's way.
- ✔ My anger says that I am greedy — I always expect to have more than others and I get mad when I don't.
- ✔ My anger says that I feel I am not being treated with disrespect.
- ✔ My anger says that I need to dominate others in all types of life situations.

✔ My anger says that I am a "special" person and thus entitled to always have my way.

✔ My anger says that I can feel another person's pain.

✔ My anger says that I am a pessimist, always expecting that things won't work out and then getting mad when they don't.

✔ My anger says that there's way too much stress in my life — I'm overloaded!

✔ My anger says that it's high time to make some positive changes in my life — there has to be a better way to live.

Do you like what you see in the mirror? If not, then it's time to do some reconstruction.

Constructive Anger

Constructive anger involves two things:

✔ Deciding where it is you want your anger to take you

✔ Arriving at that destination through a step-by-step process (which I outline in this section)

Before you begin, try saying the following statements to yourself — and believe them. Even if you don't believe that all these statements are true, proceed anyway.

✔ I need to reason through my anger.

✔ I need to put my anger into perspective.

✔ I can't do a thing about what has happened to provoke my anger.

✔ The situation that made me angry should be rectified.

✔ I need to find other ways to express my anger.

Step 1: Decide how you want to feel after you get angry

How you use anger is a choice — and with that choice, comes consequences. If you choose to use anger constructively — so that it has a positive outcome — you'll generally expect that, after you finish expressing your anger, you *will:*

✔ Have a better understanding of the person with whom you had the angry exchange.

✔ Feel better about that other person.

✔ Feel closer to resolving issues between you and the other person.

✔ Realize that things were never as bad as you initially thought they were when you first became angry.

✔ Feel that both parties came away feeling like something good happened.

✔ Have less conflict in the future.

Conversely, if you choose to use anger constructively, you will *not:*

✔ Continue to hold a grudge against that other person.

✔ Feel totally justified in continuing to dislike that other person.

✔ Feel tense and agitated around that person.

✔ Dwell on your angry feelings.

✔ Feel compelled to rehash your angry feelings (and the reasons for them) with anyone and everyone who'll listen.

✔ Be defensive in social situations involving the other person.

✔ Feel that the problem between you and that person cannot ever be resolved.

✔ Feel victimized by that other person.

✔ Feel impotent about how you dealt with the problem that caused your anger.

✔ Feel as though you're going to explode any minute.

On the other hand, if you choose to use your anger *destructively,* you should expect the opposite outcomes — more conflict in the future, more tension between you and the other person, and so on.

Step 2: Acknowledge your anger

A simple statement such as "I don't know about you, but I find I'm getting irritated about what just happened and I thought you should know that" will suffice. What you want to do is give a heads-up to the other party in the conversation, letting him know that emotions are in play here and that the emotion you're feeling is anger.

It's not enough just to acknowledge to *yourself* that you're angry — you have to articulate that feeling to the person you're angry with.

Step 3: Focus your anger on the problem, not the person

Taking a line from the movie *The Godfather,* when you engage in constructive anger expression, you need to start with the idea that "it's business — it's not personal." In other words, focus on the issue that triggered your anger, not the person on the other side of that issue.

Concentrate on the *what* not the *who.* When you begin to personalize anger (for example, saying something like, "That stupid woman . . ."), your anger will invariably turn vengeful.

Step 4: Identify the source of the problem

This step is an easy one. Why? Because the source of all your anger is *you!* Before you slam this book shut and throw it across the room, give me a chance to explain what I mean.

All your emotions are a reflection of yourself. If you're angry with one of your employees when she habitually comes to work late, the source of your anger lies in the fact that *you* believe you aren't getting a fair day's work for a fair day's pay. Similarly, if you're angry with your husband because he continues to read the paper while you're trying to tell him about your day at work, the source of your anger is *your* belief that you aren't getting the attention that you want from him. If you didn't have those beliefs, the actions of the other people would be of no consequence.

Right away, as you internalize the source of your anger (taking responsibility for how you feel — see Chapter 7 for a complete discussion on this), you begin to feel more in control of your anger. Now, the question is: Do I alter my expectations of that other person or do I clarify for them what those expectations are and what will happen if my expectations aren't met? (Personally, I suggest the latter.)

Step 5: Accept that the problem can be solved

Fixing *problems* is much easier than fixing *people*. What you have is a problem situation. Try to remain optimistic that you can solve this problem. Be open-minded — a closed mind goes nowhere; it just defends itself. Don't be afraid to try new solutions when the old ones don't work.

A client of mine, I'll call him Ted, called me saying he was in a dilemma. He started by telling me how angry he was with his son-in-law, who often verbally attacks him when he visits the family. That anger had, on more than one occasion, led to mutual hostilities, including "saying some things I regretted later on" as well as some pushing and shoving. Ted's daughter had called and invited Ted to his granddaughter's birthday party. His question was: Should he or shouldn't he go and risk further abuse? Ted saw it as a lose-lose situation — he was damned if he did and damned if he didn't! He told me that he had tried talking to his son-in-law, but this only provoked further rage on the son-in-law's part. He felt the situation was hopeless. What I recommended was, first, that Ted not have a general rule about attending family functions involving his son-in-law — in other words, Ted should decide what to do on a case-by-case basis. I reminded him that he was under no obligation to attend family gatherings and that his family was not entitled to have him show up regardless of the consequences.

I also encouraged Ted not to let his anger at his son-in-law totally foreclose any possibility of future relationship with his daughter and granddaughter. I suggested that Ted look for opportunities to visit with his daughter and granddaughter without the son-in-law present (for example, meet them for lunch, take his granddaughter for a visit to the zoo, and so on).

I told Ted that he should be prepared to exit gracefully from any family situation at the very first sign that his son-in-law was intent on verbally attacking him. The expectation shouldn't be that "If I go, I have to stay no matter what." (In combat, all good generals have an exit strategy.)

I advised Ted to share the responsibility for solving this family problem with his daughter — after all, it was she who had brought this angry man into the family. Ask her what she's prepared to do to make things better, if anything.

These were all things Ted hadn't considered before and that might work. All Ted could do was try.

Think about some anger-provoking situation you've been involved in that seems unsolvable. Write down all the things you tried to correct the situation. Now, think about some things you *haven't* tried. If nothing comes to mind, talk to someone else about it and see what that person suggests. Two minds are always better than one! After you come up with a new strategy, use it the next time you're in this situation.

Step 6: Try to see things from the other person's perspective

Anger is so subjective that it's hard to see past it, to put yourself in the other person's shoes. But seeing the situation from the other person's perspective is one of the most essential steps in using anger constructively.

The easiest way to understand why the other person thinks, feels, or acts the way she does is to invite their input. For example, Ted (see the preceding section) could say to his hostile son-in-law, "Whenever we get into a discussion, I feel insulted when you call me names. I may be wrong, but it seems like you're really angry with me, and I'd like to talk with you about how you're feeling and why." If you don't give the other person an opportunity to tell you where she's coming from, you're left to speculate — and odds are, you'll guess incorrectly.

Reverse roles. Think of yourself as that the other person and ask yourself:

✔ How am I feeling right now?

✔ What am I thinking?

✔ How would I explain my actions to another person, if asked?

✔ What could I tell someone that would perhaps make him less upset with me?

✔ What is it that other people don't know about me that they should?

✔ Am I giving them the wrong impression of who I really am and what's on my mind?

✔ Is my behavior justified in my mind and, if so, why?

Step 7: Co-op the other party

Another key step in constructive anger expression is to enlist the cooperation of the person you're angry with in resolving the problem. The question here is not "What am *I* going to do about this problem?" but "What can *we* do about finding a solution that works for both of us?" The minute you begin to share the responsibility (or burden) of resolving an anger-producing problem, the intensity of your anger decreases.

Learning from my mistakes

For several years now, I've been conducting anger-management classes in schools and, unfortunately, I've found out a lot about the things that *don't* work with angry, alienated kids. What *doesn't* work is making them feel bad for being angry. Another thing that doesn't work is assuming they're all angry for the same reasons. Assuming that they want to quit being so angry just because the school (and I) want them to doesn't work either.

What does work, I'm finding out, is to engage them in a dialogue that accepts their anger, doesn't judge it, and puts it in a big-picture perspective that fits their unique life story. In other words, stop trying so hard to change them and instead work just as hard to understand their point of view.

So, instead of telling them how they should feel, I ask them a lot of questions: What was it about the teacher asking you to be quiet that made you mad? What did you hope to accomplish by punching the other kid on the bus? Do you see any relationship between your leaving the house angry with your dad and the fact that you verbally attacked the teacher as soon as you came in the classroom? Did you ever think of any other way of handling that situation without resorting to violence?

You guessed it: These questions are the kind you can ask yourself if you want to understand your anger and deal with it more constructively

Step 8: Keep a civil tone throughout

What you say in anger isn't what causes problems — it's the tone in which you say it. If you can keep a civil tone to your conversation, you'll find that actively listening to the person with whom you're angry is easier — it's also easier to get your message across to that person. Lowering your tone will in turn cause him to lower his. Civility doesn't require that you stop being angry — it just helps you use the anger more constructively.

Step 9: Avoid disrespectful behavior

Clearly, there are some things — gestures, behaviors — you need to avoid if you're going to use anger constructively. By all means, do *not:*

- Roll your eyes when the other person is speaking.
- Sigh laudably while she's talking.
- Engage in finger-pointing.
- Lecture the other person when it's your turn to speak.
- Use critical language (words like *stupid, idiot, crazy, ignorant,* or *ridiculous*).

✔ Repeatedly interrupt or talk over the other person.

✔ Personalize your message (for example, "What a fool you are!").

Step 10: Don't be afraid to take a timeout and resume the discussion later

Don't be afraid to say to the other person, "I think we've gone as far as we can with this issue right now, but I really think we should continue our discussion at a later date. Do you agree?" Some issues take longer to solve than others — just as some destinations are farther away than others.

This strategy only works if you actually do resume the discussion later. Otherwise, all your constructive efforts were in vain!

Step 11: Make it a two-way conversation

Conflict resolution — which is a big part of anger management — requires a two-way conversation. The point here is that, when it comes to addressing your anger in a constructive way, you have to let the other person have a turn, too. Vengeful anger and simply "letting off steam" don't involve the other party except as the object of your wrath. You're trying to do something different in this case, right?

Step 12: Acknowledge that you've made progress

Old bad habits like vengeful anger die hard. So, if you're trying to begin using anger more constructively, it's important to acknowledge when progress is being made anywhere along the way. Tell the other person, "You know, I feel good about our discussion. I understand better where you're coming from, and I'm not nearly as upset as when we first started talking about this." Then ask her, "Do you feel the same way? Do you feel that I heard what you were saying? Do you feel we're closer to a resolution now than we were before?"

You hope, of course, that she says yes. But if she says, "No, not at all," that's okay. Maybe she'll change her mind in the future. (Most important, don't get mad just because she doesn't agree with you!)

No wonder I have low blood pressure

Recent studies have shown that adults who express their anger constructively tend to have lower resting blood pressure even after other known risk factors — age, smoking, obesity, family history — have been accounted for. Studies have also shown that adults can learn constructive anger expression and, when they do, they experience less hostility and decreased blood pressure. This is an example of when *anger management* translates into *medical management*.

What Goes Around Comes Around

My former professor and mentor, Dr. Charles Spielberger, at the University of South Florida, once wrote a paper with a title I like: "Rage Boomerangs." His message was simple: Humans tend to "respond in kind" when they're confronted with anger. Anger begets anger, just like kindness begets kindness.

If you engage in vengeful anger toward others, they will most likely respond with vengeful anger toward you. On the other hand, if you're constructive in how you express your anger, they'll reciprocate in a similar manner.

If you're caught up in this cycle of mutual anger, this is your chance to break out. Make your next move based on how you want the person with whom you're engaged to respond. If you want him to ratchet down the intensity of his anger, you start by toning down your end of the conversation. If you want her to better understand why you're angry, start by asking her to clarify why she's angry with you. If you don't want him to treat your anger with disrespect (see the previous section), then don't act disrespectful toward him. Believe it or not, you'll find that you have more of a positive influence on "what comes around next" than you imagined.

The most likely response

In a survey of high school students, we asked kids how they would respond if another student got angry with them. We gave them three choices:

✔ Just walk off.

✔ Get angry right back.

✔ Walk away but come back later to discuss the problem.

Guess what the most popular choice was? Forty-nine percent of the boys and 42 percent of the girls selected the second response (answer anger with anger). Even more enlightening was the finding that, among the most angry children in the school, the likelihood of engaging in mutual anger was a whopping 87 percent! These kids are caught up in a vicious cycle of reciprocal anger that dominates all of their peer relationships.

Part IV

Handling Anger from the Past

The 5th Wave   By Rich Tennant

"Let's see if we can identify some of the anger triggers in your life. You mentioned something about a large wolf that periodically shows up and attempts to blow your house down..."

In this part . . .

We tackle the toughest challenge of all: managing anger from your past. I want you to be able to dig your way out from old anger that lies just below the surface and that can be triggered at any time for any reason. To begin with, stop trying so hard to forget those old, unresolved grievances that create so much emotional harm. Your task is not to forget, but to forgive — and forgiveness is never easy. In this part, you explore what you have to do before you can get beyond your emotional past. My goal in this part is to get you to stop playing the blame game and realize that the person who benefits the most from your forgiveness is *you*.

Chapter 12

Why Is Letting Go So Difficult?

In This Chapter

▶ Understanding why anger persists

▶ Examining your fears

▶ Living without closure

▶ Deciding when time's up

Anger is an emotion, and emotions are meant to be short lived. Excitement, fear, sadness, surprise, irritation — all are emotions that pass through you throughout the day. But, for some people, anger persists, and through its persistence, anger is harmful.

Take, for example, Marilyn, a 55-year-old married woman. She continues to be angry about the mistreatment she suffered at work over 15 years ago. Marilyn was injured on the job and, as a result, she not only had to change jobs, but also endure continuous pain in her lower back. Marilyn found her employer to be woefully unsympathetic, which only gave her *more* reason to be angry. After several years of struggling, she experienced a nervous breakdown and was terminated by her employer altogether. The resentment that Marilyn has harbored over the years has all but ruined her health and has taken its toll on her marriage. She isn't just a victim in the sense of having been permanently injured — she's also the victim of her own unresolved anger.

In this chapter, I discuss some of the reasons why people like Marilyn hang on to anger. I also offer some solutions for letting go of this troublesome emotion.

Digging Out from Anger

When you get angry, do you have trouble letting go of your anger? When your anger is triggered, does it tend to consume you, transforming you into an entirely different human being? When you're mad, are you deaf, dumb, and blind to the world around you — listening only to your own hostile thoughts? Do you have trouble seeing beyond the anger so that you can focus instead on the issues behind it? Do you stand by helplessly as your mood progresses from irritation, to anger, and finally to a state of full-blown rage? If your answer to any of these questions is yes, then you need some tools to dig your way out from anger.

Resistance equals persistence

Ever try not to think about something? Try not thinking about the word *elephant* for five minutes and see what happens. The more you resist that thought, the more it persists — elephant, elephant, elephant!

It's the same with emotions like anger. The more you tell yourself, "I'm not mad, I'm not hurt, it doesn't bother me," the longer you stay mad. And, after a while, that feeling begins to fester.

Sarah had recurrent migraine headaches for most of her adult life — that is, until her husband's untimely death at the age of 60. Shortly after her husband died, Sarah's headaches stopped completely. The reason: Sarah no longer had to resist expressing the anger she felt toward her husband, a man who she says, "was angry all the time about almost everything and took it out on me." Her husband would explode with verbal rage and five minutes later, he was fine. But not Sarah. She held on to her anger for days — sometimes weeks — expressing it through silence and pain. "When he lashed out at me, I couldn't let it be. Staying angry was my way of telling him, 'You're not going to get away with this!'" But, who was Sarah really hurting by hanging on to her anger? Herself.

Isn't it time you stopped resisting both the experience and expression of anger in your life? If the answer is yes, start letting go by following these seven steps:

1. **Identify the source of your anger.**

   What person, event, or circumstance provoked your anger? How long ago was this?

2. **Acknowledge your angry feelings.**

   Say aloud, "I am angry because. . . ." Then decide how angry you are (what I refer to in Chapter 6 as *rate and label*). Rate the intensity of your emotion on a scale of 1 (mild) to 10 (extreme). Ratings of 1 to 3 translate into irritation, ratings of 4 to 6 suggest that you're mad or angry, and ratings of 7 to 10 imply a state of rage.

3. **Legitimize your anger.**

   Remind yourself that you have a right to experience anger, just as you have a right to feel joy or excitement. You don't really need to justify your anger — anger is, as one workshop participant I knew noted, "one way I know I'm alive!"

When your back pain isn't just back pain

Dr. John Sarno, author of *Mind Over Back Pain,* believes that most chronic back pain is not the result of herniated discs and pinched nerves, but rather the muscular tension and accompanying inflammation associated with suppressed anger. Dr. Sarno believes that by releasing this pent-up anger, patients can eventually relax and achieve pain relief.

I agree with him — so much so that I've incorporated an anger-management component into my chronic-pain rehabilitation program.

4. **Give yourself permission to express anger.**

   Anger has gotten a bad rap because people all too often associate it with violence, rudeness, and incivility. But, there are lots of healthy, constructive ways to express anger (see Chapter 11 if you want some examples). Constructively expressing your anger should be your goal.

5. **List three ways in which your life is better off by letting go of anger.**

   For Sarah, letting go of anger — after her husband's death — ended a lifetime of headaches, gave her peace of mind "every time I walk through the front door and don't have to worry about seeing that angry face staring back at me," and the freedom to live a life without anger. When last I checked, Sarah was off on yet another cruise adventure and enjoying life to the fullest.

6. **Decide how best to express anger without hurting yourself or others.**

   Don't get me wrong — I'm not proposing that you let go of anger by ranting and raving for the world to hear. That's neither healthy nor constructive. In anything, venting tends to *sustain* anger not *relieve* it. But, you can talk about your anger more openly (see Chapter 8), use exercise to drain away your angry feelings, or take pen to hand and "confess" your anger in writing (see Chapter 9).

7. **Proceed accordingly.**

   It's time to move forward and implement the decision(s) you made in Step 6. You'll be glad you did.

What are you afraid of?

Most people hold on to anger because of fear. Some common fears that may keep you from letting go of anger include:

✔ Fear of making another person angry

✔ Fear of hurting someone else's feelings

✔ Fear that letting go of anger will mean you forgive the person who made you angry

✔ Fear that you'll lose you reputation as a "nice" person if you express anger

✔ Fear that when you start to express anger, you'll lose control of your emotions

✔ Fear of other emotions (for example, sadness) that underlie your anger

✔ Fear that others will see you as weak or vulnerable

✔ Fear that if you let go of your anger, you're letting the other person off the hook

✔ Fear that anger will cause you to lose something you value (for example, a job or a friendship)

✔ Fear of admitting, once and for all, that you're only human

What are you afraid of?

Being nice doesn't mean being powerless

Who says "Nice guys finish last"? Pretty much everyone — because we've all learned to associate niceness with powerlessness. But, as it turns out, one does not necessarily mean the other.

The dictionary defines a nice person as someone who is pleasant, agreeable, courteous, considerate, and delightful. It doesn't say anything about your being a victim of other people's bad behavior. It doesn't mean that you don't stand up for yourself. It doesn't say you don't deserve to be respected, safe, and treated fairly by others.

If you see yourself as truly powerless, you'll tend to store up feelings of anger instead of letting them go. In an effort to be seen as ultra-nice, you'll say you're "fine" when you're actually irritated. And those irritations will linger and — slowly but surely — accumulate into a feeling of anger. How many times over the years have you read in the newspaper about someone who went into a public place and started shooting innocent people for no apparent reason? And how many times have his neighbors and friends described the gunman as a "really quiet, nice person"? Too many.

Mark was one of the nicest clients I've ever worked with. He was a man in his 60s, who was raised in the traditions of the Old South, where a gentleman never showed his temper in public. By day, Mark was a sweet, pleasant,

---

Not like my father

I loved my father and I hated my father. I loved him because he brought me into this world and he was the only father I had. I hated him because he drank too much and was always angry.

As a child, I held back on any anger I had toward my dad because, quite honestly, I was afraid he might hurt me physically. As an adult, I continued to stifle my anger because I didn't want to be like him. I wanted to be as easygoing and stoic as he was volatile. I wanted to be as approachable as he was remote and distant.

I still remember — 50 years later — the day my mother, in a moment of anger, yelled at me,

"You're just like your father!" She might as well have stabbed me in the heart — it hurt that much. Did I answer her back in anger, saying, "No I'm not. I'm not anything like him, and you know that!"? No — I just lowered my head and walked away in silence.

In order to avoid one type of anger problem (outrageousness), I had developed another ("in-rageousness"). In an understandable effort to distinguish myself from my father in how I expressed my anger, I had missed my mother's real message — like my father before me, I had a lot of anger.

---

charming, and accommodating man. No matter how badly he was treated, he would simply respond by saying, "That's fine — don't worry about it." But, by night, he was a raging tiger. While sleeping peacefully, he would ferociously grind his teeth (on the fresh meat of all those who had wronged him during the day). On one occasion, he woke up to find his bed sheet covered with blood from three broken teeth — like a scene from the movie *The Godfather*. His dental bills were huge. Despite his calm façade and cordial demeanor, Mark was a walking time bomb of rage.

Therapy changed all that. Mark found that he could continue to be nice without being powerless. So, when a friend stood him up for a luncheon appointment that had been planned for weeks, instead of waiting patiently for an hour and absorbing his irritation, Mark left after 15 minutes, went home, and called his friend to say that he didn't appreciate being stood up. The result: He stopped grinding his teeth at night altogether (much to the chagrin of his dentist who remarked one day "I don't know what's changed in your life, but it's been over a year since you've been in here with a tooth problem. If you keep this up, I'll be broke!").

If you hang on to anger today, it becomes both yesterday's *and* tomorrow's anger.

The myth of the angry black man

The media's profile of the angry black man is a myth. A study looking at the link between anger suppression and high blood pressure examined the typical anger-coping style of hundreds of black and white men and women living in a large metropolitan city. Black males were the group most likely to keep anger suppressed in response to provocation — for example, housing discrimination. Perhaps that explains why they also tend to have a much higher incidence of hypertension which, in turn, leads to higher rates of heart attacks and strokes.

Who hangs on and who lets go?

Letting go of anger in a timely manner doesn't come easy to everyone. It can be especially difficult if you are

- **Young:** The younger you are, the harder it is for you to let go of anger. As people age, they tend to get angry less often and get over it more quickly. Perhaps they find that staying angry too long takes too much energy — something that becomes more precious as one ages.

- **Female:** All across the age spectrum, women tend to hang on to anger longer than men. Men's anger tends to be more intense, but they get over it quicker. Women more often do a "slow burn" when they get mad. In large part, this may be due to the fact that, generally, women are perceived as nicer than their male counterparts.

- **An ethnic minority:** Being part of a minority group is characterized, among other things, by a tendency to suppress anger. In a hierarchical society, where power tends to be concentrated at the top, anger rarely flows upward. Those at the bottom tend to complain but otherwise "grin and bear it."

- **Too angry:** Obviously, the more intense your anger, the harder it is to let go. Letting go of irritations — or even normal anger — is relatively easy. But rage, that's a different matter altogether.

- **An intellectual:** Some folks intellectualize anger — think it to death — while others just get upset. Don't get me wrong, intelligence is a wonderful thing — unless it gets in the way of constructive anger expression.

- **The child of nice parents:** People who hold their anger in, rather than let it go, tend to have parents they describe as: loving, warm, easygoing, relaxed. In other words, nice. Those who express their anger openly and without reservation tend to have the opposite kind of parents — cold, distant, strict, and excitable. Monkey see, monkey do!

- **A certain type personality:** Introverts, avoiders, and dependent (or codependent) personalities all tend to move away from conflict and emotional discomfort. Their reluctance to experience or express anger is motivated by fear — fear of confrontation or the loss of a relationship on which they depend for their very survival. Ironically, highly aggressive personalities — those who move against the world — also tend to hang on to anger, but for different reasons. They need to stay angry in order to satisfy their aggressive, win-at-all-costs style of dealing with the world around them (and that includes you and me!).

✔ **Suffering from depression:** The legendary psychoanalyst, Sigmund Freud, thought of depression as "anger turned inward." If you feel uncomfortable expressing your anger directly at its source, you're more likely to either sit on it or turn it on yourself. Expressing anger also takes energy, and people who suffer from depression often lack energy.

✔ **Emotionally illiterate:** You may be surprised by how many adults cannot find words to adequately or accurately describe what they're feeling. If you ask them how they feel about something, they respond by telling you what they think ("He isn't being fair") or what they did ("I just walked off"). As a therapist, I find myself reminding my clients that emotions are feelings — like happy, sad, mad, glad. Just pick one!

✔ **Guilt ridden:** Guilt can be a good thing, but it should be reserved for those occasions where you've done something intentionally wrong, mean, or harmful. Unfortunately, for some people, guilt is the gift that keeps on giving, restricting the free flow of normal, healthy emotions — including anger — in all facets of life.

✔ **A believer:** If you're religious and believe in a higher power — regardless of doctrine or denomination — you've probably been taught to "turn the other cheek" when faced with hostility and that anger is "the devil's work." With this perspective, expressing anger — even irritation — can seem like an ungodly act.

My Jewish mentor

The next best thing to being Jewish is having a close friend who is. Many years ago, I found myself in a very stressful, unhappy job situation with — it seemed to me at the time — no way out. I had tenure, so the administration couldn't fire me, but they did the next best thing and made my time at work a living hell.

One day, feeling pretty beat up emotionally, I called a good friend of mine, who happens to be Jewish, and asked his advice as to what I should do. At first, he laughed and said, "You gentiles are all alike — you only read the half of the Bible that carries the good news. Read the Old Testament and call me back in a week."

I took his advice and a week later called and told him "Now that I see that I'm not the only one in the world who has struggled with adversity, I feel better."

"Good," he said. "Now get a good lawyer and go after those bastards!"

Excuse you!

Are you one of those people who is forever saying "Excuse me!" when some rude person bumps into you or engages in some other type of incivility. If so, you need to stop. Otherwise, you'll end up being one of life's many victims, whose mantra seems to be "Excuse me for living!"

Be assertive. The next time some aggressive person bumps into you or cuts in front of you in line, say "Excuse you!" instead. You'll be amazed at how good that feels and how much pause it gives other people who are within earshot.

Trying the ten-minute rant

One of the reasons people have difficulty letting go of anger is that they express it a little bit here and a little bit there over a period of time, rather than all at once.

At one of my biweekly adult pain-management groups, I noticed that all the participants were in miniconversations trashing physicians for not "fixing" their pain. There was an obvious undercurrent of pent-up anger. So, I abruptly said, "I'll tell you what we need to do here: have each one of you take a turn saying every angry, hateful thing you can think of about surgeons. Each of you will have ten minutes to get it all off your chest. No one will interrupt you, so go for it!"

The first patient vented his anger about his doctor for about seven minutes and then began to run out of steam. "Keep going," I admonished him. "You've still got three more minutes. We want to hear it all."

One after another, members of the group had their say, pretty much parroting one another. Interestingly, as we went around the group, each person had trouble filling up the ten minutes. At the end, about an hour and a half later, they were all emotionally exhausted. After that exercise, it was rare for anyone to bring up angry feelings about their doctors — apparently, there was nothing left to say!

At the end of each day, try giving yourself a ten-minute rant. One of my clients does it while taking a hot shower. She lives alone and no one is there to hear her anyway. She finds it quite refreshing. Or, you could confess your anger in writing (for details, see Chapter 9).

The anger you let go of today doesn't carry over into tomorrow.

Living without Resolution

Maybe you're the kind of person who holds on to anger until you can resolve the problem that caused it in the first place. That's a great approach if you're dealing with a solvable problem. But what if the problem can't be resolved at all — or at least not completely? What purpose does hanging on to anger serve then?

You'll encounter lots of problems, conflicts, and situations in life that, despite your best efforts, will never have a happy or satisfying outcome. These situations you have to live with — without resolution. Examples include

- ✔ Childhood abuse

- ✔ Being raised in an alcoholic home

- ✔ Sexual assault

- ✔ Birth defects

- ✔ Loss of loved ones (through death, divorce, or abandonment)

- ✔ Chronic illness

- ✔ Natural catastrophes (like floods, hurricanes, or tornadoes)

- ✔ War

- ✔ Disfigurement

- ✔ Disability

- ✔ Irreversible loss of income

- ✔ Having an addict in the family

 The next time you get angry, ask yourself these questions: Can my anger correct the situation? Can it undo what has been done? Or, is this one of those times when "after the toothpaste is out of the tube, you can't put it back!" If so, then let it go.

Time's Up: When to Let Go

Here's the $64,000 (or in today's economy, $1,000,000) question: How long should you hang on to anger? How long before it begins to hurt you? How long is too long?

The angry smoker

There is a statistical link between cigarette smoking and how long people stay angry. Smokers take longer to let go of anger than non-smokers. Or, put another way, people who have trouble letting go of anger are more likely to smoke cigarettes.

One explanation is that some people self-medicate anger with nicotine (for more detail, see Chapter 15). Another possibility is that smoking, along with the intensity and duration of a person's anger, is linked to an impulsive temperament and may reflect how one is physiologically "wired."

My answer is simple: 25 minutes at the most. Why 25 minutes, you ask? As Table 12-1 illustrates, most people let go of today's anger in less than half an hour. (This data is based on responses from 286 ordinary people I surveyed ranging in age from 13 to 83.) So it's pretty safe to consider less than half an hour the norm — thus, anger that lasts longer than 25 minutes is lasting too long.

Table 12-1	How Long People Stay Angry
Length of Time	*Percent*
Less than 5 minutes	29.4
5 to 10 minutes	27.3
Less than half an hour	14.0
Less than 1 hour	12.9
1 to 2 hours	4.9
Half a day	5.2
1 day	2.8
More than a day	3.5

Think of this as the 25-minute rule: The next time you find yourself angry, look at your watch to see what time it is. If you don't wear a watch, ask the person you're angry at for the time. Keep checking the time so that you know when 25 minutes have passed. If your anger has already subsided, good for you. But if it's still there, say aloud "Time's up!", let go of the anger, and move forward with your day. (This book is full of simple, easy, practical exercises for letting go of today's anger that you can use during that critical 25-minute window of opportunity.)

Chapter 13

Forgiving

- -

In This Chapter

▶ Understanding that you don't have to forget to forgive

▶ Letting yourself off the hook

▶ Letting go of blame

▶ Knowing that forgiveness is voluntary

▶ Conducting a cost-benefit analysis

- -

Jack is in his 50s now. His health is poor. He's disabled from work. He's lonely. And he has little to show for his life. Jack is a broken man. Looking back, Jack has many regrets. Chief among them is the fact that he alienated himself from his family years earlier. "I know now I was wrong. My family — all they were trying to do was help me. I turned them away. I needed their help, but I turned them all away. And, for that, I feel sorry," he laments.

The one thing Jack doesn't regret, however, is his life-long anger at his mother, who had to put him in an orphanage for a brief time when he was very young. "She abandoned me — left me with strangers — and I'll never forgive her for that!" he explains. Just the mention of that hurtful time elevates his voice and brings tears to his eyes — 45 years after the fact. His mother — who is now in her late 80s and suffering from Alzheimer's — came back to get him after a year, when she could provide Jack and his brother with a stable home, and she raised Jack until he graduated from high school and joined the Army. But none of that mattered to Jack. His mother had committed an unpardonable crime and he would punish her — and himself — for the remainder of his life for that one act.

The anger toward his mother that Jack carried all through life, in the end, is what broke him. He had a good job and friends, and he was surrounded by people who loved him. But his outrageous temper trumped all that. Anger, which on more than one occasion resulted in physical violence, cost him two marriages, a relationship with his only son, his job, and ultimately his health. And yet, even today, Jack is unforgiving.

This chapter offers strategies for letting go of old feelings of anger and hurt that are tied to past grievances. It provides you with both a rationale and a road map for handling yesterday's anger — which, I believe, is the most difficult type of anger to manage. As far as I can tell, there is only one antidote to anger from the past — and that is forgiveness.

Forgiveness Is Never Easy

For reasons none of us can fathom, forgiveness never comes easily to human beings. Anger, now *that* comes easy — but forgiveness, no. You were born with an instinctual capacity for anger, but forgiveness is something you have to learn. It's a skill, really — no different from riding a bicycle, playing soccer, or speaking a foreign language.

You may be one of those lucky people who was raised in a tradition of forgiveness. You learned to forgive by observing the forgiveness that your parents showed one another. Or you learned it through your participation in organized religion — in church, synagogue, or temple. If so, forgiveness comes easier for you than it does for the rest of us.

Some examples of life experiences that are most difficult to forgive are

- Childhood abandonment (by death or divorce)
- Physical abuse
- Emotional abuse
- Sexual abuse
- Rape
- Traumatic workplace injury
- Betrayal by a spouse
- Parental neglect
- Assault
- Death of a child
- Death or injury due to drunk driving
- Unexpected job loss
- Violations of trust or innocence

Support is only support if . . .

Support is only support if you take advantage of it. Your support network is the number of people you can count on to help you deal with adversity in life. Support, on the other hand, has to do with your willingness to avail yourself of that help. Some of us actually have a small network, yet we feel a tremendous sense of support as we struggle our way through life. Others have a huge network and yet feel isolated and alone. The irony is that people who are full of anger and resentment, who need support the most, are the least likely to accept it.

It takes time

Forgiveness is a process, not a thing. It's a journey, really. A magic wand is a thing — and, when it comes to forgiving those who have wronged you, there is no magic wand. The longer you've been holding on to anger, the more time you need to reach that point of resolution called forgiveness. Jack, the man I mention in the introduction to this chapter, has been angry at his mother for over 40 years. Even if he begins the process of forgiveness today, it will be some time before he completes it. The good news for him is that time is on his side. His mother is still alive and, if he can forgive her before she dies, he will undoubtedly have less guilt and remorse after she's gone.

Is today the day you're ready to start this journey — to free yourself from yesterday's anger?

It requires support

Nothing worth doing is worth doing alone. Forgiving someone takes strength, courage, maturity — and, some of that you can draw from those around you. Who do you know who can serve as your forgiveness ally? Who has already been encouraging you to let go of anger from the past? Who can serve as a positive role model — someone who has forgiven some past transgression and moved on with his life?

It's true that forgiveness is a voluntary act. No one can (or should) force you to forgive another person. As a therapist, I've never advised a client to forgive someone. What I do, though, is offer forgiveness as an option that each person should consider in her efforts to find peace of mind. But the choice is entirely hers. And, of course, I offer to support her if she makes this healthy choice.

Do you have the support you need to begin this journey?

It demands sacrifice

Now comes the hard part. In order to forgive someone, you have to sacrifice something. Something has to give. The question is, "What?" Consider the following possibilities:

- ✔ You have to give up being a victim.

- ✔ You have to give up the myth that "life must always be fair."

- ✔ You have to give up your use of anger to protect yourself from emotional pain.

- ✔ You have to give up reliving the initial grievance day after day.

- ✔ You have to give up this hold you're letting the other person have on you by keeping him foremost in your thoughts.

- ✔ You have to surrender your "right" to revenge.

- ✔ You have to give up the notion that by holding on to anger you can somehow undo the injustice that was done to you.

- ✔ You have to give up the idea that you're entitled to the good life — a life free of stress, misfortune, pain, and injury.

- ✔ You have to give up the belief that everyone — especially those closest to you — must always approve of you and treat you with consideration.

- ✔ You have to give up the idea that forgiveness is a sign of personal weakness.

Are you ready to make the necessary sacrifices?

Choosing to Forgive

As the old saying goes, "Timing is everything." Conditions need to be right before you can honestly expect to begin a journey of forgiveness.

You have to be safe

Anger does play a protective role in unsafe life circumstances — situations where mistreatment is ongoing, where you are on guard against the potentially hurtful actions of others, and where you believe your physical or emotional survival is threatened. To ask yourself to forgive someone who is actively harming you here and now is, I think, too much to ask. You have to be safe first.

I didn't forgive my father for his alcoholic, outrageous behavior until after he died. In life, he was far too imposing of a figure. And no matter how old I was, I never stopped being intimidated by the very sight of him. When I visited him on his deathbed — after years of being estranged — I saw a man who was sadly defeated by life, shrunken in appearance, and reconciled to his own death. At that very moment, my heart began to soften, and I think that's when I began to forgive him.

My mother was a different story. I forgave her for being less than the ideal parent — and that's putting it mildly — while she was still alive. But I could do so because I was safe. I was a grown man, I had achieved some measure of success in life, and I lived three states away from her. In other words, I have managed to separate myself emotionally from her, seeing myself no longer as her child but rather as her son. And because she could no longer hurt me, I could afford to love her fully, without recrimination.

Are you safe enough to start a process of forgiveness?

You have to acknowledge the frailty of human nature

The thing we mostly need to forgive others for is being human. Humans are actually very frail creatures, despite all the marvelous advancements in technology that we find around us each and every day. We make mistakes. We hurt other people's feelings — intentionally or not. At times, we're far too selfish. We say "no" when we should say "yes." I could go on and on.

Most people mean well. Most people do the best they can under the circumstances. But, often, that's not good enough. So, people end up blaming each other for what? For being human.

You probably get angry with people because they don't do what you expect of them. But do you expect too much? Nobody has the absolutely perfect parent, child, boss, spouse, or friend. And if you can't forgive yourself ("I hate myself. I'm a loser. I never do anything right."), is that because you hold yourself to an unrealistic, all-or-nothing standard of performance?

In the immortal words of humorist Woody Allen, "We are all bozos on the same bus." Some of us are poor bozos, some intelligent bozos, some beautiful bozos, some inconsiderate bozos, some difficult bozos — but, in the end, we're still bozos.

Isn't it time you looked at the person you've been unable to forgive simply as a "bozo" — maybe a big bozo — instead of some evil person who deserves your vengeance?

How to ruin a good marriage

Professor John Gottman, a leading expert on the dynamics of healthy marriages, has concluded that the primary cause of divorce is a feeling of utter contempt by one or both partners toward each other that expresses itself through a variety of demeaning behaviors. Contempt implies that one person is better — more worthy — than the other, that one person has fewer (if any) character flaws or faults, that one person is indeed superior to his mate in all respects. Contempt leaves no room for equity or parity in intimate relationships — it's simply a matter of who is master and who is slave.

Doing a Cost-Benefit Analysis

If you're going to forgive someone, there definitely has to be something in it for you. You have to believe that it is in your self-interest to let go of yesterday's anger. And, that basically comes down to two questions you need to ask yourself:

- ✔ Who are you letting off the hook?
- ✔ Do you deserve to be happy?

Who are you letting off the hook?

I would argue that the primary beneficiary of your forgiveness is you. Forget about the other person — do it for yourself! Forgiveness should be about *your* anger, not *her* bad behavior. In fact, the thought that you're doing something good for a bad person can only serve as an obstacle to starting this journey.

So, let's see what it's costing you to hang on to old anger as compared to how you might benefit if you let go. Here are some of the costs of hanging on:

- ✔ You constantly relive the painful past.
- ✔ Old anger finds its way into your present and future relationships.
- ✔ You feel drained as a result of all that anger.
- ✔ You continue to feel like a victim.
- ✔ You lose sight of the positives in your life.
- ✔ You remain in a constant state of mourning.
- ✔ Your health is compromised.
- ✔ You have difficulty also forgiving yourself.

The gift of forgiveness

A good friend of mine got angry with me years ago and didn't speak to me for a long time. Looking back, I can now see that he had good reason for his anger, but that can't make up for all the good times we lost because of it. Hard as it was, I accepted that our relationship was over and I grieved both for what was and what might have been.

And, then one day — completely out of the blue — my friend reopened the door and gave us a second chance. That day continues to be one of the happiest of my life and not a day goes by that I don't feel grateful for his gift of forgiveness.

✔ You remain in a constant state of tension.

✔ Your unresolved anger turns into bitterness and hostility.

And here are some of the benefits of letting go:

✔ Your energy is freed up for constructive use.

✔ Your life is now focused on the present rather than the past.

✔ You no longer feel so vulnerable.

✔ Your outlook becomes much more optimistic.

✔ When you forgive, others tend to forgive you.

✔ It becomes easier to forgive yourself — for being human.

✔ Your health improves.

✔ You experience an inner peace that you haven't felt before.

✔ You have a newfound sense of maturity.

✔ You move beyond the pain of past transgressions.

Isn't it time to let yourself off the hook?

Do you deserve to be happy?

I would argue that, of course, you deserve to be happy. But the answer to that question is really something you have to decide for yourself. If you agree, then you have to let go of the recurrent memories of past wrongs, the blame you attach to the other person's behavior, your desire for revenge — all that baggage. You see, bitterness and happiness are incompatible. If you keep one, you lose all chance for the other.

Is there some reason you feel you don't deserve a chance at happiness?

Accepting the Finality of Being Wronged

Another obstacle on the journey of forgiveness has to do with accepting the finality of being wronged in some way. Have you ever thought in an angry moment, "I'm going to stay angry until I get justice, until things are set right again, or until I can somehow even the score"? Well, good luck, because that day will never come. What in the world can a parent do to truly even the score when his child dies at the hands of a drunk driver? How does the wife of an unfaithful man get true justice? How do you set right the fact that your employer went out of business, causing you to lose the best job you ever had? How do you make up for parents who neglected or abused you?

When I say that in order to forgive someone you have to accept that he did you wrong, I'm not suggesting that you overlook what he did — absolutely not! Nor, am I suggesting that you approve of his hurtful behavior. And I'm not asking you to pardon him of his sins. No need to. But you do have to accept what was done and move on.

You don't have to forget the past

Now that I'm over 60 years old, I find that I try more and more to convince myself that there must be some blessings associated with late life. And then it came to me — the one good thing about Alzheimer's disease is that you finally forget all the bad things in your life. Short of Alzheimer's, however, I'm afraid that forgetting the past just isn't that easy.

The age of forgiveness

Forgiveness requires a certain amount of maturity. And maturity, ideally, comes with age. Young children can be quite unforgiving because they deal in what Dr. Bernard Golden, author of *Healthy Anger: How to Help Children and Teens Manage Their Anger*, calls "child logic," logic that is self-centered, unrealistic, and dominated by emotion. The same can be true of adolescents, who for the first time begin to see that the adult world is complex, imperfect, and at times unfair — but still a world in which we have to live. This, in large part, accounts for the heightened levels of anger in these early years (more about this in Chapter 2).

As you grow older, forgiveness is more of an option. Child logic no longer prevails. You have a more balanced, realistic view of yourself and your fellow human beings. You come more and more to acknowledge and accept the fact that we're all frail creatures. The world is not simply a matter of black and white. We hurt each other, intentionally or not, as we journey through life. Forget that it shouldn't be that way — it *is* that way! Maybe the ability to forgive is the *real* gift of age.

When clients who have suffered some trauma come to me, often the first question they ask is "Doctor, when will I get over this?" My honest answer, one that none of them likes or at first understands, is "Never." I then explain that human beings don't get over bad things; if they're lucky (or get the right kind of help), they just get *beyond* those things. Bottom line: You'll never forget whatever it is that you have trouble forgiving. But you don't have to. The memory will linger. What you have to do is get to the point where you can remember without anger. And the only way to do that is forgiveness.

The harder you try to forget something — the more you try not to think about it — the more you remember it. Try this: Close you eyes and try really hard not to think about cucumbers for ten minutes. See what happens? Cucumbers on the brain.

Choose pain over anger

Most people hang on to old anger as a way of avoiding pain. That makes perfectly good sense — because anger (particularly rage) is such a strong emotion and it can mask even the most severe physical and emotional pain. But sooner or later, you're going to have to deal with the pain anyway. It's like the old saying, "You can run but you cannot hide!"

Mandy's family brought her to see me because they were facing yet another difficult Christmas after the untimely death of Mandy's youngest daughter. Clearly, the woman didn't want to be sitting in my office, and she did everything she could to appear pleasant, assuring me that she didn't have any psychological problems. That is until I asked about her daughter, whereupon Mandy suddenly became visibly angry and snapped, "I don't want to talk about my daughter. That's none of your business. She died and there's nothing else to say."

I asked a few more questions about her death — how long ago it happened, what time of year it was, the cause of her death — and she became increasingly agitated. Then I asked her to verify what her family had said about how, every Christmas, she brings out all the wrapped presents for her daughter that were under the tree four years earlier at the time of her death. She acknowledged that she did that, so I asked her why. She burst out in rage, "So she'll have her presents when she comes back!" "What do you mean 'comes back'?" I replied. "She's dead." The pain on that poor woman's face was obvious, as she yelled, "Don't you say that! Don't you ever say that! My daughter is coming back to me. If not this Christmas, then next. And her presents are going to be there — right where they were when she went away."

The woman stormed out of my office with her distressed family in tow, and I never saw them again.

Mandy wasn't full of forgiveness. She couldn't forgive the fact that her daughter was gone forever. She couldn't forgive God for letting this terrible thing happen to her and her family. She couldn't forgive her family for trying to get her to move on with her life. She couldn't forgive her husband and remaining children for not wanting their Christmas ruined. She couldn't forgive herself for being a mother who couldn't protect her child from a life-ending illness. And she couldn't forgive me for confronting her with the reality of her tragic loss. All these things that she couldn't forgive left her consumed with anger. The only way Mandy can get beyond the anger is to let herself feel the pain of losing her daughter — which is what grief counseling is all about.

Part V
Lifestyle Changes That Improve More Than Your Anger

The 5th Wave   By Rich Tennant

"We've tried adjusting your diet and practicing meditation to manage your anger. Now let's try loosening some of those bolts and see if that does anything."

In this part . . .

I argue that emotions, like anger, do not occur in a vacuum. To the contrary, your emotions say a lot about how you live your life — how much sleep you get, what kinds of chemicals (like nicotine or caffeine) you ingest throughout the day, how well you're handling stress, whether you have a balanced lifestyle, how spiritual you are, and your prevailing mood. The techniques I offer in this part are intended to make you a happier, healthier person, not just someone who is less angry. You'll discover which types of stress are toxic, how to be a more responsible drinker, how much caffeine is too much, how to create healthy pleasure, how faith can be a weapon, how to calculate your positivity ratio, how anger revitalizes a sluggish brain, and more.

Chapter 14

Managing Stress

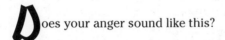oes your anger sound like this?

> "Get off my back, dammit!"
>
> "You'd better back off — I've had all I can take!"
>
> "Give me a break for God's sake! How much crap do you think I can take?"
>
> "I'm not going to tell you again — leave me alone!"

If so, your problem isn't anger — your problem is stress. You either have too much stress or the wrong kinds of stress, but either way, you're stressed. Anger is just your way of expressing it. Some people withdraw and get quiet under fire; others lash out. Unfortunately, neither strategy works well and both strategies end up endangering your health (see how in Chapter 3).

This chapter shows you what to do when your plate gets too full and you see the warning signs of impending anger. I tell you how to identify those stress carriers who, if you weren't feeling irritated before you encountered them, you will afterward. I tell you how to avoid stress burnout and why it's the little hassles of everyday life that do you the most harm. And, most important, I show you how to thrive under stress — how to be a hardy personality. It's easier than you think!

Distinguishing Stress from Strain

Believe it or not, your great-grandparents didn't get stressed out. Well, maybe they *felt* stress, but they didn't call it that. *Stress* and *strain* are engineering terms that were first applied to human beings in the 1930s.

Stress is a normal part of daily life. It's what fuels that built-in fight-or-flight response that you have for help in defending yourself against things — people, circumstances, events — that threaten your survival. Stress isn't a choice — it's a gift (even though it doesn't feel like one!).

Here are some of the changes that occur in your body every time you feel stressed:

- ✔ Your pupils dilate.
- ✔ Your blood sugar rises.
- ✔ Your blood pressure increases.
- ✔ Your blood clots faster.
- ✔ The muscles throughout your body tighten.
- ✔ You breathe more rapidly.
- ✔ Your heart rate increases.
- ✔ Your pituitary gland is activated.
- ✔ Your hypothalamus gland is activated.
- ✔ Adrenaline flows freely.
- ✔ Your palms become sweaty.
- ✔ Your blood cortisol level rises. (*Cortisol* is a stress hormone that enhances and prolongs your body's fight-or-flight reaction.)
- ✔ Fat is released into your bloodstream.
- ✔ Your liver converts fat into cholesterol.

Strain, on the other hand, is what happens to your body when you become *over*stressed — that is, when you experience too much of a good thing. Think of a bridge (I told you this comes from engineering!) that has cars constantly crossing it year after year. Because of their weight, the cars stress the bridge. The more cars that pass over, the greater the stress. Now, imagine that after a few years, cracks begin to appear under the bridge — small at first, but larger as time goes on. These cracks threaten the integrity of the bridge. The cracks represent the strain that inevitably occurs from too much stress. The bridge is you — your body, your health.

My fuse is getting shorter

People ask me all the time: "I've always had a short fuse, but it seems to be getting shorter all the time. Why is that?" In most cases, the answer is that they're experiencing more and more strain as they struggle through life, first with one thing and then another. As the stresses accumulate, so does the strain. Life begins to weigh heavily on them. Their tolerance decreases and their reactivity increases, as indicated by the length of their fuse. Bear in mind, this doesn't happen under conditions of normal stress — only when stress becomes extreme.

Now imagine the bridge creaking and groaning as it begins to show signs of strain. You can see the role that anger plays in communicating to the world just how much strain you're under. Anger is simply your way of creaking (showing your irritation) and groaning (flying into a rage).

Staying Away from Stress Carriers

Do you know someone who, when he walks into the room, seems to disrupt everything around him? Before that person arrived, people were in a good mood, laughing, talking, getting their work done, enjoying life — and this person changed all that. The laughter stopped, moods changed, and tension suddenly permeated the air. That lovely person is a *stress carrier*.

You can tell a stress carrier by the person's:

- ✔ Tone of voice (rapid, pressured, and grating)
- ✔ Body posture (it communicates aggression [for example, hands waving] or defensiveness [for example, arms crossed in front of chest])
- ✔ Tense facial expression (clenched jaw, frown, or narrowing around the eyes)
- ✔ Fist clenching
- ✔ Use of obscenities
- ✔ Tendency to talk over other people in a conversation
- ✔ Jarring laugh
- ✔ Fixed, angry opinions
- ✔ Rapid eye-blinks

Limit your exposure

I used to have a business partner who was a big-time stress carrier. Everywhere he went, he left a wake of uneasiness, hostility, unhappiness, and worry. The tension finally got to the point where the other partners and I consulted with our lawyer about what to do with our business. His counsel was simple: Limit your exposure to the guy. "How do we do that," we asked? Dissolve the partnership. So, we did.

✔ Sighing

✔ Dark circles under the eyes

✔ Head-nodding

✔ Excessive perspiration

✔ Finger tapping

✔ Jerky body movements

✔ Tendency to walk fast

✔ Tendency to eat fast

✔ Tendency to frequently check what time it is

✔ Tendency to hurry up the speech of others by interjecting comments such as "Yeah," "Uh-huh," "Right," and "I know."

✔ Talking or listening to you while the person's eyes continually scan the room

Stay away from stress carriers as much as you can. Their stress is contagious — if you're around them very long, you'll feel stressed, too. If a stress carrier's stress spills over into anger, guess what will happen to you? You'll find yourself angry — and you won't know why.

You may be a stress carrier yourself. Check out the list in this section, and see if you have any of those stress-carrier characteristics. If you're really brave, ask someone who knows you well to examine the list and tell you what he thinks. You may not be the best judge of your true self.

Identifying the Sources of Your Stress

Stressors — those people, events, and circumstances that cause you stress — come in all sorts of sizes and shapes. Some are physical (noise, pollution), some social (noisy neighbors, meddling in-laws), some emotional (death of a loved one), some legal (divorce), some financial (bankruptcy), and so on.

Some are even positive — getting a new job, getting married, graduating from college — and they excite your nervous system no less than the negative experiences do.

Psychologists tend to group stressors into two primary categories: minor irritants (or hassles) and major, critical life events.

Minor day-to-day stressors that you're likely to experience and that can eventually set the stage for anger include the following:

- Hurrying to meet a deadline
- Being interrupted while talking
- Finding that someone has borrowed something without asking your permission
- Being disturbed while taking a nap
- Seeing that someone has cut ahead of you in line
- Driving in heavy traffic
- Misplacing something important
- Caring for a sick child
- Having unexpected company
- Having to deal with car repairs
- Developing a cold sore
- Seeing that a bird has unloaded on your brand-new car
- Having an appointment with someone who shows up late
- Hearing a rude remark directed at you
- Having too *much* time on your hands (You read that right: People with too much time on their hands get bored. Scientists call it underutilization when it occurs in the workplace, and I think the same is true for teenagers stuck at home. It inevitably causes problems of one kind or another if it persists.)

Major stressors — which can have a much more significant impact on your life — include the following:

- Being fired from your job
- Being sentenced to jail
- Having a chronic or life-threatening illness
- Experiencing the death of a close friend
- Having the bank foreclose on your home loan
- Separating from your spouse

My God, what a score!

There's a psychological test that measures the amount of major stress a person has been under for the past year. It lists 42 different stresses and gives each one a score or *impact value.* The total score, it turns out, is a fairly good predictor of future illness — everything from a common cold to a heart attack. The cutoff score for toxic stress is 300. Anything less than that is probably not going to compromise your health. I gave it to a client who came in saying, "I'm not sure why I'm here, but I just don't feel good." Her score was 2,292 — unbelievable! Oh, and by the way, she was a *very* angry woman.

- ✔ Getting pregnant
- ✔ Your children leaving home
- ✔ Moving
- ✔ Winning the lottery
- ✔ Losing your job
- ✔ Starting a new job
- ✔ Being promoted at work

Which type of stressors — minor or major — would you guess are the most unhealthy? If you're like most people, you said the major ones. But the reality is that you're much more likely to be undone by the small things in life. Why? Precisely because they are small and they occur on a daily basis. People see minor stressors as so universal ("Hey, that's just part of life, right?") that they don't take them seriously — and that's a mistake! The good news about major stressors — the ones that potentially affect your life in some critical way — is that they don't occur that frequently and you tend to marshal all of your resources to effectively deal with them. In other words, you take the major stressors more seriously, so they're far less harmful.

Knowing Which Types of Stress Are Toxic

Each person has a finite *carrying capacity* for stress — that is, the amount of stress she can accommodate without showing signs of strain. Even the most resilient people can find themselves overloaded from time to time. That's when you need to take stock of what's going on around you and work to restore some semblance of balance in your life (see Chapter 16).

Stress can become an addiction. If you can't remember the last time you didn't feel overwhelmed by the demands of your day; if you enjoy the adrenaline rush or high that goes along with meeting one challenge after another; if you seem to invite and sometimes create stress where there is none; and, if you find yourself restless and bored when things are too quiet, consider yourself a stress addict.

If you're a stress addict, you need to start weaning yourself off stress, with small steps. You can start by setting aside one otherwise busy evening a week to just hang out with a close friend who isn't competitive and who doesn't require a lot of conversation. Try taking off your watch in the evenings and for portions of your weekend — say, Saturday afternoon from noon until 6 p.m. (and work up to longer periods over time). Sign up for a yoga class or spend a few minutes in a Jacuzzi three or four times a week.

Some types of stresses — regardless of their magnitude — are more poisonous to your life than others. I like to refer to these as the Four Deadly C's.

Cumulative stress

Cumulative stress is stress that — you guessed it! — accumulates over time. It's one thing adding to another, and another, and another, until you can't take any more.

That's how Henry feels. Recently retired, Henry thought he was beginning to live out his golden years. He had a secure income and a paid-for home, and both he and his wife were in good health — or so it seemed. Now Henry is concerned. His wife of many years is starting to forget where she puts things, occasionally gets disoriented, is unable to master simple tasks, and has to have things repeated over and over so she won't forget. Henry told her a week ago, for example, that he would be out one evening at a volunteer meeting. The very next morning, she asked, "When is it that you'll be out for the evening?" Henry told her again, giving her the benefit of the doubt. The next morning, she again asked, "And when is it that you're going to that meeting?" Now clearly frustrated , Henry told her for the third time. Same thing again the next day. Finally, after six consecutive days of having to repeat himself, Henry finally erupted in a state of rage. He yelled, she ran to her room in tears, and both were left feeling bad afterward. Henry wasn't stressed because his wife asked when his meeting was — he was stressed because she kept asking over and over. One or two times, fine; six times, no.

Chronic stress

Have you ever found yourself confronted with a stress that just won't go away? You wake up to it every morning and go to bed with it every night. That's *chronic stress* — it's with you all the time. Many of my clients deal with chronic stress in the form of enduring back pain. Injured on the job in their middle years, they're sentenced to a life of unremitting pain that can't be fixed by the medical profession. No wonder they stay in such an irritable state and are quick to get angry when confronted with any little problem that arises!

Other examples of chronic stress include

- Debt
- Poverty
- Noisy neighbors
- Obesity
- A dead-end job
- Domestic violence
- An unreliable car
- Living in a high-crime area

Catastrophic stress

Events such as terrorist attacks, tsunamis, or hurricanes devastate people — particularly if you're one of those most immediately affected. They represent the most horrific, life-altering kind of stress — *catastrophic stress.* Some people never recover from catastrophic stress (for example, Vietnam veterans who almost 50 years later are still reliving that war as part of a Post Traumatic Stress Disorder); those who do recover from catastrophic stress usually take a long time to heal.

Control stress

Human beings love to control things. People feel safer, stronger, and more competent when they have a handle on their lives. Problem is, life doesn't always afford us that opportunity.

Take Michelle, for instance. She's a bright young woman, who had a great head start on a promising career in marketing before the corporation she worked for went into major reorganization. Michelle found herself with no immediate superior, a doubled workload (with no additional compensation), and too few resources to meet the demands of her job. Worst of all, she no longer had time to devote to the activities she did best. Normally, Michelle was an energetic, positive, dynamic personality, but since her company's reorganization, she found herself exhausted all the time, dreading going to work, irritable, and suffering from migraine headaches and stomach pains. Michelle's life was out of her control, and she was experiencing control stress.

The love of your life

Not all mental health professionals would agree, but I believe that the death of the love of your life is a catastrophic loss, particularly if you've been together for 20 years or more. Those kinds of strong attachments, once broken, cause great personal pain.

Grief is not something that always comes quickly or ends quickly. For example, men widowed after a long and loving marriage are most vulnerable to stress-related illness (heart attack) between 6 and 12 months after the loss of their wives. Women, on the other hand, appear fine for the first two years, before finally showing signs of illness that can be traced back to the death of their husbands.

Grief over the loss of a loved one is one type of stress where professional counseling or a community support group can make a big difference in alleviating suffering. Reach out and get some help after you suffer such a loss — even if you don't feel like you need it.

Avoiding Burnout

Burnout is a form of strain that inevitably results from prolonged, intense, and unresolved stress. The dictionary defines burnout as "the point at which missile fuel is burned up and the missile enters free flight." Guess who the missile is? You. The fuel — that's your physical and psychological energy. And, the free flight — that's all the disorganized, erratic, and inefficient behavior that you find yourself engaging in lately.

The best way to avoid burnout is to see it coming. How many of the following symptoms do you have? If the answer is five or more, you're well on your way to burnout.

- ✔ Chronic fatigue
- ✔ Loss of appetite
- ✔ Insomnia
- ✔ Headaches
- ✔ Heartburn, acid stomach, or indigestion
- ✔ Anxiety
- ✔ Depression
- ✔ Cynicism
- ✔ Hopelessness
- ✔ Feeling bored and unmotivated
- ✔ Abusing alcohol

- ✔ Missing work

- ✔ Being accident-prone

- ✔ Suicidal thoughts

- ✔ Hostility and resentment

- ✔ Agitation

- ✔ Telling sick jokes

- ✔ Spontaneously crying

- ✔ Feeling up one minute, down the next

- ✔ Sudden bursts of temper

- ✔ Loss of passion for your work or life in general

- ✔ Feeling just as tired on Monday morning as you did on Friday night

- ✔ Poor concentration

- ✔ Confusion about routine things both at work and at home

Here's a bit of irony: The people most likely to burn out in any walk of life are the ones most likely to succeed — people who are most passionate about their work, are most liked by superiors and co-workers, are seen as being the friendliest, most energetic, most motivated, most conscientious, most confident, most assertive.

This book offers several strategies that can help to buffer you from the full brunt of the stresses you're currently under, including: shifting to a Type B personality (Chapter 10); moderating your use of stimulants (Chapter 15); relying on friends and co-workers for support (Chapter 16); getting enough sleep (Chapter 17); and participating in spiritual activities (Chapter 18).

But there are other things you can do as well. Find a solution to your chronic stress. For instance, Michelle (see the "Control stress" section, earlier in this chapter) needs a new job. She's fighting a no-win battle. All she can conceivably do is continue to lose ground, spinning her wheels but getting nowhere.

Taking stress breaks throughout the day also helps. Stress breaks don't typically solve the problem, but they do eliminate the *chronic* aspects of stress. I'm amazed at how few people I know who steal a few minutes here and there for themselves just to relax away some of the built-up tension. I can hear the Type A's yelling, "But, I don't have time to relax!" The answer: Make time.

If you want to avoid burnout, try to be more realistic about what you can expect from the situation you find yourself in as well as your own abilities. Burnout usually occurs when there's too big a discrepancy between those two. Forget how things "should" be and deal with them as they really are. And quit demanding more of yourself than is reasonable. Believe me, whatever your job is, it's not to save the world (or the company you work for) single-handedly. Try backing off a little and setting some limits to protect yourself.

The Dutch experience

I was fortunate to spend a year as a guest professor at the University of Nijmegen in the Netherlands toward the end of my academic career. One of my favorite Dutch experiences was a ritual that occurred every single day in the psychology office where I worked. Midway through the morning, everyone — and I mean everyone — put down whatever important piece of work they were engrossed in and gathered for coffee and sweets in a communal area. Secretaries, faculty, students, administrators — everyone was present. We spent about 20 minutes talking about anything other than psychology. How absolutely civilized — how absolutely un-American!

Discovering How to Be Hardy

My aunt Lillian, bless her heart, was a hardy soul. She grew up in an orphanage after her parents both died suddenly in a flu epidemic. Vivacious and athletic, she was almost killed in a head-on collision with a drunk driver in her early 20s — an accident that left her with a mangled knee and stiff leg for the remainder of her life. An attractive woman, she had few suitors due to her injury, and she ended up marrying a much older man. She wanted children but couldn't have any, so she became the patron aunt of a host of nieces and nephews — including myself. She worked full time for all of her adult life, long before women were liberated from the confines of home. She and her husband managed a modest living, although money was always a concern. Following a severe stroke, she spent the last ten years of her life in a nursing home, paralyzed on one side of her body and strapped to a wheelchair. She died quietly in her sleep at age 88.

The remarkable thing was that Lillian never complained about life being unfair or about her physical limitations. She refused to adopt the role of a disabled individual. To my recollection, she never — not once — displayed any anger toward anyone, even if the person deserved it. Instead, she was legendary for her forbearance, her good humor, her forgiving ways, and her optimistic, anything-is-possible outlook.

Psychologist Salvadore Maddi made a career studying people like my aunt, who he described as having a *hardy personality*. According to Maddi, hardiness was an amalgam of three separate traits: control over our own lives, commitment to the things and people that matter to us, and our ability to face a challenge with a positive attitude. These traits, when combined, cut a highly stressed person's likelihood of becoming physically ill by half — even more when combined with other healthy behaviors like regular exercise.

Hardy personalities are more likely to utilize *transformational coping strategies* (transforming a situation into an opportunity for personal growth and societal benefit) when faced with stress. They're also less likely to try to deny, avoid, or escape the difficulties at hand. In older people, being hardy also reduces the risk of stress-related illness — colds, flu, headaches, upset stomach, and nervousness.

People who lack hardiness tend to feel alienated from the world around them. They don't have the support and feeling of being socially connected that their hardy counterparts enjoy — that connectedness goes a long way toward minimizing the impact of stress in their daily lives. Because their lives are devoid of value and purpose, they have no real incentive to solve their problems — it's just easier to be mad.

There appears to be no gene for hardiness — it's a style of dealing with stressful life circumstances that is a byproduct of life experience. In other words, it's learned — and if you haven't learned it already, it's not too late!

Be the master of your own destiny

In order to have the kind of hardy personality that'll help you cope with stress, you need to believe in your own ability to deal with adversity. Call it self-esteem, self-confidence, self-efficacy — call it whatever you want — it comes down to being the master of your own destiny.

What do you do when you're on the wrong end of some major stress? Do you run and hide, avoiding even thinking about the problem or how you can resolve it? Do you distract yourself with a cigarette, a beer, or some serious shopping at the local mall? Or, like my Aunt Lillian, do you ask yourself "What can I do to make things better for myself?" and then act accordingly. If you're like Lillian, you have one of the three critical elements of a hardy personality — a sense of internal control.

Practice thinking like a hardy personality by repeating to yourself statements such as the following:

- People get the respect they deserve in life.

- Good grades in school are no accident — they're the result of hard work.

- Luck has little or no effect on how my life turns out.

- Capable people become leaders because they take advantage of opportunities that come their way.

- What happens to me is my own doing.

- With enough effort, voters can wipe out political corruption.

To choose or not to choose

Maybe you like to choose your own destiny. You want to decide how best to deal with problems, conflicts, challenges, and stresses. Good for you! You are what psychologists call a *self-directed personality*. The more options you allow yourself (or others allow you), the better.

But, believe it or not, not everyone wants choice. In fact, you might get confused, upset, or paralyzed with indecision if you're forced to decide how best to cope with some major life stress. You are an *other-directed personality* — which means you need help from outside sources (family, professionals) to decide what you should do. So, ask!

✔ I can fight city hall!

✔ People only take advantage of me if I let them.

Be a player, not a spectator

Hardy people have a deep sense of involvement and purpose in their lives — the commitment component of a hardy personality. In the game of life, you have to decide whether you want to be a player or spectator.

While non-hardy folks are waiting idly by for life to improve (that is, become less stressful), hardy personalities do the following:

✔ Vote at all levels of government — local, state, federal

✔ Join civic groups that have a mission to help people

✔ Run marathons

✔ Beautify highways

✔ Volunteer for community service

✔ Tackle projects at work that nobody else wants

✔ Find meaning in the smallest things

✔ Have a willingness to make mistakes in order to develop new skills

✔ Assume leadership positions

✔ Pray actively for themselves and others

✔ Take classes to better themselves (or just for the fun of it!)

✔ Become totally involved in family activities

✔ Get regular health checkups

✔ Have strong political opinions

✔ Seek out new relationships

✔ Find something interesting in everyone they meet

Transform catastrophes into challenges

Life is forever changing. Sometimes these changes are in your favor; other times they're not. Either way, they're stressful. What matters is whether you see these changes as catastrophes or challenges. People respond actively to a challenge, and retreat from catastrophes.

Two people unexpectedly lose their jobs. One thinks of this as the end of the world as he knows it. He goes home, gets drunk, loses his temper with his family, and spends the next two weeks sleeping and watching TV. The other man tells himself, "Great, now I can look for an opportunity in something that has more security and pays better," and then he develops a plan (with his family's support) for what to do next.

When you're hit with some major stress in your life, which person are you?

The next time you have to deal with a major stress, and you start thinking it's the end of the world and wanting to retreat, try taking these steps:

1. **Clearly define the problem.**

   Did you lose your job? Did your youngest just leave home, leaving you with an empty nest? Is your spouse gravely ill?

2. **Ask yourself: What is the challenge?**

   If you've lost your job, you have to go find another one. If your house is soon to be empty of children, you'll have to find other things you're passionate about. If a loved one has just been diagnosed with a fatal disease, you'll have to prepare to grieve over that loss and to handle life more on your own in the future.

3. **Determine whether you have enough support to meet the challenge.**

   Support is all-important in dealing with major challenges in life. Figure out how much support you have on your side. Ask yourself: "Who can I count on to help?", "How can they help — give moral support, lend a hand, tell me I'm okay?", "Is their support up close and personal or long-distance?", and "Do I need to find new sources of support — for example, legal assistance or counseling?"

4. **Develop an action plan.**

Laughter eases the pain

Before being subjected to pressure-induced pain in an experimental setting, men and women were allowed to listen to one of three audio tapes — one that made them laugh, one that relaxed them, and one that was on an educational topic. Pain tolerance, it turns out, was greatest in those who shared a good laugh. The next time you're feeling pained (challenged) by some stressful event or circumstance, find someone or something to make you laugh — it's good medicine!

Ask yourself: "What specific steps do I need to take to meet this challenge?", "Where do I start?", "Where do I want to end up — what's my goal?", "How will I know when I've met the challenge?" Set some timelines for each of the individual steps. Reward yourself along the way as you complete each step. Celebrate when you've completely met the challenge — and your life becomes less stressful.

These steps work whether you've experienced a true catastrophe (a hurricane has destroyed everything you own, your family has died in a plane crash) or you're facing something more common. What matters isn't whether the event was a true catastrophe — what matters is that is *feels* like a catastrophe to you, and you can transform the catastrophe into a challenge. The more traumatic the event, the more help you'll need in facing the challenge. But you *can* get through it, no matter what it is.

Coping with Stress: What Works and What Doesn't

Everything you do to get through the day — every thought, every deed — is an act of coping with stress. Going to work, getting drunk, paying off debts, laughing, crying — all are acts of coping. Some ways of coping with stress are aimed directly at the source of stress; other ways of coping have more to do with the strain that is produced by this stress.

Here are some examples of coping strategies that feel good and provide some temporary relief from stress, but that *don't* resolve the problems that do you the most harm:

- ✔ **Avoiding:** Avoidance basically means dealing with stress by *not* dealing with it (for example, by eating, smoking, or drinking alcohol).

- ✔ **Blaming:** If you cope with your stress by assigning blame, you either point the finger at other people, or you beat up on yourself.

The happiest time of life

As I write this chapter, I just finished seeing a 70-year-old client who is the happiest he's ever been in his life. He told me about a number of recent stresses he's dealing with — financial problems with his son, a meddlesome sister-in-law, chronic back and leg pain — all without getting angry.

What is noteworthy here is the fact that this man spent his entire adolescent and adult life getting angry at every problem that came his way. If the cows got out of the fence, he got angry. If his dog was barking, he got angry. If his wife wanted him to do something and he was tired, he got angry. When his kids didn't always obey him, he got angry. If there was a problem at work, he got angry.

But, at age 60, he decided to change all that. Now, he can see that he doesn't need anger to cope with stress — and, he never did! He just *thought* he did.

✔ **Wishing:** Some people sit around and try to imagine their problems away.

✔ **Acting on impulse:** When in doubt, some people shoot from the hip. They don't think — they just act.

Here are some *effective* coping strategies for dealing with stress:

✔ Try to find out more about the situation.

✔ Talk with a spouse, relative, or friend about what's bothering you.

✔ Take things one step at a time.

✔ Pray for guidance or strength.

✔ Draw on past experiences of a similar nature.

✔ Seek professional assistance (from a doctor, lawyer, or clergy member).

✔ Try to see the positive side.

✔ Focus on the problem, not your emotional reaction.

✔ Be patient — don't look for the quick fix.

✔ Persist — keep trying no matter how long it takes to reach a solution.

✔ Accept feelings of uncertainty while you work toward a solution.

✔ Develop several options for problem solving.

✔ Keep communication lines open.

✔ Be willing to compromise.

✔ Be optimistic.

Chapter 15

Managing Your Chemistry

· ·

· ·

For all my angry clients, I have three prescriptions:

✔ Stop smoking.

✔ Lay off the caffeine.

✔ Cut back on alcohol.

Otherwise, you're only fueling the fire.

In this chapter, I show you how to effectively manage anger by creating a less anger-friendly *internal* environment — the environment within your body. I show you how common chemical substances such as nicotine, caffeine, and alcohol affect your body (and your anger). And I help you understand the connection between impulsivity, anger, and substance abuse.

Just Because It's Legal Doesn't Make It Healthy

Most people — myself included — confuse issues of legality with that of health. If something is legal, we tell ourselves it can't harm us. But common sense tells us otherwise.

Raise your hand if you use drugs

Some years ago — when I still had school-age children — I was asked to address a group of middle-school parents about why kids take drugs. To my great surprise, the auditorium was filled to capacity, full of moms and dads hoping to hear something that would reassure them that drugs would never be a problem in their families.

To start what I hoped would be a lively, back-and-forth discussion, I asked the parents to raise their hands if they were drug users. Needless to say, not one person raised his hand. In fact, most people had a rather startled look on their faces.

Then I asked how many had smoked a cigarette that day. Lots of hands went up. Next, I asked how many had had a cup of coffee, tea, or some type of soft drink. Almost everyone's hand went up. Lastly, I asked how many had had some alcohol. Some more hands went up.

I reminded them that caffeine, alcohol, and nicotine are all drugs — legal drugs but drugs nevertheless.

Then I asked my original question — How many of you are drug users? — and every hand in the auditorium was raised. Why this exercise? Because illegal drug use among children is highly influenced by the drug use — legal or illegal — of their parents and by the fact that our culture sanctions the use of drugs as an integral part of what's called the "good life."

For example, cigarettes are legal, but everyone knows that nicotine is an addictive drug and that smoking leads to the untimely death of millions of people. Alcohol is legal, but when it's used in excess, it contributes to everything from domestic abuse and fatal traffic accidents, to heart attacks and liver disease. And caffeine — perhaps the most popular common-use drug of all — is certainly legal, but it interferes with brain chemicals that promote good sleep (see Chapter 17), raises blood pressure, and increases the risk for miscarriage, stillbirth, and low-birth weight babies in pregnant women.

One big problem, I think, is that most people don't think of common-use chemicals as "real" drugs — certainly not in the same way they think of heroine, cocaine, amphetamines, and marijuana. Maybe you consider them "safe" drugs that have no ill effects on your health and well being. Most people don't really know the connection between what I call the "chemistry of everyday life" and emotions such as anger.

These so-called "harmless" chemicals, as it turns out, can lower your threshold for anger arousal in a number of ways:

> ✔ **Caffeine and nicotine stimulate the central nervous system, making it more reactive to environmental provocation.** *Translation:* If your nervous system is ramped up, you'll have a harder time staying calm when that guy on the freeway cuts you off.

Self-medicating anger

Margo, a 43-year-old divorcee, has struggled with a drinking problem and intermittent depression for years. Every time she thinks she has loosened the grip that alcohol has on her life, something upsets her and she instantly falls off the proverbial wagon.

"I was doing fine — no alcohol for months — and then my boyfriend really hurt my feelings over the weekend. I'm so depressed," she said crying. "Now all I can think of now is getting drunk."

Margo's core problem is suppressed anger. She's furious at her boyfriend — she says he's insensitive, uncaring, and unsupportive — but she feels hurt instead. Alcohol — her drug of choice — is her way of medicating the emotional pain she feels. Its appeal, of course, is its anesthetic quality. Where Margo needs help is in recognizing and dealing with her deep-seated, unexpressed anger, not only toward her current boyfriend but also to all those men in her life (and there have been many!) who have similarly mistreated her. Until she accomplishes that, Margo has no chance of remaining sober for any significant length of time.

✔ **Alcohol, even in small quantities, can cloud or exaggerate a person's perceptions, causing an intoxicated person to misread the actions and intentions of others.** *Translation:* If you've had too much to drink, you may think your girlfriend is flirting with that bartender when she's really just asking where the bathroom is.

✔ **Alcohol tends to make a person less inhibited (emotionally and behaviorally), allowing a person to feel and act in ways he wouldn't if he were sober.** *Translation:* When you're sloshed, you're much more likely to lash out or throw a punch at someone you're upset with. (Bars have bouncers for a reason.)

✔ **Caffeine and alcohol, if used excessively, disrupt sleep patterns and lead to increased irritability (see Chapter 17).** *Translation:* All that coffee may help you stay up late cramming for a final exam, and the alcohol you drink to celebrate when finals are over, may feel good at the time, but there's a reason you're tired the next morning.

✔ **Alcohol can affect a person's mood, especially in terms of depression, which in turn affects emotions — such as sadness and anger (more about this in Chapter 18).** *Translation:* If you've ever ended up crying into your beer stein only moments after you were toasting your friends, it may be because the alcohol has wreaked havoc with your mood.

How Much Is Too Much?

When it comes to common-use chemicals like caffeine and alcohol, the less the better. In moderation, these substances have no affect on your emotional state — but when used to excess they do. The trick is to know when enough is enough. What's a safe dose of caffeine? What constitutes responsible drinking? (For more on smoking, see "Eliminating Your Favorite Cigarette," later in this chapter — if you figured I would tell you to quit, you're right.)

On average, adult human beings can tolerate approximately 250 mg of caffeine daily without experiencing adverse physical, emotional, and behavioral consequences. Table 15-1 illustrates some common sources of caffeine and the concentration levels of each:

Table 15-1	Sources of Caffeine
Source	*Amount of Caffeine*
Brewed coffee, 8 ounces	85 mg
Instant coffee, 8 ounces	60 mg
Decaffeinated coffee, 8 ounces	3 mg
Brewed tea, 8 ounces	50 mg
Instant tea, 8 ounces	30 mg
Soft drink, 12 ounces	32–65 mg
Cocoa, 8 ounces	6–142 mg

Note: Prescription and over-the-counter medications may contain caffeine as well. Read the label or check with your pharmacist to find out how much caffeine your medications contain.

The length of time caffeine remains active in the nervous system is between three and seven hours. Because of its lingering effects, concentrations can build up to toxic levels throughout the course of the day.

Caffeine should come with a warning label — evidence suggests that it can become addictive even at low dosages. If you're a heavy user, you can expect physical withdrawal symptoms — headaches, fatigue, irritability — when you lay off the caffeine. If you're thinking, "Oh come on, how bad can the consequences of too much caffeine really be?", consider the following list of potential side effects:

✔ Tachycardia (an abnormally fast heartbeat)

✔ Disturbances in cardiac rhythm

- ✔ Elevated blood pressure

- ✔ Muscle contractions

- ✔ Rapid respiration (breathing rate)

- ✔ Drowsiness

- ✔ Increased anxiety

- ✔ Restlessness

- ✔ Tremors

- ✔ Flushing

- ✔ Insomnia

- ✔ Depression

- ✔ Irritability

- ✔ Lightheadedness

- ✔ Headaches

- ✔ Stomach pain

- ✔ Frequent urination

- ✔ Indigestion

- ✔ Hives

- ✔ Burning feet syndrome (it is what it sounds like — your feet ache and feel like they're burning)

The rules of safe, responsible alcohol consumption are simple:

- ✔ Don't have more than two alcoholic drinks per day (one if you're female).

- ✔ Don't consume more than four alcoholic drinks at one sitting (three if you're female).

Note: By one drink, I mean 12 ounces of beer, 5 ounces of wine, or 1½ ounces of hard liquor.

If you stay within these guidelines, your alcohol consumption shouldn't have a negative effect. Responsible drinking does not mean abstinence — in fact, medical science has suggested that people who consume up to 3 ounces of alcohol daily enjoy better health over a lifetime and live longer than teetotalers, presumably because of its relaxation effects. But drinking in moderation is not always easy — as many people can attest!

Type A's drink more

Individuals with a Type A personality (see Chapter 10) tend to drink alcohol more frequently than their Type B counterparts. Roughly half of Type A's report consuming alcohol "nearly every day" or "every day." One possible explanation for this lies in the fact that Type A's have more difficulty relaxing than Type B's, and Type A's use alcohol to help them relax. A second explanation has to do with the fact that Type A's tend to be more extroverted and outgoing and find themselves in social situations where drinking is not only possible, but expected. My own theory is that their alcohol consumption pattern is just another part of their overall "aggressive" style of interacting with the environment.

Keeping Track of Your Substance Use

There are three good reasons for keeping track of your daily use of chemicals such as nicotine, caffeine, and alcohol:

✔ You may not have the faintest idea of precisely how much you ingest on a regular basis, which means you're unaware of the potentially influential role such substances play in your emotional life.

✔ Simply paying closer attention to your substance use patterns can be an effective way to cut back. (Psychologists call this the *self-monitoring effect.*)

✔ It helps you begin to appreciate how the substances you take in may be linked to the likelihood of your losing your temper.

Keep a daily record of your all the cigarettes you smoke, as well as all the caffeine and alcohol you consume, for one week. Be sure to include all three. In addition to noting the time of day you engaged in each type of behavior, also indicate whether you were irritated, angry, or in a rage before or after you smoked a cigarette, drank a cup of coffee, or had a beer. Table 15-2 illustrates a hypothetical record of one person's daily use:

Table 15-2		Substance Use Diary	
Time of Day	*Substance*	*Feeling Before*	*Feeling After*
7:30 a.m.	Coffee (8 oz.)	No anger	No anger
7:45 a.m.	Coffee (8 oz.)	No anger	No anger
9:30 a.m.	Coffee (8 oz.) and cigarette	Irritated	No anger
12 p.m.	Cigarette	Irritated	No anger

Time of Day	Substance	Feeling Before	Feeling After
1:45 p.m.	Coffee (8 oz.) and cigarette	Irritated	Angry
3 p.m.	Cigarette	Angry	Irritated
6 p.m.	Beer (12 oz.)	Irritated	No anger
6:45 p.m.	Beer (12 oz.)	No anger	No anger
7:30 p.m.	Beer (12 oz.) and cigarette	Angry	Angry

Two things are apparent from this record:

✔ The person uses caffeine to self-medicate anger — that is, when she's angry, she usually has a cigarette, a cup of coffee, or a beer.

✔ Her approach appears to work. She's usually less angry or completely anger-free immediately afterward.

The problem is that appearances can be deceiving. This diary suggests that self-medicating anger works in the short run, but that doesn't necessarily mean that it works in the long run. These substances may provide an immediate benefit to you when you're angry, but over time you may find yourself needing more alcohol, more cigarettes, and more caffeine to have the same effect. First you're hooked on anger, and then you become hooked on substances. In addition, caffeine and nicotine are stimulants that have the capacity to overstimulate your nervous system, thus making it easier for you to get angry the next time you get frustrated or provoked. In effect, you end up in a vicious cycle where anger leads to chemicals and chemicals lead to anger.

Why do I have a hangover?

How bad your head hurts the next morning may, to a large extent, be a function of just how angry you were when you were drinking the night before. My friend and colleague Dr. Ernest Harburg at the University of Michigan found that "angry drinkers" have far more hangover symptoms — stomach discomfort, tremors, diarrhea, anxiety — than "non-angry drinkers" do. The difference was particularly pronounced for men, who were twice as likely to fit the profile of the angry drinker. Even more fascinating was the fact that the amount of alcohol they consumed made little difference. Bottom line: Anger and alcohol are not a good mix! If you're angry, don't drink; if you drink, be cool.

Eliminating Your Favorite Cigarette

The best way to stop (or cut back on) smoking is to start by eliminating your favorite cigarette of the day. For most people, this is the after-dinner cigarette. The second-most-favorite cigarette is the one "first thing in the morning." (Interestingly, the latter is more typical of smokers who are nicotine addicted.)

Smoking is a *habit* (a predictable behavior that is conditioned to repeat itself without any conscious, deliberate thought or intent on the part of the smoker). Smokers light up basically because they have the urge to do so and that urge is stronger at certain times of the day than others. The logic here is simple: If you can eliminate the strongest urge in your day, it will make all the other weaker urges throughout the day easier to overcome.

After you decide which is your favorite cigarette of the day, develop a plan of action for outlasting the urge. As part of your plan, you may want to:

✔ **Spend the time you normally allocate to smoking a cigarette on some alternative form of pleasure.** Despite its health hazards, there is no denying that smokers derive pleasure from ingesting nicotine. So, what you're looking for here is a substitute.

✔ **Talk yourself through the urge.** My favorite mantra is "This too shall pass." The stress-inoculation technique in Chapter 22 will come in handy.

✔ **Rely on a higher power to help you find the strength to resist the urge to smoke.** Do you have sufficient faith in yourself to overcome the urge to smoke?

✔ **Lie back, close your eyes, and engage in some positive imagery.** Give you mind something to do other than focus on smoking a cigarette. Picture yourself doing something you enjoy where you typically don't smoke.

✔ **Have a piece of hard candy rather than a cigarette.** This strategy works with anger, why not smoking? (See Chapter 4 for details.)

✔ **Take a minute for some journaling.** This is a perfect time to spend a minute or two — as long as it takes for the urge to pass — to write down how you're feeling at the moment. It's okay to confess that you miss having a cigarette!

The smokers who are the most successful in quitting (or cutting back) are those who devise their own self-help program. So, if you're committed to this as part of your overall anger-management program, then the odds are in your favor. Don't be afraid to be creative! Think outside the box — you never know what might work.

Counting Your Caffeine

Controlling caffeine is all about numbers. The human body can absorb and make use of 250 mg of caffeine a day. All you want to do here is get your consumption — using the numbers in Table 15-1 (earlier in this chapter) — down to or 250 mg or less. Try the following:

✔ Switch from coffee to tea as your beverage of choice. (Both have caffeine, but tea has less.)

✔ Alternating between caffeinated and decaf coffee.

✔ Try drinking "half-and-half" coffee — half caffeine, half decaf.

✔ Cut back on your use of over-the-counter medications, such as Bromo-Seltzer, Excedrin, or NoDoz.

✔ Rather than soda, order water with lemon in restaurants — it's trendy!

✔ Limit yourself to no more than two soft drinks a day.

✔ Go through the day counting caffeine just like you count calories.

✔ Limit yourself to two units (cups of coffee, glasses of iced tea, soft drinks) at one sitting — anything more you can think of as "caffeine bingeing."

Caffeine has an active half-life of three to seven hours. If you want a good night's sleep (see Chapter 17), avoid caffeine four hours before bedtime.

Adopting a New Drinking Style

Unless you have a definite drinking problem, a few common-sense rules about how to drink responsibly will hold you in good stead. Here's my 12-step program:

✔ **Avoid drinking alone.** Married people are less likely to smoke, drink, and drink heavily than unmarried people. As crazy as this may sound, you're also less likely to abuse alcohol when you're in good company than when you're by yourself.

✔ **Eat plenty of food before you drink and while you're drinking.** Food absorbs alcohol and lessens its effect on your nervous system (especially high-protein foods such as meat and cheese).

✔ **Alternate between alcoholic and nonalcoholic drinks.** That way, you'll cut your alcohol intake by half!

Letting the impulse pass

Call it an urge, a craving, a hunger — whatever. You ingest most substances based on impulse. An impulse is your body's way of signaling you that it wants (or needs) something and your job is to satisfy that impulse. The whole process is mindless!

Some people have too many impulses to eat — and they end up obese. Some have too many urges to consume alcohol — and they end up alcoholics. Some have too many urges to smoke cigarettes — and they end up with lung cancer. Some have too many urges to buy things — and they end up broke.

The number of urges you have throughout the day to do something reflects just how much a part of your life is defined by that want or need. For example, in Chapter 2 I talk about the difference between folks who only occasionally get irritated versus those who fit the profile of a chronic rager. The same distinction can be made between a chipper (someone who only occasionally smokes a cigarette) and a four-pack-a-day smoker. So, here's my question: Do you want your life to be defined by chemicals of this sort?

The good news about impulses are that they're transient — they come and go, passing through your nervous system if you let them. Each time you experience the impulse but don't act in a way that satisfies it, the strength of the impulse weakens. If you're a smoker, think of your favorite cigarette. Each time you *don't* smoke that cigarette, it becomes a little less important until one day it's not your favorite cigarette at all. The same strategy works when you're trying to get sober — each time you intentionally put yourself in a situation where you always drank alcohol in the past, and don't drink, the connection between that place and alcohol weakens until you can go there with no urge to have a drink whatsoever. (That's why traditional 28-day sobriety programs generally don't work. They isolate you from the real world for a few weeks until you dry out and then send you right back out there where the situational urge to drink is just as strong as ever. You don't have a chance!)

✔ **Drink slowly.** Aggressive drinkers drink everything faster and, as a result, end up having more drinks. Try to make each drink last one hour (the time it takes for your body to eliminate that same drink).

✔ **Volunteer to be the designated driver once in a while.** Your friends will love you and you'll feel much better than they do in the morning.

✔ **Always let someone else pour.** People are far more generous in the amount of alcohol they use per drink when they make it for themselves.

✔ **When you go out, decide in advance how much money you want to spend on alcohol.** With the price of a drink somewhere between $4 and $8, it won't take long to reach the limits of your pocketbook. (Better yet, pay cash — if you're like most people, you have less of that than you do credit!)

The blessing of old age

Temperament changes with age. My studies of community residents, ranging in age from adolescents to folks in their 80s, suggests that as people age, they tend to be less impulsive, less emotionally reactive, and more independent (who would have guessed?). This most likely also explains why people smoke less and get less angry in their later years. There's no known cure for aging, but at least this information gives us something to look forward to!

✔ **Never drink when you're in a bad mood.** *Remember:* Even though most people think of alcohol as a stimulant (it loosens us up and gets the social juices flowing!), it's actually a depressant. The truth of the matter is that, after a brief period of euphoria, your mood will take a downturn. If you're suffering from clinical depression (see Chapter 19), you should never — and I emphasize *never* — drink alcohol!

✔ **Let someone else in your group be the drunk.** Competing to see who can drink the most or get drunk the quickest is a child's game — and a dangerous one at that.

✔ **Don't drink before you drink.** Having a drink (or two) before you leave home, get on the road, and head off to an evening of socializing (and more drinking!) only adds to the amount you're drinking.

✔ **Drink like you're a woman — whether you are or not.** Women have a lower tolerance for alcohol and require fewer drinks to feel intoxicated. Find some other arena to prove your manhood — like on the golf course or in the executive boardroom.

✔ **If you do all this and you still drink too much, consider seeking professional help.**

Chapter 16

Adding Balance to Your Life

. . . .

In This Chapter

▶ Adopting a balance-sheet approach to life

▶ Identifying the barriers to a balanced lifestyle

▶ Overcoming extremes

▶ Figuring out how to be multidimensional

. . . .

*W*ho says anger management can't be fun? Of course it can and, in this chapter, I show you how. Basically, it comes down to one simple thing: adding balance to your life.

Is your personality too one-dimensional — work, work, and more work? Do you live life mostly at the extremes? Does everything you do have an all-or-nothing quality to it? Too much socializing, too little solitude? Too much parenting, too little canoodling? When's the last time you experienced some healthy pleasure — and, do you even know what that is? Are you well connected socially? How uplifted have you been lately?

If you answer these questions the way I think you will (and, unfortunately, the way most people do), then your lifestyle is definitely out of balance. To fix this, I show you how adopting a balance-sheet approach to life leaves little room for anger.

Counterbalancing Stress

Thirty years ago, Dr. Stewart Wolf, a pioneer in the field of stress research, introduced the concept of "counterbalancing stress" to the world of modern medicine. Up until that time it was inconceivable that human beings could protect themselves from stress-induced illness by their own voluntary actions — for example, by maintaining strong religious beliefs, fostering family solidarity, and striving for an interdependent (working collaboratively with others) lifestyle.

You're not being serious

You may be surprised at how many people find the idea of living a balanced lifestyle unthinkable and unacceptable. One rather obsessive-compulsive gentleman — always thinking, always doing — came to me for stress management and ended up getting quite belligerent when I suggested that he needed to learn to "just sit and watch the grass grow." He said indignantly, "That's it? That's all you have to offer? I don't think you're taking my problem seriously and that pisses me off!" No matter how hard I tried to explain that I was just suggesting a principle we might pursue — to balance off his constant striving for accomplishment with some old-fashioned relaxation — it was to no avail. He left angry.

No longer did we have to wait for the stresses of everyday life to make us sick (or angry!) — we could counterbalance that stress and thereby remain healthy. So, how do you do that? In the following sections, I provide the information you need.

Adding uplifts to your life

In Chapter 14, I tell you about the harm that minor irritants (hassles) can have on both your temperament and your health. What about the flip side of that stress-illness relationship? Just as you encounter all kinds of small stresses day to day, you probably also encounter a variety of small positive, uplifting experiences. *Uplifts* involve people, events, circumstances, and activities that create in you a sense of joy, hope, optimism, faith, relief, and release — all antidotes to stress. Here are some examples of uplifts you may have in your daily life:

- Engaging in regular exercise
- Spending time with children
- Working on hobbies
- Enjoying a beautiful day
- Reading for pleasure
- Shopping
- Making a new friend
- Hearing some good news
- Enjoying free time
- Meditating
- Giving and receiving love

✔ Smelling pleasant aromas — vanilla, lavender, the smell of fresh bread

✔ Being entertained

✔ Spending time with pets

✔ Contributing to a charity

✔ Doing volunteer work

Uplifts affect you in the opposite way that stress does. Stress expends energy and can lead to a condition known as *vital exhaustion* (see Chapters 3 and 17), whereas uplifts create energy and revitalize you physically and mentally. Stress irritates your nervous system — hence, its connection to anger. Uplifts have a relaxing effect and release stored-up tension, leaving the door open for feelings of peace, tranquility, and inner harmony.

The more hassles — as well as major stresses — you have in your life at the moment, the more you need to be uplifted. But you can't rely on the chance that these positive experiences will find you — you have to seek them out, make them happen, go looking for them. In other words, you have to take the initiative. Believe me, you'll be glad you did. Start by making sure you have at least one uplifting experience each day — no exceptions!

Living an unbalanced life can be painful! For the past 25 years, I have worked tirelessly to rehabilitate clients suffering from chronic, disabling back pain. One of the things I find most interesting is that the first thing these folks do after they're injured is eliminate all the uplifting social and recreational experiences from their lives. They quickly decide to give up having sex, going to church, visiting friends, attending their youngsters' sporting events — all because of pain. Yet, strangely enough, even with pain, they continue to complete domestic chores — vacuum, rake leaves, carry in the groceries. No wonder 70 percent of them become clinically depressed. Their lives are lopsided — all they have left are pain and chores.

Creating a favorable ratio

When my daughter, Rebecca, was in high school, she had to conduct a project to compete at the science fair at the local community college. Being the helpful father I was, I suggested she study the relationship between daily hassles, uplifts, and illness among young people her age. She loved the idea!

She set about surveying a sizable number of her peers, asking them to indicate how often they experienced a wide range of standard hassles and uplifts within the past month, and also had them complete a self-report illness measure.

What she found was intriguing: It turned out that the best predictor of illness wasn't either the hassles or uplifts score alone, but the ratio of the two. The more positive the ratio (uplifts divided by hassles), the fewer health complaints.

Moving away from the extremes

Are you one of those people who lives life at the extremes? Everything you do is either all or nothing. You think too much and act too little. Your daily routine is full of a long list of have to's (have to go to work, have to pick up the kids, have to pay the bills, have to mow the grass) with no room left for any want to's (want to take a nap, want to sit quietly and drink a glass of wine, want to listen to some classical music, want to call an old friend and catch up). Your life seems mostly about others and not about you. (That may get you into heaven, but it makes for a very stressful time on earth!)

Well, if you want to counteract stress, it's time you moved to the center. Add more diversity to your day — mow the grass and then have your glass of wine! Make that long-distance call to your old friend during your lunch break at work. Pick up the kids at school and then, while they run off to do their thing, you do yours — take a bubble bath while listening to your yoga tape.

Basically, what I'm advocating here is that it's possible to literally have your cake and eat it, too. Make a concerted effort to engage in at least one "want to" experience as part of your daily routine. Doesn't matter what it is or how little time it takes — just do it!

Creating Healthy Pleasure

One thing is for certain: Human beings are creatures who constantly need and seek pleasure. Without a sufficient amount of joy and pleasure in our lives, we inevitably end up feeling irritable, moody, tense, and, worst of all, dull. Seeking pleasure in everyday life is just as natural for your brain as avoiding pain. That's right: The rather large, extremely complex brain you have operates on what is called the *pain-pleasure principle* — and, it continually strives (with or without your help) to strike a favorable balance between the two.

The brain doesn't distinguish between healthy and unhealthy pleasure — from a neurological standpoint, it's all the same. The good news is you can achieve the same high from running a marathon as you can from smoking pot. The former is an example of healthy pleasure (pleasure without adverse consequences); the latter, not so much. Have you ever known anyone who lost all her initiative, became uncoordinated, had trouble driving a car, and developed memory problems from running a marathon? Ever heard anyone called a "marathon head"? How about with pot?

A pleasure a day

For the past seven years, I begin each day — without fail — by having breakfast at a local restaurant. I'm there even on the weekends and holidays, like clockwork. I sit quietly, eat a modest breakfast, read my paper and then my AA devotional, and have that precious 20 minutes with myself before taking on the challenges of the day. It's something I look forward to, much like I used to look forward to a stiff drink at the end of a tiring day. It took me most of my adult life to appreciate simple pleasures like this and how they set the stage for whatever comes next.

I'm going to assume you have a good bit of experience with unhealthy pleasures — drinking too much alcohol, taking in too much caffeine, gambling on sporting events, driving way above the speed limit, having unprotected sex, and engaging in shop-'til-you-drop consumerism. But do you often engage in healthy pleasure? Here is a list of possibilities:

✔ Attend a jazz festival.

✔ Savor a cool glass of lemonade.

✔ Go crabbing in the backwaters of Galveston Bay. (Boy, do I miss that!)

✔ Walk your dog.

✔ Watch birds cavort through the trees in the springtime.

✔ Enjoy an expensive meal.

✔ Help someone less fortunate.

✔ Get a new car. (I know they're expensive, but still. . . .)

✔ See the Grand Canyon for the first time.

✔ Ride in a hot air balloon.

✔ Spend a week on Maui.

✔ Watch your favorite football team score the winning touchdown in the last second of the game.

✔ Look at the horizon and picture God's handiwork.

Spend some time — it doesn't have to be much — each day indulging in some form of healthy pleasure. (Careful, you might get addicted!)

Go with the Flow

Do you ever get so involved in something that nothing else seems to matter and you lose track of time? This is the question that Dr. Mihaly Csikszentmihalyi, professor of psychology at the University of Chicago, asks countless numbers of people in the study of what he calls *flow* — a state of consciousness that occurs when you find yourself immersed in one of those "best moments of my life." Csikszentmihalyi, interestingly, finds that only 20 percent of people answer yes, that this happens to them on a daily basis. Fifteen percent say no, that it never happens — and, these, I'm willing to bet, are the folks most likely to experience toxic anger.

So, how do you get into this healthy state of mind? Actually, it's not that difficult. Here are some tips:

- ✔ **Flow comes from active involvement in some aspect of daily life.** Flow is not some mystical, magical, spiritual state that falls over you — if you're lucky — like mist from the heavens above. It only comes when you're actively involved in life. Passive activities — watching TV, listening to music — won't do the trick. For me, writing books provides a constant state of flow. For you, it may be a hobby — stamp collecting, bird watching, experimental cooking, gardening, chess, or recreational sports like golf and tennis.

- ✔ **Flow requires positive motivation.** Flow is a byproduct of a "want to" activity. If you don't really *want* to play golf today, and you're just doing it because your boss wants you to, you may shoot a low score, but you won't experience flow. Again, using myself as an example, I write because I want to, not because I have to — and that makes a big difference!

- ✔ **Flow requires your full attention.** Flow requires a full commitment on your part. Your mind cannot be elsewhere while you are actively engaged in something that has the potential to produce flow. Mentally speaking, you and the activity have to be one. A client of mine who has been suffering from extensive pain throughout his body every minute of the day for over 20 years puts it this way: "When I can't stand the pain anymore — when it's absolutely killing me — I go up into my computer room and get into the computer. I don't get *on* the computer, I get *into* it. I get lost in there, and for a couple of hours, I am completely pain free."

- ✔ **Flow activities have to be challenging.** Doing something that is easy, that doesn't take much in the way of skills, energy, or concentrated effort, won't produce flow. Flow comes from activities that are challenging, even though they may seem effortless when you're doing them. Repetition makes us dull! If you start out achieving flow from a particular activity, over time — if you don't change the activity in some way to make it more challenging or complex — it will lose its effect. That's why, for my entire 40-year career, I have made it a practice never to be redundant in what I do at workshops or in my writing — I'm trying to stay in the flow.

What do you want to do Saturday?

One day when I was venting to my therapist, who was doing all he could to help me out of this state of intense and prolonged depression, about all the things that had bugged me lately, he interrupted and asked me, "Doyle, what is it that you want to do next Saturday?" Somewhat startled, I immediately answered, "I have to go to my son's Little League game, my wife wants to go shopping. . . ." He interrupted again and said, "I didn't ask you what your son, wife, or daughter wanted you to do next Saturday — I asked what *you* wanted to do."

I didn't know what to say, so I sat there quietly and began to feel angry. I realized in that moment that at age 45 — having had a highly successful career and having been a good husband, father, son, son-in-law, friend, brother, neighbor — I didn't know anything about myself, who I was, and what I wanted out of life. My whole life had been in the service of others and I was a complete stranger to myself. My life was totally out of balance! And it was on that day that I started on the road to recovery.

✔ **Flow comes from activities that produce immediate reward.** You achieve flow in the process, not in the outcome. It happens while you're actively engaged, not later on down the road. Whereas most of the rewards in life comes from sustained effort — nose to the grindstone — flow occurs in the here and now. And it begins to subside as soon as you stop whatever you're doing to produce it. A lot of people ask if flow leads to happiness. The answer is yes, but happiness is the end product of lots of moments of flow that accumulate over time.

✔ **Flow activities don't always present themselves — sometimes you have to create them.** I hear people say all the time, "I just never seem to have the time to do the things I really enjoy. I can't remember the last time I had an opportunity to sit and play the piano — my favorite thing. I wish God would just give me a day off." What I hear less — maybe because I work with very distressed folks — is something to the effect of, "I know the dishes need washed and I still haven't vacuumed the downstairs, but, what the heck, I'm going to stop and play the piano a while. I need to get into the flow." Make time for flow. Make it a priority in your life. Be one of that top 20 percent of the population that understands what Dr. Csikszentmihalyi is talking about.

✔ **Flow comes from knowing yourself.** You experience flow when you commit yourself to spending time in your favorite activity. So I ask you, what is your favorite activity? You may not be able to readily answer that simple question. That's in part because you don't know enough about yourself to actually know what your favorite activity is. Spend some time experimenting with different activities that appeal to you a little bit and see which ones you have the most fun with.

Table 16-1 lists examples of activities that do and don't produce a state of flow.

Table 16-1	Activities That Do and Don't Produce Flow
Activities That Produce Flow	*Activities That Don't Produce Flow*
Working or studying at something you are interested in	Doing housework
Preparing a creative meal	Eating that meal
Driving or traveling	Watching TV
Taking part in hobbies	Sitting and thinking
Playing recreational sports	Resting and relaxing
Playing a musical instrument	Listening to music
Having conversations with interesting and stimulating people	Having idle conversation
Having stimulating sex	Having routine sex
Taking part in creative activities	Doing mindless activities

Ask yourself, "What is my favorite activity? What do I do that is effortless? What is it that I like to do that makes time stand still?" Now, make sure you engage in that activity at least once a week.

Maintaining Meaningful Social Ties

Human beings are social animals. Like dogs, we are what are commonly referred to as *pack* or *companion* animals and it isn't in our nature to live alone. That isn't to say that you can't survive all by yourself; it just means that you'll find it much more tedious, burdensome, and difficult to do so — even more so when life becomes too stressful.

Strive for quality not quantity

Often, people confuse social *support* with a social *network*. Support has to do with the *quality* of your relationships with those closest to you — family, spouse, friends, children, neighbors — and, at its best, reflects a state of intimacy or emotional connection with others. A network, on the other hand, simply defines how *many* such relationships you have (the quantity).

Some people have a rich support network, with only a small number of individuals. Others have literally a zillion friends and acquaintances, yet are hard-pressed to name one they can call on in a time of need. Of course, it's okay to have casual acquaintances in your life — people you hang out with once in a while — as long as you have strong support in other relationships. It is these more enduring and *meaningful* relationships that protect and sustain you during hard (more stressful!) times.

Assemble your support team. Here's how:

1. **Make a list of people you think you can call on when life becomes too stressful.**

2. **Next to each name, list whether these people are local (within driving distance) or long-distance (only an e-mail or phone call away).**

3. **Make a note of how long it's been since you had contact with each person — two days, six months, longer than that?**

4. **If it's been too long since you last touched base, call or drop each person a note and reconnect.**

5. **Decide what type(s) of support you can get from each member of your team.**

   Examples include

   • Emotional support: A hug, the chance to vent

   • Tangible support: Transportation, a loan, fixing something for you

   • Informational support: Advice, counsel

   • Appraisal feedback: Constructive criticism, praise

Now, you're prepared for whatever life throws at you.

Support is a two-way street

Support is a give-and-take process. If you only take and never give, you find fewer people available for support as time goes on. You have to reciprocate — be there when they need you, be at the ready with some sage advice, lend a helping hand, and so on.

Reaching out *to* help is just as important as reaching out *for* help. Think of it as an investment in your future. Plus, helping other people is a good way to balance out your life.

Support is only good if you accept it

If you're like most people, you have lots of potential support that you never fully take advantage of. What possible good does the help of other people do you if you don't accept it?

A chronic-pain client of mine — I'll call him Andy — sat in the men's pain group week after week, complaining that since he was injured and lost his job all of his so-called friends had abandoned him, something that seemed, at least to him, to justify his abiding anger. What Andy didn't want to talk about — and would get even angrier if I brought it up — was the fact that he had systematically avoided all overtures by his friends to support him. He steadfastly refused to return their phone calls, wouldn't answer the door when they came to call (or hid in the bedroom and had his wife tell them he wasn't at home), and always said no when they invited him to join them in activities that he used to enjoy. Who had abandoned whom here? The fact that, yes, they eventually — slowly but surely — quit offering support said more about Andy than about any of his friends.

Having people who support you isn't enough — you have to accept that support when they offer it. If you have trouble asking for and accepting help, you'll find it easier if you give to others — when you see that giving feels good, you'll have an easier time accepting the same from your friends and family. Don't deny them the joy that comes from giving.

Understanding Why Your Life Is Unbalanced

In today's demanding, fast-paced, opportunistic world, it's easy for life to become unbalanced. All kinds of factors can contribute to an unbalanced life, primary among them the ones I cover in the following sections.

Age

As with any skill, you find how to balance out your life by living. As you get older, you get wiser. Young people have a tendency to be one-dimensional. They put their energies into one thing or another — relationships, careers. Older folks are more diversified, more balanced in their use of energy. Life has taught them the fallacy of an all-or-nothing relationship with the world around them.

Gender

Women generally tend to be better at balancing their lives than men. Why? Simple: They *have* to because of the many, varied demands that culture places on them. Women no longer have to choose between a domestic life (being a homemaker, raising children) and having a career — in today's world, they're expected to do both, as well as tend to elderly parents (and in-laws).

Personality

Introverts have a much harder time reaching out for support when they're under stress. Type A personalities, because of their overly hostile nature, tend to alienate others and, as a result, do not enjoy the same level of social support (and connection to the world around them) as Type B's do (see Chapter 10). Hardy individuals, on the other hand, have no difficulty taking the initiative in keeping their lives balanced and committing themselves wholeheartedly to activities that keep them in flow. (Turn to Chapter 14 to discover how to be a hardy personality.)

Time constraint

In my opinion, time management is the single biggest challenge facing human beings today. The average person has more money than he does time. The culture has bought into the 24/7 mentality and many people work ten-hour days, six or seven days a week.

Overemphasis on independence

In most western cultures, there is a strong emphasis on independence. Society tells you that you should control your own destiny without much, if any, help from others. To reach out for support is seen as a sign of weakness. Success comes from individual effort and initiative. Interdependence — doing *with* others — has become a lost art. When you're pressured to be independent, you take on too much work yourself, and your life goes out of balance.

A reliance on unhealthy pleasure

Make no mistake — unhealthy pleasure sells! By *unhealthy pleasure,* I mean that buzz or jolt you experience with caffeine, that thrill of victory that accompanies work accomplishments, the high that people get from a friendly sports bet or compulsive gambling, the eager anticipation that awaits your next encounter with a fast-food restaurant, and the passion of unsafe sex. The problem, unfortunately, with unhealthy pleasure is that it comes with a cost — gambling throws your bankbook out of balance, too much caffeine throws your physiology out of balance (Chapter 15 tell you how much is too much), and unsafe sex leads to disease and pregnancy — which only adds to the stress in your life.

Stress

Einstein was right about the theory of relativity — everything in life is relative. By yesterday's standards, life today is extremely stressful, exhausting, and unbalanced. But by today's standards, all of that is normal. People today don't know how really stressed they are — so they don't appreciate the need to balance out their lives. You've probably come to accept that burdensome feeling of having too much to do in not enough time as normal, usual, and customary.

Technology

You live in a marvelous technological age. There are more gadgets than ever, and life has never been more easily managed (from a production standpoint) than it is today. But, technology is a double-edged sword. Because it makes life easier, it (in its own seductive way!) makes you want to do more with your life. Because we have automobiles, we want to go more places. Because we have computers at our disposal that make information more available, we expect to accomplish more in a given workday. Because we have cellphones, we no longer have any real sanctuary from the stressful world around us. If you're not calling them, they're calling you — constantly!

Affordability

People in most corners of the world today are more prosperous than ever before. Despite our complaints to the contrary, the standard of living and the amount of disposable income for most people has dramatically increased over the last century. What this means is that we can literally afford to live an unbalanced lifestyle. Thanks to the credit card industry and dual-income families, you can create mounting levels of personal debt that are burdensome, to say the least. And to make matters worse, the more you can afford (or *think* you can afford), the more you want. So, you spend more hours working and fewer hours engaging in flow, maintaining meaningful social ties, and indulging in healthy pleasure.

Too much freedom

No one (except dictators!) would argue that freedom is a *bad* thing, but too much of a good thing can be bad. Without doubt, people have more options, opportunities, and choices to make than ever before in the history of mankind. Trouble is, I think, most people try to exercise as many of those options as they can. By wanting it all, you overload yourself with demands, commitments, and obligations that you can't possibly satisfy. (As the cartoon character Pogo said, "We have met the enemy, and he is us.")

Lack of perspective

Most people seem to live for today. In your parents' or grandparents' day, a favorite saying was "I'm waiting for my ship to come in," meaning that you work hard while looking ahead and hope that one day some good fortune will come your way. Your parents or grandparents "saved for a rainy day," waiting until they could afford to pay cash for something before they bought it — an idea that by today's standards seems absolutely abhorrent.

Today, if you want something, you're supposed to get it now. If something feels good, do it now. Don't think about it, don't weigh the pros and cons, don't put things in perspective — go for it now!

How does this lack of perspective lead to imbalance? It creates future stresses — like debt! — that become burdensome later on. In effect, too much pleasure today can cause too much pain tomorrow.

Making Self a Priority

Living an unbalanced life can be more about neglecting yourself than it is about being too selfish. Most people are good, decent, and well meaning — but they get caught up trying too hard to satisfy the unending needs of the people they love and the people they work with.

No time for this . . .

The principal of a middle school where I had conducted an anger survey asked that I make a presentation of the findings to parents attending a PTA meeting. She thought they would want to know just how angry their children were and my thoughts about how this impacted their education. I agreed.

So, a few weeks later, I stood up in front of hundreds of parents to share my thoughts and get their response. I was amazed by what I saw as I looked out across their faces — blank, expressionless looks and absolutely no energy.

When I finished, the principal asked if there were any questions or concerns. There were none — not a single hand was raised. These poor families, it was plain to see, were exhausted from the day's work and all the chores that still lay ahead — and, they simply had no time to find out anything about their kids.

The town of Roseta

Dr. Stewart Wolf and his colleague John Bruhn, both behavioral scientists working in the field of medicine, discovered a small Italian community in eastern Pennsylvania that, they believed, unlocked the secret to the epidemic of heart disease that began in the United States in the early 1900s. What they found unique about Roseta was the fact that one person had died of a heart attack over a period of 16 years — despite the fact that Rosetans smoked cigarettes, had a diet high in animal fat, had elevated cholesterol levels, and were sedentary and obese.

So, why were they immune to heart disease? Wolf and Bruhn found the answer in how Rosetans lived their lives. They had somehow maintained the old-world family structure, with a great deal of intergenerational interdependence. And, this was also true throughout the community as a whole. They were an extremely cohesive people. Everyone literally made it their business to help everyone else. Social support was abounding. There was no poverty or crime, and the elderly were held in high esteem — they were listened to and respected. Rosetans were hardy souls. Rosetans emphasized religious beliefs over materialism. They shared a group identity and what they accomplished as individuals mattered less. Each member of the town knew his place in a highly structured society and felt self-satisfied and secure.

Unfortunately, time marches on and Roseta was the ultimate victim of the new world order. Their young people began to choose values and behavioral patterns that conflicted with the previous well-integrated social structure. Instead, they actively pursued their own individual advancement and status, spent far less time participating in religious activities, preferred country clubs to social clubs, and became increasingly dependent on life outside Roseta — new relationships, new opportunities.

With these changes came heart disease — not surprisingly linked to anger. In wonderfully descriptive clinical cases of two Rosetan men who died of heart attacks, Wolf and Bruhn noted that both were volatile individuals who were under constant stress, had few supportive relationships, were Type A personalities, and were angry most of the time. One man openly expressed his anger and died at age 39 on a day in which he earlier had a fistfight with a drunk. The other kept a lifetime of anger — at his family of origin, his spouse, his unfulfilling job, his lack of education — suppressed until the day he died suddenly, at age 41, working selflessly on a project for his wife, whom he despised. Characterized as "misfits" in an otherwise balanced society, they had lost their immunity from this dreaded disease.

Brenda is a good example. She came into my office one day and instantly started crying. She had awakened from a nightmare early in the morning and hadn't been able to calm herself down ever since. I asked her what the dream was all about. She replied that it was about a totem pole, which she explained was something that symbolized all the highpoints in a person's life after they were deceased. In her dream, she was reviewing all the elements on her totem pole from the top down — her husband, daughter, parents, in-laws, siblings — and, as she got to the bottom, she suddenly realized that she was "nowhere on the pole." Translation: She had never been a part of her own life, only a part of *other people's* lives. The fact that this revelation came about when she was almost 60 years old made it all the more disturbing. Brenda was a truly selfless person, but also a deeply depressed, rather hopeless woman. The two were linked. For Brenda to become free of depression, she would, we agreed, have to begin to live for herself and not just others (at least some of the time) — in other words, achieve some balance in her life.

Challenge yourself by asking some simple, but important questions: Are you worth it? Do you deserve some relief from stress? Do you deserve to experience flow some time in your life? Are you worth overcoming all the obstacles that keep you from living a more balanced life? I hope the answer is yes!

Chapter 17

Getting a Good Night's Sleep

. . . .

. . . .

I'm sure you've seen a child, out in public, screaming and thrashing about, totally at odds with everything going on around him. The child is tired and angry. Nothing his parents do suits him. And if he can hold still for one second, he falls into a deep sleep, hanging on his mother's arm like a rag doll.

Fast-forward this scenario 20 or 30 years, and you can see countless adults doing the same thing — acting cranky because they're exhausted and behind on their sleep. Poor and inadequate sleep increases irritability, which is a crucible for impending anger.

In this chapter, I talk about the vital role that rest and proper sleep play in anger management. I tell you how to maintain good sleep hygiene — and what that means. You discover how to listen to your body's signals, telling you it's time to give it a rest. With the information in this chapter, you won't always find yourself getting up on the wrong side of the bed.

Understanding What Sleep Does for You

Contrary to what you may have always thought, sleep is *not* a waste of time. Sleep is an essential tool in the human nervous system's effort to survive. In an evolutionary sense, sleep protects you by removing you from an otherwise harmful environment — your cavemen ancestors were at a distinct disadvantage at night compared to the predators of the day. Sleep also plays a restorative function, both physically and psychologically. It helps you to recover from the events of the previous day and prepares you to meet tomorrow's challenges. Most important, sleep restores lost energy. Finally, sleep plays a crucial role in physical development, especially in children and adolescents — for example, during sleep the pituitary gland releases a growth hormone.

Perhaps the easiest way for you to appreciate what sleep does for you is to see what happens when you're sleep deprived. The following are just a few symptoms of chronic sleep deprivation:

- Suppression of disease-fighting immune system function (in other words, you're more likely to get a cold or the flu)
- Increased irritability
- Impaired creativity
- Difficulty concentrating
- Impaired memory
- Obesity
- High blood pressure
- Reduced problem-solving ability
- Inefficiency at work
- Being prone to accidents
- Driver fatigue
- Road rage
- Pessimism and sadness
- Early signs of diabetes
- Slurred speech
- Lower tolerance for stress
- Impaired coping abilities
- Slower reaction time
- Impaired decision-making abilities
- Rigid thought patterns (not being able to look at a situation in more than one way)
- Hallucinations
- Emotional outbursts

Why torture yourself?

The Geneva Convention, the United Nations Convention on Torture, and Amnesty International all consider extended sleep deprivation a form of torture, which should be outlawed by all civilized societies. Yet, ironically, millions of human beings torture themselves willingly day after day by not getting the proper amount of sleep. Who is there to protect them — against themselves?

✔ Increased potential for violence

✔ Reduced muscle strength

✔ Loss of stamina/endurance

To figure out if you're suffering from sleep deprivation, ask yourself the following eight questions. If you answer yes to *three or more,* you're definitely behind on your sleep.

✔ Is it a struggle for you to get out of bed in the morning?

✔ Do you often fall asleep while watching TV?

✔ Do you fall asleep in boring meetings at work?

✔ Do you often fall asleep after eating a heavy meal?

✔ Do you have dark circles around your eyes?

✔ Do you typically sleep extra hours on the weekends?

✔ Do you often feel drowsy while driving or riding in an automobile?

✔ Do you often need a nap to get through the day?

People who suffer from Attention Deficit/Hyperactivity Disorder (ADHD), sleep apnea, alcoholism, or clinical depression, as well as those who do shift work, are at high risk for sleep deprivation.

Knowing How Much Is Enough

The amount of sleep you need depends in large part on how old you are. Table 17-1 shows you how much sleep is required, on average, by different age groups.

Negative energy and anger

In one study, I asked 68 employees at a local company two questions about energy:

✔ Do you feel fresh and rested when you wake up in the morning?

✔ Do you ever feel like a battery that has lost its charge?

I then compared their negative energy scores (no to the first question, yes to the second.) to how angry they were. Those who admitted to "chronic rage" had a negative energy score more than twice that of employees who acknowledged getting only "intermittently irritated" (see Chapter 2 for information on these different types of anger experience).

Does this mean that people who are angry all the time use up too much of their energy on emotion, or does it mean that people who are tired all the time are more apt to go into a rage? At this point, I can't say for sure, but I do believe this link between energy and anger is worth pursuing.

Table 17-1	Average Hours of Sleep Needed
Age Group	*Sleep Needed (in Hours)*
1–24 months	16–18
2–11 years	10–11
12–20 years	8–9
21 or older	7–8

The need for nighttime sleeping is somewhat less for older adults, but they tend to make up for it by taking daytime naps. It turns out that the idea that you require less sleep in late life is a myth.

My uncle Aubrey lived to be 98 years old. And up until his death, he slept soundly for eight to nine hours a night. He remained physically active — planting apple trees all by himself — and lived independently to the end. His mind was sharp, and he always displayed good humor. I never remember seeing him get the least bit irritated. He was a testimony to what good sleep can do for you!

Rating the Quality of Your Sleep

Even more important than the number of hours of sleep you get is the quality of your sleep. Just because you spent eight hours in bed doesn't necessarily mean that you got a good night's sleep. Ask anyone who's slept off a big night of drinking if she feels refreshed when she wakes up the next morning. Odds are, the answer is no!

To determine the quality of your sleep, all you have to do is rate how rested and refreshed you feel on a 10-point scale, where 1 is not at all and 10 is extremely rested. Concentrate on how you feel when you first wake up in the morning (before you even head off to the bathroom!). Do that for a period of ten days and then figure out your average (add up all ten numbers and divide by ten). This number will tell you if you're usually getting a good night's sleep. If your average sleep rating is 7 or above, you're in good shape. If your average rating is below 7, you're in trouble.

Sleep quality is directed related to *sleep hygiene* — maintaining healthy sleep habits (just like oral hygiene is maintaining healthy habits for your teeth and gums). Some examples of *poor* sleep hygiene includes the following:

- Taking daytime naps lasting for two or more hours (with the exception of those age 60 or older)
- Going to bed and getting up at different times from day to day
- Exercising just prior to bedtime
- Using alcohol, tobacco, and caffeine within four hours of bedtime
- Participating in some kind of stimulating activity (for example, computer activity) just prior to bedtime
- Going to bed angry, upset, or stressed

Vital exhaustion

Dutch psychologist Ad Appels and his colleagues at the University of Maastricht have demonstrated a potent link between loss of physical and psychological vitality (known as *vital exhaustion*) and the risk for heart disease, sudden cardiac death, and stroke. Interestingly, of the three components that make up vital exhaustion — excessive fatigue, increased irritability, and demoralization — the one that puts people at greatest risk is the "tiredness" factor. Apparently, what those who suffer from exhaustion can't do is fall asleep easily and remain asleep throughout the night without repeated awakening. This leaves them suffering from chronic sleep deficit — which no doubt explains their increased irritability and depression.

Ask yourself the following five questions:

- Do you often feel tired?
- Do you feel weak all over?
- Do you lately feel more listless than before?
- Do you sometimes feel that your body is like a battery that is losing its power?
- Do you ever wake up with a feeling of exhaustion and fatigue?

The more of these questions you answer yes to, the more likely it is that you're suffering from vital exhaustion.

✔ Using the bed for things other than sleep and sex (like work or watching TV)

✔ Sleeping in an uncomfortable bed

✔ Sleeping in an uncomfortable bedroom environment (one that's too bright, too warm or cold, too noisy, and so on)

✔ Actively engaging in important mental activity while in bed (This is not the time to rehearse the speech you're going to give at tomorrow morning's staff meeting.)

Improving the Quality of Your Sleep

Improving the quality of your sleep is one area where you can definitely make a difference. Rather than continuing to be a victim of poor sleep (read: exhausted and irritated!) — and before considering the use of sleeping pills — begin practicing some good sleep hygiene. In the following sections, I show you how.

Listening to your body

Fatigue isn't a state of mind — it's physical. Fatigue is your body's way of telling you — without words — that it's low on energy. Just like hunger tells you that your stomach is empty and thirst tells you that your body is dehydrated, fatigue is your body's way of saying, "Get thee to bed!"

Energy is a fixed commodity. You have a certain amount to use each day to accomplish whatever you need to. As long as the demands you face are within the limits of your energy supply, your mind and body don't show signs of strain. (In Chapter 14, I fill you in on the difference between stress and strain.) Think of fatigue as a warning sign that you're starting to run out of energy. Your body is letting you know it's time to begin conserving energy. Exhaustion — the most intense state of fatigue — is a sign that your tank is near empty. It's time to stop expending energy and begin a process of recovery.

Take a few seconds once every hour throughout your day and monitor your energy level. Rate your present energy level on a scale of 0 to 10 and record the data in a notebook. At the end of the day, plot the numbers on a piece of graph paper hour by hour. Do that for a week. Do you see any patterns? For example, does your energy seem to decrease as the day goes on? At what point in the day does your energy level drop to a rating of 5 or less (fatigue)? Does it ever get as low as a rating of 1 or 2 (exhaustion)? ***Remember:*** The lower your energy level, the more likely you'll begin to feel strained; one common indicator of strain is irritation, and the next step after irritation is anger.

When are you most positive?

Research studies demonstrate that positive mood fluctuates throughout the day and is highest during the middle of the day. Human beings are their least positive selves when they first wake up in the morning (between 6 and 9 a.m.) and at the end of the day when they're preparing for sleep (9 p.m. to midnight). The good news is that if you wake up on the wrong side of the bed, it won't last. (My theory is that we're all more likely to be in a good mood when we're engaged in meaningful activity and around people, which is less the case early and late in the day.)

You're also more likely to be hostile early in the day — between 6 and 9 a.m. — than any other time. You're your least hostile self midday — noon until 3 p.m. And then you begin getting grouchy again right before bedtime. So next time you need to have an important (potentially stressful) conversation with someone, arrange for a lunch meeting. You'll be less likely to get upset than you would if you talked over breakfast or just before bed.

Getting physical

Regular physical exercise is an essential part of good sleep hygiene. But, the benefit of exercise on sleep only comes when you:

- ✔ **Engage in moderate, nonstrenuous exercise.** What you want to do is to tire the body out and relax it without overstimulating it at the same time. Any type of prolonged or intense exercise — which makes you sweat — prior to going to bed will be counterproductive. Consider doing 10 to 15 minutes of light weights, slow walking on a treadmill, slow pedaling on an exercise bike, or stretching exercises.

- ✔ **Exercise in the late afternoon or early evening.** The benefits of exercising early in the day are long since past by the time you're ready for bed. But you also don't want to wait until the last minute — an hour or two before retiring — because of the overstimulation effect. Late afternoon or early evening is the optimal time to exercise if you want a good night's sleep, because your body will be rebounding (cooling) a few hours later, which promotes good sleep.

- ✔ **Adjust your exercise to your age and overall fitness level.** If you don't, you'll stress your body and produce a sense of physical restlessness, which will keep you awake.

- ✔ **Make exercise part of your pre-sleep routine.** Exercise should be but one step — albeit an important one — in preparing you for optimal sleep. Most likely, because of timing issues, it will be either the first or second step, depending on your use of stimulants (see the "Avoiding stimulants" section).

Why Type A's never rest

Type A's — competitive, impatient, hostile — never rest because they never get tired. Or, does it just seem that way? Actually, Type A's fatigue just like Type B's do — they just fail to recognize it. Dr. David Glass, psychologist at the University of Texas, was the first to note the tendency of Type A personalities to suppress feelings of fatigue while engaged in any sort of competitive task (which with Type A's means most everything they do!). This, more than anything, explains why they can relentlessly pursue unreasonable deadlines and continue to give 120 percent effort until they reach their goal. Type A's have tunnel vision, focusing only on the end game, with no appreciation whatsoever of normal bodily sensations having to do with things like hunger and fatigue. This trait no doubt also explains why Type A's also deny the early signs and symptoms of an impending heart attack and delay getting necessary medical treatment.

When I first joined the faculty at Duke University Medical Center and was the psychologist assigned to the Coronary Care Unit, a male patient was admitted, having just experienced a severe heart attack. I met with his wife, who was understandably quite upset. She said, "I just don't understand how he could just suddenly have a heart attack and fall over like that in the middle of the day." After I talked with her, it quickly became evident that her husband had been symptomatic for several days. She now remembered that he had walked around the house rubbing his chest and complaining of a feeling of pressure, which he interestingly (albeit typically) attributed to having a cold or just being tired. He also seemed not to have his usual stamina and complained of shortness of breath, which again he chalked up to "this thing that's going around." And, last but not least, he was more irritable than usual. In typical Type A fashion, he went to work early the day of his heart attack after arguing with his wife that he couldn't stay home sick — there was too much business to be done!

Avoiding stimulants

The two main stimulants that you should avoid four hours prior to sleep are caffeine and nicotine. Both activate the central nervous system — your brain — and promote alertness, which isn't what you want to do when you're getting ready to go to sleep.

Caffeine

When it comes to caffeine use, there are several things you want to keep in mind:

- ✓ **Caffeine is available in many forms — coffee, tea, soft drinks, chocolate, over-the-counter drugs (for example, cold and allergy medication).** So just because you're passing up coffee after dinner doesn't mean that you're not getting caffeine in the form of that triple-chocolate cake you had for dessert.

A word about alcohol

Although alcohol is considered a depressant rather than a stimulant as far as its effect on the nervous system, keep in mind the following:

✔ Smokers report that the most likely situation in which they smoke is when they're also using alcohol.

✔ Alcohol has been shown to increase anxiety and nervousness shortly after it is ingested.

✔ Alcohol use may lead to emotional outbursts (read: *anger*), which in turn make it difficult for you to relax into sleep.

Bottom line: Drinking alcohol within four hours of bedtime is not conducive to good sleep. Avoid hitting the bottle before hitting the hay.

✔ **The body can only handle about 300 mg of caffeine in a 24-hour period.** Exceeding that amount isn't difficult — one cup of regular coffee contains between 100 and 220 mg of caffeine!

✔ **The half-life of caffeine (the time it takes your body to get rid of it) ranges between three and seven hours.** So the cup of coffee you drank at 8 p.m. can still be actively stimulating your nervous system when you hit the sack at 11:30 p.m.

✔ **Caffeine affects people differently.** If you're prone to anxiety and nervousness, you only become more so with caffeine use.

✔ **If you're a heavy caffeine user (by that, I mean you routinely exceed 300 mg/day), caffeine withdrawal may be a problem when you abstain from caffeine four hours or more before bedtime.**

✔ **Evidence shows signs of sleep disturbance even in those folks who claim that caffeine has no effect on their sleep.**

Nicotine

Nicotine, just like caffeine, stimulates the nervous system, leading to increased heart rate, elevated blood pressure, and generalized muscle tension — hardly conducive to good sleep. Smokers take longer to get to sleep, on average, and are much more likely to awaken repeatedly through the night. Interestingly, many smokers' first thought when they wake up is to smoke a cigarette. Smoking researchers attribute this to conditioned nicotine withdrawal — in other words, your brain wakes you up because it needs a fix.

Try not to let your favorite cigarette of the day — all smokers have one — be the one after dinner. Unfortunately, 40 percent or more of heavy smokers as well as so-called chippers (those who smoke fewer than five cigarettes a day) enjoy that after-dinner smoke the most.

Step away from the cellphone

At the very time I'm writing this chapter, late-breaking medical news suggests that cellphones stimulate the brain by literally heating up the "stimulation center" of the brain, leading to increased tension and restlessness. The researchers who made the finding say talking on a cellphone is no different from having a cup of coffee.

The stimulant effects of nicotine and caffeine are additive, and they combine to ensure poor sleep. Bottom line: A little bit of both adds up to a lot when it comes to activating the nervous system.

Setting up a pre-sleep routine

Your nervous system craves routine. It works best — and to your advantage when it comes to being healthy — when you carry on day to day in much the same way. *You* may find living a routine life boring, but your *body* loves it!

So, if you're looking to get a better night's sleep (and you're wanting to manage your anger), you need to have a pre-sleep routine. That routine should begin four or more hours before you actually try to go to sleep — when you have your afternoon or early evening workout, stop using caffeine and drinking alcohol, and eat your last big meal of the day (you want your body to complete the work of digestion before bedtime!) — and ends only when you turn out the lights. It's good not to go to bed on an empty stomach. An hour or so before you go to bed, have a light snack — some yogurt or a piece of fruit, not six slices of pizza or an ice cream sundae!

Creating a positive sleep environment

When it comes to creating a sleep environment with reduced stimulation, it's not just a matter of what you eat, drink, and smoke that counts. It also includes the physical environment itself. Ideally, you want a place to sleep that doesn't just make getting a good night's sleep *possible,* but very likely.

Here are some tips on how to create a positive sleep environment:

- ✔ **Use curtains and window shades to cut down on intrusive light from the outside.**
- ✔ **Avoid temperature extremes.** The ideal temperature for sleeping is between 54° F (12°C) and 75°F (24°C).

- ✔ Lower your body temperature by taking a hot bath two hours before bedtime.

- ✔ Use earplugs if the person sleeping next to you has a snoring problem.

- ✔ Use background noise — a ceiling fan, a radio on low volume, or your radio's white noise or nature settings — to mask more disruptive sound.

- ✔ **Spend some money on a good mattress.** You want one that fits your body size (you don't want your feet hanging off the end of the bed) and provides adequate support.

Eliminating competing cues

The human brain works on the principle of association — if two things occur in time and space often enough, your brain makes a connection. When that connection is made, one part of that association will trigger the other. (That's why when you walk into a Mexican restaurant, you immediately think about having a cold beer — the human version of Pavlov's dogs!)

Your brain should have only one connection — one thought, one impulse, one craving — when it comes to the sleep environment and that is: "Hooray, *finally,* I can get some sleep!" If you're saying, "What about sex?", don't worry: Sex is the one other activity that the brain can connect with the bedroom, but sleep is the primary reason for being there.

You may have a problem getting to sleep in your bedroom simply because your brain has too many connections to other activities that compete with sleep. For example, your bedroom may be the place where you:

- ✔ Watch television

- ✔ Argue with your spouse

- ✔ Eat late at night

- ✔ Have your last, favorite cigarette of the day

- ✔ Consume the last alcohol of the day

- ✔ Work

- ✔ Listen to loud music

- ✔ Study for a class or upcoming test

- ✔ Talk with your housemates about what you did today

- ✔ Plan for tomorrow

- ✔ Roughhouse with your pets

- ✔ Have late-night phone conversations

If using your bedroom as a multipurpose room sounds familiar, no wonder you have trouble sleeping and are tired — and irritable — all the time. These are all activities that you can — and should — do elsewhere. Where? Anywhere but where you sleep. Your bedroom should be a place of sanctuary — a place where your mind and body can rest and recover.

What if you live in a studio (one-room) apartment? Try to separate your sleeping area from the rest of the room with bookshelves, a screen or room divider, or something similar. Then vow to keep your non-sleep activities to the other areas of your space.

Distancing yourself from work

For many people, work has become an all-consuming daily activity (some argue that it's an obsession!). If you're not actually at work, it's on your mind and in your home. In fact, the most likely competing cues (see the preceding section) that interferes with your sleep is work.

When I first started practicing behavioral medicine at Duke University Medical School in the early 1970s, a man came into our clinic complaining of chronic insomnia. He had apparently tried everything to solve this problem, and nothing worked. As I was interviewing him about his sleep environment, I quickly identified the problem: The man was an artist, and he painted "with a passion" until it was time for bed. Then he stopped abruptly, turned off the lights, and fell onto a cot he had sitting next to his easel. He was, in effect, sleeping in his *office* — the place where he worked.

To make matters worse, he wasn't allowing any time between the highly creative and stimulating activity of painting and trying to go to sleep. His brain was still very much *on* when his head hit the pillow. I suggested two changes:

- ✔ That he begin to sleep only in his bedroom, a room separate from his studio
- ✔ That he stop painting at least an hour before he retired

During that time, I also recommended he get out of the house and take a short walk to clear his mind, do some light reading (something that had nothing to do with his chosen profession), and just plain relax. He came back a week later and, with some amazement, reported that he was sleeping soundly for the first time in years.

If work is filling your every waking moment, you need sufficient time to disconnect or unplug your mind from work activities before you can have any hope of getting to sleep. I recommend starting to pull away from all things work related four hours prior to sleep. If four hours seem impossible, at least give yourself one hour of separation time between work and sleep — but keep in mind that more is better.

Uncluttering your mind

Another reason you may have difficulty getting a good night's sleep is that your mind is too cluttered with psychological "junk" at bedtime. The instant things get quiet and the room gets dark, your brain begins to focus on all the unsolved problems, grievances, anxieties, worries, and frustrations that make up your psyche.

As part of your pre-sleep routine, you might try writing down things you have in mind to do the next day. (Keep a notebook handy by your bedside table just for this purpose.) That way, the list will be there for you in the morning and you won't have to toss and turn all night, worrying that you'll forget.

Considering sleeping pills

Many people — frustrated from days, weeks, months, or years of bad sleep — think that sleeping pills are a good option.

Using sleeping pills to get a good night's sleep and reduce fatigue and irritability is not something you should do without consulting your doctor. Many types of sleeping pills produce negative side effects (daytime drowsiness, anxiety, rebound insomnia when you stop taking them). Plus, using them may only reinforce the idea that you're a victim of a disorder over which you have no control — which is far from true. No credible evidence says that over-the-counter sleep aids improve sleep by any objective measure.

The one type of pill that might help you get a good night's sleep, but without the usual concerns about addiction and rebound effects, is an antidepressant. Antidepressants can be prescribed at lower dosages to promote sound sleep. Consult with your physician before deciding whether taking antidepressants to help with sleep is appropriate in your case.

Chapter 18

Looking to a Higher Power

. . . .

In This Chapter

▶ Exploring the link between spirituality and emotional health

▶ Viewing faith as an anger-management tool

▶ Striving to be humble

▶ Substituting compassion for contempt

. . . .

*T*he peace of mind that comes from a belief in a higher power is an anti-dote to anger. When you believe in something more powerful than your-self and act in accordance with that belief, you tend to feel less helpless about life's struggles, less hopeless, and more optimistic about your future. You can relax into your problems because you feel support from above.

In this chapter, I make a case for why I think spirituality — which may or may not involve regular participation in religious activities — can lead to a more anger-free life. This chapter is not meant to repeat information provided in other chapters having to do with confession (Chapter 9), forgiveness (Chapter 13), and what some might see as "sinful" substances like caffeine, alcohol, and nicotine (Chapter 15). Instead, it addresses other traditional ele-ments of spiritual belief such as faith, compassion, gratitude, and humility — common to all organized religions — that you can also bring to bear in defus-ing anger.

Reaching Up rather than Out

Support is essential to human survival. And for most of us, that support comes from other human beings with whom we're closely connected — your spouse, family members, friends, children, members of your church or temple.

But what if those usual sources of support aren't readily available for some reason? What do you do in situations where you've exhausted all the sup-portive resources at your disposal? What do you do if the people who typi-cally support you are angry at you? In other words, what do you do when you can't reach out for help when you need it the most?

Showing up — it doesn't matter where

If you want to minimize the odds that you'll suffer from the health problems in which anger plays a significant role (see Chapter 2), take my advice and attend a religious service at least once a week. Medical studies have repeatedly shown, for example, that churchgoers have about half the risk for coronary heart disease as do non-churchgoers. As a group, churchgoers also have lower blood pressure — regardless of their age, whether they smoke, their weight, and their socioeconomic circumstances.

Apparently, participating in religious activities can be the remedy for what the great psychologist William James called the "sick soul" of mankind.

Remember: There is no evidence to suggest that one religion — Christianity, Judaism, Islam, Hinduism, Buddhism, and so on — conveys more health protection than any other, so it really doesn't matter where you go — just that you show up somewhere!

You reach up instead. You turn your thoughts to a higher power. You pray. You take respite from the burdens of the world by turning your problems over to that unseen, invisible, spiritual entity in whose hands you now feel safe and secure. Then you can relax. You no longer need to defend yourself against adversity — which means you don't need to carry around all that fear and anger.

According to the New Testament, even Jesus reached up to his heavenly father, when faced with the ultimate destiny of his painful crucifixion, by praying: "Father, all things are possible unto thee; take away this cup from me; nevertheless not what I will, but what thou wilt" (Mark 14:36).

Don't be afraid to be enthusiastic. *Enthusiasm* means "having a godly spirit within." Try to remain especially enthusiastic when you're faced with life's many problems.

Using Faith as a Weapon

In my work, I've met many people who are incredibly angry because they suffer from some type of chronic-pain disorder (for example, a back injury). Believe me, I know they have a lot to be angry about — medical treatments that haven't worked, unsympathetic employers and insurance companies, loss of income and status. What impresses me, though, is the intensity of their anger and how long they hang on to it. Someone suffering from chronic pain isn't just irritated about his life and health situation, he's extremely angry — to the point of rage. And he stays that way day after day, year after year, which only heightens his pain and leads to secondary psychological problems, such as depression. Many chronic-pain sufferers are caught up in a vicious cycle — the more they hurt, the angrier they get, and the angrier they get, the more they hurt.

Another thing that typifies this group is their loss of faith — in their employers, insurance companies, physicians, family members, friends, even in themselves. And more than a few lose faith in God, because they believe God has abandoned them. For chronic-pain sufferers, anger seems to be their weapon of choice. As they see it, anger is the *only* way they have to fight back against pain and injustice.

But faith can be a weapon, too — and just as powerful as anger. Faith can be an antidote to fear, isolation, and depression. Faith can be comforting. And as long as you have faith in some higher power (no matter how you conceive of that power), you're never truly alone.

No one can make you have faith. It isn't something that you earn. Believing in something you can't prove and over which you have no control is simply a personal choice. For example, you need a lot of faith to believe that an angry, defiant teenager will actually grow up and amount to something in life. You need a lot of faith to work your way through some unexpected crisis in your life — a loving spouse who is suddenly diagnosed with cancer, a major hurricane that destroys everything you've worked hard for over your lifetime, the loss of a child to a drunk driver. Faith is a way of telling yourself that things will get better even when all objective evidence points to the contrary. Having faith is what keeps you from despair — and despair can be a breeding ground for anger.

Keep the faith

It was 2:30 a.m. and Art sat at his dining room table contemplating taking his own life. He did so while his wife of 25 years slept soundly in the other room. Art had suffered from chronic pain for almost 15 years, and he was tired of always hurting, being unemployed, and being severely limited in his routine, day-to-day activities. He was angry — not angry because of anything that had happened in the last day or two, but angry about the endless struggle with pain that had been forced on him by a work injury years before. He felt totally alone with his pain and suffering; even his wife, who loved him, couldn't understand why he couldn't get well.

The decision he had before him that morning was whether to end his suffering (he had the revolver on the table) or to begin a whole new approach to life that very day. At 54 years of age, Art's life was full of nothing but uncertainty — the only thing he was certain of was that he would experience pain every minute of the day ahead of him.

After hours of going back and forth, he finally decided to stay alive and become a "born-again" person in terms of how he lived his life. That was over a decade ago and Art remains in chronic pain, but he is, by all accounts, a reasonably happy man. He built a new house, travels, works in his yard from time to time, even plays a little golf — all while in pain. And all it took to move from that old, tragic life into this new one was a little faith!

Hardiness and religion

Interestingly, studies show a link between religious attendance and being a hardy personality. Hardiness involves a sense of inner control, an active commitment to life, and the ability to view adversity as a challenge rather than a catastrophe. Does attending a religious service make you hardy or does it simply reinforce that which is already part and parcel of your personality? Who knows? But because the two seem inextricably connected, why not give it a try?

Faith is a weapon that helps you deal with an uncertain future. It's a means to an end — survival, a happier time, the resolution of a problem. Like most human beings, you probably hate uncertainty because it elicits fear — and fear, in turn, can lead to anger. Is anger your way of fighting off uncertainty ("Damn it, why can't things settle down and go right for a change?")? If so, embrace the uncertainty of the situation (see Chapter 14 for tips on how to become a hardy personality) and transform a crisis into a challenge.

For the most part, anger is about defending yourself from adversity. Faith, on the other hand, is a coping strategy, which Dr. Avery Weisman, author of *The Coping Capacity,* describes as a "strategic effort to master a problem, overcome a problem . . . that impedes our progress" through life. Anger is reactive — faith is proactive.

Praying Prayers of Gratitude

There are many forms of prayer. Some people pray for understanding, some for forgiveness, some pray to God to "fix" things in their lives that have gone wrong, some for pain relief, some for opportunity, and so on. These all represent prayers of *supplication* — you want something! Such prayers always begin with the word *please.*

Asking God for something is fine, but if you want to get something out of you prayer life, it helps to think in terms of thank you. It's hard to be angry when you're giving thanks.

Anger has a lot to do with feeling that you're not getting what you want (or what you feel entitled to). You're not getting recognition at work or making the money you feel you should. Your kids don't show you the respect you feel entitled to as a parent. Your dog doesn't come when you call him. So you get mad.

Gratitude, on the other hand, has to do with being thankful for what has already been given to you. Some years ago, when I was trying really hard to overcome a major episode of depression (accompanied by lots of anger), I decided one morning to no longer ask God for anything for myself. I continued to ask him to watch over my children as they learned from their successes and failures, over my wife (the love of my life), over my brothers and their families, over my friends, over my clients, and even over my bassett hounds. But I figured that God had already given me more than I ever expected in life. My thinking was that if God wants to bless me with more good things in the years I have left, okay. And if not, that's okay, too. Either way, I'm grateful — and, I rarely get angry anymore.

Start each day with a prayer of gratitude. Make a mental list of all your blessings — people, events, whatever — and recite them to yourself (silently or out loud) so that God knows that you remember the good things that have been bestowed on you and you are, indeed, thankful. And then see if you don't feel a sense of inner peace as you take on the challenges of the day.

Practicing Compassion

All world religions, regardless of their differences, have one thing in common — they teach and preach compassion. When the Bible talks about doing unto others as you would have them do unto you, it's not talking about anger and violence — it's talking about love of your fellow man and woman (or, for that matter, your cat!).

Table 18-1 highlights some differences between two opposing ways of treating other human beings: compassion and revenge.

The apple doesn't fall far from the tree

The difference between revenge and compassion is illustrated by a wonderful story told by the legendary golfer Chi Chi Rodriguez. Chi Chi was born into a poor Puerto Rican family. Even though his father worked hard, he still had difficulty feeding his family.

One night, his father heard someone prowling around in the backyard. When he went, machete in hand, to investigate, Chi Chi's father discovered his neighbor — also very poor — picking up bananas off the ground. Instead of getting angry with his neighbor and attacking him for his theft, he took the machete and cut off a big stalk of bananas, handed them to his neighbor, and told him that if his family needed something to eat he shouldn't steal it but instead come and ask him for help.

That lesson in compassion set a standard for Chi Chi's whole life — and no doubt accounts for his well-deserved reputation of sharing with those much less fortunate the wealth he has gained from playing professional golf.

How are you?

During the five years I struggled my way through a cloud of clinical depression, I often found myself despondent and weary. And then a wonderful thing would happen — the telephone would ring and one of my close friends would say, "Doyle, I just had a free minute in my day and I wanted to see how you are." Often, my answer was, "Not too well!" My friend would then spend a couple of additional minutes trying to lift my sagging spirits, but most of all they let me know that somebody out there cared about me. I honestly think those little interventions of compassion saved my sanity, if not my life. I will go to my grave remembering their calls with a never-ending sense of gratitude.

Remember: One way you can manage your own anger is by helping those around you. Start paying attention to your friends and family and how they're feeling. If you get your focus off of your anger and onto helping someone else, you may just find your anger abating.

Table 18-1	Revenge versus Compassion
Revenge . . .	**Compassion . . .**
Is born out of anger or hatred.	Is born out of love.
Has the goal of hurting someone.	Has the goal of helping another person.
Heightens conflict.	Eases conflict.
Is judgmental.	Is nonjudgmental.
Says, "They're wrong."	Says, "They need help."
Says, "I'm against them."	Says, "I'm for them."
Is destructive.	Is constructive.

Make a pact with yourself not to let a day go by without finding some way in which you can show compassion to your fellow man. You might be surprised at how small acts of compassion — a kind word at exactly the right time — can salvage someone's day. Professor Shelly Taylor at UCLA sees such acts as examples of what she calls "tending and befriending," a form of positive psychology (more about positive psychology in Chapter 19) that allows everyone to better survive hard times. (Interestingly, this trait is much more common in women than it is in men. Maybe this is why women live much longer?)

Being Humble — It Helps

Developing a sense of humility is yet another antidote to toxic anger. Being humble is the opposite of

- Being arrogant

- Feeling entitled

- Seeing yourself as superior

- Adopting an attitude of contempt toward all those you see as not as good as you are

All of these opposites of humility tend to incite anger. Have you ever met a Type A personality who was humble? Probably not! Type B's, on the other hand, have a refreshing sense of humility (see Chapter 10).

I remember hearing about the world-renowned stress researcher Dr. Hans Selye who, when asked why he wasn't stressed by the infirmities of his advanced age (hobbling up and down from a stage to lecture about stress) and the fact that not everyone in the medical profession agreed with the conclusions of his life's work, replied simply, "Because I never took myself that seriously." Talk about being humble!

Humility is born out of adversity. No one gets humble on the way up the ladder of life — humility is what you experience on the way down. Being in the business of human suffering, people ask me all the time, "Why does God let bad things happen?" Not wanting to speak for God, I instead offer them my personal theory of why such things happen and that is: "Because, I think, that's the only way we learn to be humble — which is God's plan." Who knows if I'm right? But it does seem to ease their suffering a bit.

Type A personalities and religion

It turns out that Type A personalities are more often churchgoers than Type B's. This little bit of trivia is intriguing given the observation that Type A's are *less* likely to believe in a loving and forgiving higher power.

The cynical explanation for the link between church attendance and Type A behavior is that being a churchgoer, like having a high income and occupational status, is a sign that people have achieved ultimate success. One could certainly argue, on the other hand, that Type A's attend church in an effort to fill the "spiritual void," which the originators of the Type A concept — Dr. Meyer Friedman and Dr. Ray Rosenman — say typifies them.

Each day, look for ways to be humble. Remind yourself of what the comedian Woody Allen says, "We're all bozos on the same bus!" You may be the driver of the bus or just a passenger — either way you're a bozo. Every time I think about that, I feel a profound sense of relief — and it makes it so much harder to get angry throughout the day. Try getting involved in a community task without being the person in charge. Find some fairly menial ways to make the world a better place. (**Hint:** Beautify your community by collecting trash on the side of the highway. Or spend a day working for Habitat for Humanity.)

Having a Blessed Day

One of my most memorable chronic-pain classes included three women, all of whom had suffered from agonizing back and neck pain for many years. Unlike the majority of my pain clients who respond to my cheerful "How are you doing this morning?" greeting as they walk through the door either with a silent shrug or a hostile retort — "How do you think I'm doing?" — these ladies always came back with "I'm blessed — hope you are." And when they left four hours later — sometimes after painful, strenuous fitness training — the last thing they said was, "Have a blessed day!"

At first, I wasn't sure how to respond to their "blessing." Not only was it not a typical response for patients, it almost seemed incongruent with the agenda of that setting — pain management. But I soon got used to it, began responding in kind ("I'm blessed — I hope you are."), and realized that this was why these three women weren't as angry, bitter, depressed, and frightened by ongoing pain as most of my other clients. Rather than dwell on the painful part of their day-to-day lives, they were able to view pain and injury as only a part of an otherwise blessed life. They felt blessed to be alive, to have caring friends, to have supportive families, to still be mobile enough to attend church on Sunday — in effect, to have what it took to effectively live with their pain.

Start your day by saying to the first ten people you meet, "Have a blessed day." Watch how they respond. And see if they don't answer, "You, too!" every time. Along the same line, try ending conversations you have with particularly hostile people with a "Have a blessed day!" and see how they respond. I'm betting it takes some of the steam (and sting) out of their hostility. It's hard to be a jerk to someone who just gave you his blessing!

My three black angels

At the end of the five-week chronic-pain class (see "Having a Blessed Day" in this chapter), the same three ladies, all of whom are African American, surprised me with a gift. They wanted me to know how much they appreciated all my hard work in helping them find a way to continue having a meaningful life despite their endless pain. Their gift was quite unique — three wooden black angels. "We wanted you to know that no matter what comes your way in life — especially hard times — you always have three black angels looking out for you."

I couldn't have been more touched — I did feel truly blessed. I then mused, "I wonder how many white guys have three black angels looking over them?" and we all had a good laugh and hugs all around. I keep those angels prominently displayed in my office as cherished mementos. And, on days when I'm down or irritated and fully prepared to snap someone's head off, I look at them and instantly feel much better.

Chapter 19

Staying in a Good Mood

. . . .

In This Chapter

▶ Finding ways to stay in a good mood

▶ Identifying a mood disorder

▶ Linking anger to depression

▶ Exploring effective treatment options

▶ Revitalizing a sluggish brain

▶ Knowing when to seek professional help

. . . .

A strong link exists between anger and a bad mood — you can't be angry and in a great mood at the same time. But this link goes beyond a bad mood: If you're depressed, anger comes all too easily. In this chapter, I cover the reasons that depression and anger are so closely connected — including an alteration in brain chemistry, a pessimistic outlook, and loss of meaningful relationships. Suppressing anger can also lead to depression — for example, when you fail to speak out in anger (Chapter 5) or harbor old grudges (Chapter 13). And, finally, just as with substance use or abuse — nicotine, alcohol, caffeine — anger can be a way of self-medicating a mood disorder.

A participant in one of my anger-management workshops, when asked to define anger, described it as "one way I know I'm alive." Given her rather depressed tone of voice, I surmised that without the energy surges that anger provided her, she felt otherwise "emotionally dead" — which, to my way of thinking, is an apt way to define severe depression.

In this chapter, I also suggest the important role that prescription medication — antidepressants — can play in anger management. Les, a 47-year-old mechanic, is a good example of what can happen when you combine so-called "happy pills" with all the other strategies for reducing toxic anger (all the ones I outline in this book). Les referred himself for treatment following an incident where he assaulted his wife. This was the first time he had expressed his anger physically, but his temper had been an ongoing problem since his early childhood — as had depression. In addition to having difficulty controlling his anger, Les also reported having trouble concentrating, worrying constantly, experiencing spontaneous crying spells, and feeling "blue" most of the time — all of which had progressively worsened in recent years.

At first, Les was skeptical about taking medication — he thought that his problem with anger would either correct itself or get "fixed" by talking to a therapist. What he didn't count on was just how much better he would feel when his antidepressant kicked in — approximately four weeks after he began taking it and sooner than he could derive any lasting benefit from counseling. As he put it, "I wasn't ever happy before — I am now. I wouldn't talk with my family when I got mad before — I do now. I couldn't get a good night's sleep before — I can now. I was always tense before — I'm not now." All these changes had led to a reduction in the frequency of Les's angry outbursts, both at home and at work.

E-lim-inate the Negative: Maintaining a Positive Mood

Have you ever noticed how some people *always* seem to be in a good mood, no matter what's going on in their lives? I had an aunt like that. She lost her parents to illness when she was a young child; was raised along with my mother in an orphanage; was crippled by an injury from a head-on collision when she was in her early 20s; was never able to have children; struggled financially all her life; had a massive stroke in her later years, which left her partially paralyzed; and spent the last ten years of her life in a nursing home — and, the whole time, she was positive, never complained, never got angry, and had something good to say about everyone. Her positive spirit was indestructible!

For years, psychologists really haven't understood people like my aunt. They were far too busy studying the *opposite* kind of people — those who seem to lack whatever qualities my aunt had that allowed her to transcend life's many difficulties. But that's all beginning to change with the advent of what is called *positive psychology,* which identifies and strengthens the assets a person has (things like optimism, resilience, wisdom, hardiness) to thrive in the face of adversity and achieve optimal success in life.

In the following sections, I tell you about some behaviors that promote and maintain a positive mood. Then I tell you what you can do to correct a bad mood — things like laughing, being optimistic, finding benefits, and creating an emotional climate in which you can flourish.

Laughter: It really is the best medicine

Laughter is (literally) a painkiller. It can kill both physical and emotional pain. Studies comparing some type of neutral distraction, relaxation, and laughter found laughter to be most effective in raising a person's pain threshold. Bottom line: Laughter reduces pain sensitivity.

The same is true for *anger sensitivity* — how touchy you are and how easily you can be provoked to anger. In other words, you're less likely to be annoyed by something if you're in good humor than if you're not. Think of humor as a shield that protects you from the stinging impact of someone else's bad behavior.

Some people seem to have been born with a keen sense of humor. They don't have to *try* to be funny or make themselves and other people laugh — it just comes naturally. Other people have to look outside themselves to find something to make them laugh. Some years ago, I had a client who spent time each day cutting out cartoons from the newspaper and magazines and then handing them out as "gifts" to people she met throughout the day — I always got one when she came for therapy. She claimed it not only helped her feel less depressed about her back pain; it actually made her hurt less. Even after I quit seeing her for treatment, she would come by my office regularly to drop off a few cartoons and brighten up my day. Here are some other ways you can bring some laughter into your life:

- ✔ If you have a friend with a good sense of humor, spend time with that person as often as you can.

- ✔ Avoid the serious stuff on TV — especially the news! — and watch things that are lighthearted, even to the point of being silly.

- ✔ Find some movies that make you laugh and watch them repeatedly — think of it as therapy!

- ✔ Eat out in places where people tend to be loud, raucous, and having fun. (When I'm in a down mood, I always head straight for a Mexican restaurant!)

- ✔ Spend time with pets. When you get to know them, they can be a riot.

- ✔ Go to a bookstore and buy a joke book. (In the long run, it might do you as much good as a book on anger management!)

- ✔ Watch late-night TV. It's all silly and stupid — just what the doctor ordered at the end of a long, stressful day.

- ✔ Involve yourself in activities that provide good-natured fellowship. You won't believe how much laughter floats down the stairs when my wife meets with her bridge group. I can hardly hear the television!

- ✔ Keep visual reminders in your home and office of fun times with friends and family.

- ✔ Close your eyes and revisit a situation where you laughed until your sides burst.

My gift to the world

It's ironic that, while I rarely laugh myself (I'm too serious for my own good!), I've always been able to make other people laugh. When I was a kid, I learned to use this "gift" as a way to make friends and deal with my enemies. I was one of those skinny, weak geeks whom the rest of the boys liked to bully, and I quickly learned that as long as I made them laugh, they left me alone. Even today, when I have a few free minutes in my day, I often go visit a colleague or call a friend long-distance and lighten up their day. They laugh, and that makes me feel good — not a bad trade-off!

Hanging around with optimists

There is a direct link between your attitude about life and your mood. Optimists — people who believe that things will generally turn out for the best — tend to be in a more positive mood than pessimists. Pessimists are always expecting things not to turn out well (just wait, you'll see!) and, as a result, they're more apt to find themselves anxious, worried, and ready to be angry when their negative expectations are met.

Attitudes like optimism are formed early in life. They may even, as some people would argue, reflect inherited dispositions handed down from one generation to the next. Regardless of their origin, however, they remain fairly stable from cradle to grave. Even when life seems to be conspiring against you, if you're an optimist you tend to envision a more hopeful day somewhere in the future.

Attitudes are contagious. If you hang around with people who have a positive outlook on life, you're more likely to feel the same way. The reverse is true if you hang with a bunch of naysayers who see the worst in everything.

This *contagion effect* was readily apparent in two groups of chronic-pain clients who participated in my five-week rehabilitation program. The first group had five participants — four men and a woman. The woman, despite her painful injury and greatly altered lifestyle, began the program with a very optimistic outlook. She laughed, was cheerful throughout the morning, and was eager to involve herself in all aspects of the rehab experience. The men, on the other hand, were negative from the outset — hostile, reluctant to participate "because it won't do any good as far as my pain goes," and argumentative. Unfortunately, by the end of the five weeks, the female patient had caught the men's negativity — she no longer laughed, was quiet much of the time, and less energetic in her participation. They had, in effect, won her over to their all-negative way of thinking!

In the second group — three women and a man — the reverse was true. The women were all positive, and the poor negative guy didn't have a chance — by the third week, he was beginning to smile, laugh, and actually look *forward* to the classes. He had been converted to a more positive outlook, not just on pain but on life itself.

I've seen this pattern repeated time and time again, and I'm convinced that one requisite to staying in a good mood is to surround yourself as much as possible with positive thinking people. It's the next best thing to being a naturally optimistic person yourself!

Finding the good in the bad

Psychologists have a new name for finding something good in a bad situation — it's called *benefit-finding*. Studies of patients with a variety of catastrophic, disabling illnesses — heart disease, breast cancer, rheumatoid arthritis, multiple sclerosis — suggest that most people can identify at least *one* benefit they derive from being ill. The possibilities include

- ✔ An enhanced sense of spirituality (see Chapter 18)
- ✔ A greater appreciation for what life offers
- ✔ Deeper, more meaningful interpersonal relationships
- ✔ A heightened sense of compassion
- ✔ Greater introspection — examining one's inner self
- ✔ Greater willingness to openly express emotion
- ✔ Improved mood
- ✔ Less tension, anxiety, and anger
- ✔ Greater sense of mastery in dealing with day-to-day stress
- ✔ Increased vigor and activity
- ✔ Reduced fatigue-inertia
- ✔ Better future health

Being able to find the silver lining was a key to Ann's ability to endure chronic neck and back pain. Ann, a divorced mother of three, was only 36 when she was permanently injured while employed as a nurse. Asked one day during group therapy by another pain client why she continued to be so upbeat despite intense pain, she said, "Hey, had I not been injured, I would just be another working mom who rarely got to spend time with her kids. At least now I can be part of their lives in a more meaningful way. And that's a good thing."

Find benefit now — find relief later

In a study of 96 women undergoing treatment for breast cancer — including radiation, chemotherapy, and reconstructive surgery — those who could identify a potential benefit of their cancer experience were much less anxious, angry, and depressed when reassessed seven years later. This is yet another good example of how what you do today may affect tomorrow's anger.

Calculating your positivity ratio

Proponents of positive psychology point out the critical role that emotions like joy, love, and contentment play in helping human beings flourish in the course of everyday life. Flourishing is the opposite of languishing, which suggests that someone is in a rut, going nowhere, and feeling bad. Languishing is something I see in all the kids in my school-based anger-management classes. These are kids who, in addition to being terribly angry and aggressive, aren't taking advantage of the positive activities available to them — scholarship, sports, and organizations requiring cooperative behavior with schoolmates. I'm not sure they appreciate it when I tell them, "No wonder you're all so angry — you're not part of the good stuff!"

According to Dr. Barbara Fredrickson (of the University of Michigan) and her colleagues, there is a *critical* positivity ratio of roughly 3-to-1 (positive emotions over negative ones) that is necessary if you're to flourish at any point in your life. Think of it like a recipe — three parts joy/love/surprise to one part irritation. Anything less than that and it's a recipe for languishing.

Once a week, take a 24-hour sampling of your emotions — both positive and negative. Find a quiet time and circumstance, preferably at the end of the day to review Table 19-1. Circle any feelings or emotions you experienced that day. Now, count up the positive feelings and divide by the number of negative ones. This is how you derive you positivity ratio. If the value is below 2.9, you're in trouble! If it's 2.9 or above, you're more than okay.

Table 19-1	Feelings You Experienced Today
Positive	*Negative*
Appreciated	Afraid
Contented	Angry
Curious	Annoyed

Positive	*Negative*
Excited	Anxious
Happy	Ashamed
Interested	Dejected
Joyful	Disinterested
Loved	Frustrated
Respected	Guilty
Satisfied	Irritated
Surprised	Sad
Validated	Worried

If you're a little short on the positive feelings, think of some activity, pastime, or social situation that can make you feel more appreciated, valued, and excited — and then go for it!

When Your Mood Becomes a Problem

Mood becomes a problem when it is negative, when it persists, and when it is severe enough to adversely affect your life. All three elements must be present. No one comes to a mental-health counselor complaining of a persistent, disabling case of joy or happiness. You don't seek professional help, nor is your life changed significantly, because of one bad-hair day. And it's unlikely that your lifestyle will be greatly altered by one or two mood-related symptoms — sleepless night, low energy level.

But, if you're like Lisa, mood is a problem. In her wildest dreams, Lisa would never have pictured herself feeling the way she does when she wakes up every morning. "I just dread getting up. I wake up tired even after sleeping all night, and all I want to do is go back to sleep," she says. "I just want to run away, go somewhere where no one can find me. I just hate my life!" Describing how she feels is enough to make Lisa cry — which she does quite often lately. Lisa eats, but she has no appetite. And she can't relax — "I feel like there's a clenched fist in my chest all the time."

Looking for the last time you felt good

You can tell how long a person has been depressed by asking a simple question: When is the last time you really felt good — positive, happy, relaxed, satisfied — for a sustained period of time (say, one month)? If you answer with statements like "I don't know — it's been so long," "Oh, at least a year or more," or "Before my father died, five years ago," that's how long you've suffered from depression.

In the normal course of life, moods vary quite a bit, ranging from brief periods of exhilaration and joy to episodes of momentary despair and gloom. In between these extremes, you can also experience the everyday blues, mild excitement, or a feeling of neutrality — neither positive nor negative. If you visit all these different mood states on a fairly regular basis, the people who know, love, and work with you probably describe you as "moody." And — as you may have guessed — moody people are more prone to anger.

Lisa is suffering — and I do mean suffering! — from clinical depression, a condition so prevalent that some have called it the "common cold of mental illness." To determine if you're depressed, think about how you've felt the past two weeks and answer the following questions:

✔ Do you feel sad at times?

✔ Do you not enjoy things the way you used to?

✔ Are you discouraged about your future?

✔ Do you find yourself less interested in other people than you used to be?

✔ Do you cry for no apparent reason?

✔ Do you wake up early and have trouble getting back to sleep?

✔ Have you lost your appetite?

✔ Are you more irritated than usual?

✔ Does it take extra effort for you to get started doing something?

✔ Do you feel tired or exhausted most of the time?

✔ Do you ever think about harming yourself?

✔ Are you less interested in sex than you used to be?

If you answer yes to at least four of these questions, you may be suffering from a mood disorder. Consult with a physician or mental-health professional to see if this is something for which you need treatment.

The Anger-Depression Link

Psychiatrist John Ratey and colleague Catherine Johnson, in their book *Shadow Syndromes,* say, "Most people would rather be angry than terribly sad." They go on to describe how anger can unwittingly be used to wake up a "sluggish brain." In short, angry outbursts can be a way of self-medicating a mood disorder.

I find this true much more for men than for women, basically for two reasons:

 ✔ It is more acceptable for men to display anger openly (it's often regarded as a sign of strength) than to appear sad or depressed (perceived as a sign of weakness).

 ✔ Just the opposite is true for women — being depressed seems quite natural for women (by virtue of its association with childbirth, the so-called empty-nest syndrome, and menopause) whereas public displays of anger are seen as unusual and unladylike.

Grief — a feeling of deep, intense sorrow or mourning over the loss of a significant attachment — is a normal emotion. It can mimic depression, but it isn't the same thing. If you suffer the loss of a loved one, you should grieve. It means you loved that person and you miss him — your life will take some readjusting because your loved one is gone. In fact, if you didn't grieve over someone you loved or were attached to, that would be curious.

When my sister died at age 40, after years of poor and declining health, I was fine (or so I thought!) for a few months until suddenly, out of the blue, I found myself crying uncontrollably, raging uncontrollably, drinking uncontrollably, unable to sleep, with my head full of strange, foreboding thoughts. I wrote in my diary at the time,

> I'm calm for the moment, but probably that will change any time. Woke up this morning feeling *not* rested and felt shaky inside — agitated. Quickly got upset and on the defensive with family this morning even though things started off well. As the morning progressed, my emotions began to bounce all over the place, even to the point of tears a couple of times. I'm crying for help and no one hears me!

My condition worsened and progressed over a period of years. People don't grieve over the loss of a loved one for five years, no matter how much they loved the person. But as I found out (the hard way!) normal grief can quickly transition into a state of clinical depression, which, unfortunately, in some cases can last forever — or at least seem to.

The most dramatic illustration of how long a mood problem can persist comes from a client — a very nice woman in her mid-50s — who came to me for help some years ago. When she sat on my couch, I asked her "How are you today?" She began to sob uncontrollably and did so nonstop for the next 20 minutes.

My second question to her was, "How long have you felt this bad?" She replied, "Sixteen years!" and began to cry again. When she once again stopped, I asked her, "Why in the world did you wait so long to get some help?" With the saddest look on her face that I think I've ever seen, she said, "I just kept telling myself that it would get better — but it never did."

The more depressed you are, the more negative your view of the world. In fact, in extreme states of depression, people can become paranoid — harboring a fixed belief that everyone, even those closest to them, is out to cause them harm. Depressed folks are more apt to read malicious intent into the actions of others ("You did that on purpose!"). And, because of lack of sleep, decreased energy, and an increasingly self-critical attitude — all symptoms of depression — they struggle more in keeping up with the demands of their day and, thus, are more easily frustrated. It's amazing how, when you're no longer depressed, the things that used to set you off into a tirade now, at best, only annoy you.

Psychologist James Averill at the University of Massachusetts has noted that only about 10 percent of people act out their anger publicly (for example, by yelling at, pushing, hitting, and smashing things and people). These are the so-called *outrageous* people. The remaining 90 percent do just the opposite — they keep their anger in. These folks I call "in-rageous."

Keeping anger inside may sound like good news to you — that is, until you find out just how toxic anger turned inward can be. The anger-health checklist in Chapter 3 provides a host of examples of how anger literally makes people ill to the point of shortening their lives. As noted in this same chapter, in-rageousness can also:

✔ Rob you of your energy

✔ Contribute to poor health habits like overeating, smoking, and abusing alcohol

✔ Increase the likelihood that you'll engage in risky sexual behavior

✔ Adversely affect your career

✔ Precede road rage

✔ Lead to divorce

✔ Take all the joy out of life

✔ Poison the health of all those around you

Anger and depression share a common chemical pathway in the brain — a neurotransmitter called *serotonin*. My former colleague at Duke University Medical Center, Dr. Redford Williams, has researched this chemical connection and in his excellent book *Anger Kills* (coauthored with his wife, Virginia) he argues that what he has called the Hostility Syndrome — high levels of anger and aggressive behavior — could, in fact, be a "serotonin deficiency disorder." A wealth of psychiatric research shows that a chemical imbalance involving a shortfall in serotonin is similarly a root cause of depression. Finally, a shortage of this important brain chemical is also associated with smoking, increased appetite and weight gain, and alcohol consumption — which are symptoms of both toxic anger and depression. These commonalities should make you consider the possibility that rageful tantrums (anger out) and depression (anger in) are basically two sides of the same chemical coin.

Fixing the Problem

So, what do you do if you find yourself in a depressed mood? Simple: You get help. The good news is that psychiatrists probably know more about how to treat depression than they do any other mental-health problem. (For a complete and comprehensive discussion of depression and its treatment, turn to *Depression For Dummies* by Laura L. Smith, PhD, and Charles H. Elliott, PhD [published by Wiley].)

No single method has been proven most effective in providing relief from depression. I suggest a range of therapies that, when used alone or in combination, enhance your mood — and, thus reduce your anger. The more intense your depression, the more necessary it is to combine treatment strategies — for example, when I see folks who are moderately to severely depressed, I always recommend a course of psychotherapy along with antidepressant medication. My years of clinical experience have taught me that when clients are that depressed, counseling or drugs alone will most often prove ineffective. Finally, there is no magic wand when it comes to treating depression — believe me, I wish there were! — so therapists, patients, and their families all have to find how to be patient with the process.

Despite what some well-meaning mental-health researchers suggest, I don't believe that most human beings *spontaneously* recover from episodes of clinical depression. What I have found to be true, however, is that depression is a progressive illness and the longer you go without appropriate treatment, the worse you feel. Bottom line: The sooner a depressed person seeks help, the less that person suffers in the long run.

Taking the "happy pill": Antidepressants

More people rely on antidepressant drugs to "fix" their mood than any of the other forms of therapy available. In part, this is because we live in a world where we have a pill for everything and society tells us that pills can fix anything — cheaply and quickly.

I've been waiting for your call

When I experienced my first bout of depression, I quickly sought help from a psychiatrist I knew from my days at Duke University Medical Center. As it turned out, I wasn't that depressed so after three or four visits I felt much better. Sensing my "flight into health," my therapist told me I needed to make a decision — whether to stop now and hope the symptoms didn't return or continue on with therapy to better understand why I had gotten depressed in the first place and prevent it from occurring again. I took the low road and quit going. Less than a year later, when all the emotional wheels fell off at the same time, I called him frantically asking for help. I'll never forget what he said over the phone — "I've been waiting for your call."

You could see how much better Polly felt by her increased sense of humor. When she first came for treatment, she was so depressed that she basically spent the counseling hour mostly crying and talking negatively about herself. But three months later, she was one funny lady. I remember commenting on how nice she looked one day by saying, "That's a pretty dress — you look nice today." Her instant reply was, "Prozac — the Prozac made me buy it!" And then we both laughed. Another time, I commented on how unique her earrings were — again she responded, "Prozac — the Prozac made me buy them!" Another good laugh. Polly would be the first to tell you that counseling helped her get her life back together and put an end to her suffering, but at the same time she acknowledged the important role that medication played in her recovery.

Depressed patients make two big mistakes when they take antidepressant drugs:

- ✔ They don't take the medication long enough to achieve the desired pharmacological benefit. Typically, it takes four weeks before you begin to notice any type of sustained improvement in your mood and six months before you obtain the full, lasting relief you hope for.

- ✔ As soon as they feel the least bit better, they quit taking the pills — and then all too soon they're back to square one.

Tyler was a businessman, which meant that he was used to achieving results quickly. When I told him I thought he was sufficiently depressed to warrant a trial of medication, he was skeptical but went along anyway. He came in a week after he started the medication and the first thing he said was "I don't think the pills are helping me at all." I reminded him that antidepressants typically take two to four weeks before you begin to notice any difference in your mood. The second week, he came in saying the same thing — "They're not working!" Third week, same thing — and so on. Until the eighth week, when Tyler came in looking very upbeat and said, "Doc, I don't know what happened, but all of a sudden I feel a whole lot better than I have in months. I'm sleeping better, laughing more, have more energy, you name it." All of a sudden, he was a believer. The good news is that he hung in there all those weeks and gave the medication a chance to work.

Because antidepressants act as sedatives, they can have a more pronounced effect on people who are 50 years old and up. Physicians specializing in *geropsychiatry* are best able to manage antidepressant medications in the over-50 crowd.

All medication — even aspirin — has side effects. If you're taking medication for depression, be sure to ask your physician (or your pharmacist) what to expect — dry mouth, weight gain, hypersensitivity to the sun — when you take the drug. And don't be afraid to call the doctor if you think you're having some unusual side effect — that's what doctors are there for!

Antidepressant medication only works if you follow your doctor's orders about when and how to take the pills. Following instructions assures maximum effectiveness. Antidepressants aren't like most other types of medication — they aren't designed to be taken "as needed." To restore a healthy and balanced brain chemistry, you have to take the pills every day — regardless of how you feel. Otherwise, they don't have a chance to build up in your brain to the point where they do you some good.

The talking cure: Psychotherapy

Therapy works! I don't say that simply because that's how I've made my living for the past decades — I say it because I've been on the receiving end of the so-called talking cure. Psychotherapy is a process that not only saved my life, it changed my life for the better. In essence, I got much more benefit than I ever bargained for.

When most people think about counseling, they conjure up this Freudian image of lying on someone's couch and regressing back to childhood in order to relive all the painful experiences of the past (see the discussion on catharsis in Chapter 5). In today's world, nothing could be farther from the truth. Counseling is primarily about helping people who suffer from depression — and too much anger — gain insight into all those things that helped them get sick in the first place and then eliminating as many of those things as possible so that they can get well. Much of the information in this book would — and should — be part of what counselors and clients talk about. The emphasis should be on what you're doing *today* that is keeping you in a bad mood — not what you were thinking, feeling, or doing 30 years ago.

Cognitive therapy (examining how you think about life and how that in turn affects your mood) is one of the more popular strategies for defeating depression. Thoughts like "I have to be perfect in everything I do or else people won't love me" and "It's wrong to ask people for help — that only lets them know that you're weak and incompetent" can slowly, but surely, lead you into a mood disorder.

A shrinking network

Recent surveys indicate that the typical size of our social support network — those folks who can serve as confidantes, whose advice we trust, and who love us no matter what — has shrunk drastically. For example, in 1985, Americans reported having an average of three close friends. By 2006, the number had dropped to two. Even more troubling is the fact that 25 percent of those surveyed indicated that they had no one — not one living soul — whom they could turn to in a time of need. All of this has transpired at the same time that rates of depression have skyrocketed. Coincidence? I don't think so.

By all means, if you're in a funk or having the proverbial bad-hair day, reach out to friends and loved ones for support and comfort. But if you're suffering from clinical depression, you need more than what friends can provide.

Healing through exercise

A plethora of scientific evidence supports the fact that regular physical exercise improves mood in non-depressed people and, more important, can facilitate recovery in someone who is clinically depressed. What is also clear is that:

- ✔ **It doesn't matter what type of exercise you choose.** I heard someone ask a friend of mine who owns and operates a gym, "What's the best kind of exercise?" His response was, "The kind you'll agree to do!"

- ✔ **It doesn't have to be strenuous to be effective.** The key seems to be that you incorporate it into your lifestyle so that it's not just an add-on — doing it only when you have time or feel like it.

When it comes to using exercise to enhance mood, the best regimen seems to be a combination of:

- ✔ Aerobic exercise, such as walking or jogging, for endurance
- ✔ Weight-lifting for strength
- ✔ Stretching exercises for flexibility

If you're depressed and you choose to exercise regularly (three times a week), you can expect to:

- ✔ Be better able to concentrate
- ✔ Sleep better
- ✔ Show a greater interest in sex
- ✔ Have more energy

✔ Be less tense

✔ Enjoy life more in general

✔ Feel less alienated from those around you

✔ Make decisions easier

✔ Be more optimistic

✔ Complain less about minor physical ailments

✔ Be less self-absorbed

✔ Think more clearly

✔ Be less obsessive

✔ Be more active

✔ Be less irritable

Ironically, people who need to exercise because they're depressed are the ones most likely to quit sooner rather than later. One thing about depression is that it keeps people from being disciplined and persistent — sticking with things. Here's where having an exercise buddy — someone who understands where you are emotionally — comes in handy; that person's job is to keep you going.

Depressed people tend to be more isolated and spend far too much time alone, which only makes their negative mood persist. For that reason alone, I recommend that you do your exercise in a fitness facility (such as a gym or your local YMCA) where you're in contact with lots of people. Even if you don't talk to anyone, just being around other human beings will make you feel better.

Type A's and exercise

A former student of mine, Dr. James Blumenthal, who has since become a prominent figure in the field of health psychology, conducted a study at Duke University Medical Center, in which he recruited Type A's and Type B's who were free of coronary heart disease to enroll in a supervised ten-week exercise program consisting of a combination of stretching exercises and continuous walking/jogging.

He and his colleagues found that exercise led to a significant reduction in Type A behavior — including a 36 percent reduction in hostile/competitive behavior — which was comparable to that achieved with more conventional psychological therapy. Exercise didn't affect the Type B folks, but then they were more relaxed and easygoing to begin with.

Honey, you need a dog

I love animals, particularly bassett hounds, and I found myself quite distraught some years ago after one of our hounds got hit by a car and died. For weeks, I moped around the house, staying to myself, and talking myself into the idea of never ever having another dog — it's just too painful when you lose them.

One evening, my wife came home to find me sitting and staring at the television set. She announced, "Honey, we need to get you another dog." The tone of her voice suggested that she wasn't asking me if that's what I wanted to do, but telling me that that's what we were going to do — and, we did. Given my history of depression and the fact that our children had long since left home, that was a pretty smart move on her part. She prevented what could easily have become another bout of depression. Just one more reason I'm glad I married her!

Re-placement therapy

Depression is often described as the emotion of meaningful loss. Freud called it *melancholia* — a feeling of loss expressed through sadness. The more meaningful the loss — such as the death of a loved one, a child leaving home to go to college or get married, the loss of the best job you ever had — the more severe and persistent the resulting depression. One strategy for coping with this type of unwanted, negative change in life circumstances is what I like to call *re-placement therapy*. I'm not suggesting that you replace that which you've lost (you probably can't — otherwise, you would). What I'm suggesting is that you re-place the energy, sense of commitment, and feeling of emotional connection you had in that past relationship, job, or role as parent into something else that has a future. Otherwise, you'll spend each day mourning — as well as being angry over — what's not in your life rather than appreciating what is.

I was once asked to help a young woman who had lost her 8-year-old daughter to illness. The girl had died just before the Christmas holidays three years earlier, and each year after her death, the woman ruined the family holiday by dragging out the gifts that she had under the tree at the time the little girl died. It made her other children terribly sad, and her husband spent most of his time drinking as a way of not dealing with the whole thing. I suggested that she think about finding a new home for those gifts (in effect, re-placing them)— for example, as gifts for underprivileged kids. Talk about anger — she came close to physically assaulting me, all the while shouting, "Those are my daughter's gifts and they're going to be under that tree when she comes back!" She was fully intent on continuing to deny the reality of her child's death and was perfectly willing to remain severely depressed as a result.

Another client's story had a more positive outcome. Like the other woman, Fred lost his teenage son to a tragic illness. He had progressed from grief to a full-blown episode of depression by the time he finally took his family and friends' advice to get some professional help. Interestingly, one of the things he decided to do — after medication gave him more energy — was to use his skills as a photographer to take pictures of all the youngsters who were in his son's high-school class. He did this free — as a gift to those young people who were healthy and had outlived his son. He felt connected again in a small way to his son, which helped reduce his feelings of loss. Fred knew he could never replace his son, but he came to learn — through therapy — that he could re-place his love in other young people and make a difference in both his life and theirs.

Part VI
Managing Anger in Key Relationships

The 5th Wave   By Rich Tennant

"Right now I'm working on my anger management through medication, meditation, and limiting visits from my pain-in-the-butt neighbor."

In this part . . .

You'll see the effects of toxic anger on three types of key relationships: career, family, and loved ones. Is your workplace a battleground? Are you a loser when it comes to effective parenting? Are you locked into a loving, but angry relationship? If so, this part of the book will provide you with everything you need to know to avoid counterproductive work behavior, improve your negotiating skills, create an anger-free family atmosphere, adapt to the changing role of a parent, avoid ending up being an angry couple, inoculate yourself from abusive anger, and keep your cool when loved ones are losing theirs. In effect, this part is a guide to turning hostility into harmony with all the key players in your life.

Chapter 20

At Work

● ●

In This Chapter

▶ Realizing that it's not all about you

▶ Seeking win-win solutions

▶ Competing without confrontation

▶ Getting beyond impasse

● ●

*I*n this chapter, I highlight the role that anger management plays at work — the place where most people spend the majority of their time. But before diving in, consider these questions:

> ✔ While you're at work, do you often find yourself daydreaming rather than doing your job?
>
> ✔ Have you ever come to work late without permission?
>
> ✔ Have you ever made fun of a co-worker's personal life?
>
> ✔ Have you ever told someone outside work what a lousy employer you have?
>
> ✔ Have you ever done something at work to make a fellow employee look bad?

If you answered yes to any of these questions — and, don't worry, these situations are common — you're engaging in what occupational psychologists call *counterproductive work behavior* (CWB). CWB is any behavior by an employee that is intended to harm the organization or its members; it ranges from idle workplace gossip to acts of physical violence. The cost of CWB to industry: a whopping $200 billion in direct costs (such as theft) as well as untold billions in indirect costs (having to do with employee inefficiency). The number-one cause of CWB? You guessed it: anger!

In this chapter, I tell you how CWB plays itself out in the workplace, which types of personalities are most prone to CWB, how you can be competitive at work without being counterproductive, and how you can be more civil in your dealings with co-workers — by being an anger-free employee.

Recognizing Counterproductive Work Behavior

Recognizing counterproductive work behavior — in yourself and in others — can be tough. In part, that's because we think of much of it as "normal" at-work behavior — coming to work late or taking a longer break than you're allowed to. In addition, the majority of CWB is passive and nonviolent in nature. Here are some typical examples:

✔ Failing to report a problem and allowing it to get worse

✔ Ignoring someone at work

✔ Withholding needed information from a colleague

✔ Staying home and saying you're sick when you aren't

✔ Trying to look busy when you aren't

✔ Refusing to help a co-worker

✔ Intentionally coming late to a meeting

✔ Working slowly when things need to be done fast

✔ Refusing to accept an assignment

✔ Leaving work earlier than you're allowed to

✔ Avoiding returning a phone call to someone you should

✔ Purposely failing to follow instructions

Am I late? Sorry

Edith, a 51-year-old senior vice-president of an ad agency, knew that all employees — especially the executive staff — were supposed to attend the midday meeting, where the new CEO would be introduced. But Edith was angry — and she had been since the news of a major reorganization had been announced some weeks earlier and, along with the others, she was told that she would have a new boss. Edith had been trying not to let her anger show. But here she was coming into the packed auditorium 15 minutes late, distracting everyone from the CEO's opening remarks as she made her way down front. It was quite a show! There was no mistaking the message Edith was conveying — "Screw you all!" No one made any mention of her tardiness that day, but no one was surprised when she submitted her resignation (after being asked to) three weeks later.

Less often, CWB constitutes more active destructive or injurious behaviors such as:

- Purposely damaging a piece of equipment
- Stealing something belonging to your employer
- Insulting a co-worker's work performance
- Starting an argument with a co-worker
- Making an obscene gesture to a co-worker
- Threatening another employee with violence
- Hitting or pushing someone at work
- Purposely wasting supplies/materials
- Intentionally doing your work incorrectly
- Starting a harmful rumor about another employee
- Playing a mean prank on someone at work
- Acting nasty or rude to a customer or client

Sound familiar?

In a survey of 74 employees at one worksite, the following question was posed: How often have you observed each of the following behaviors on your present job? Here are their top 15 responses, starting with the most common:

- Complaining about insignificant things at work
- Coming to work late without permission
- Taking longer breaks than allowed
- Ignoring someone at work
- Being nasty/rude to a client or co-worker
- Daydreaming rather than doing work
- Leaving work early without permission
- Trying to look busy when they aren't
- Blaming colleagues for errors that they made
- Telling people outside work what a lousy place they work at
- Insulting fellow employees about their job performance
- Refusing to help out at work
- Avoiding returning phone calls that are important
- Making fun of people at work
- Verbally abusing a co-worker

Interestingly, I find almost the identical same list (and rankings) every time I conduct a survey of CWB, regardless of the type of work involved.

Look at the lists of counterproductive work behaviors and make note of which ones you've engaged in lately — say, the last three weeks. Do you engage in any of these behaviors on a fairly regular basis — once or twice a week? Pick one of these and tell yourself, "I'm not going to express my anger this way anymore." Then use some of the anger-management strategies outlined later in this chapter instead.

Avoidance versus aggression

CWB is an employee coping strategy. It's one of the ways you deal with work stress. The motivation behind CWB is always retaliation — which makes sense because the number-one cause of this kind of behavior is anger. When someone makes you mad at work, CWB is your way of leveling the playing field. And each time you make someone else angry, you're giving that person a reason to engage in CWB.

Most CWB is the result of interpersonal conflict — between co-workers and between supervisors and employees. The more conflict there is, the more counterproductive behavior you can expect. Conflict resolution and CWB go hand in hand.

Employees typically adopt one of two response styles when they engage in CWB: avoidance or aggression. Avoidance means you *disengage* in a variety of ways from getting the job done — coming in late or ignoring someone. Aggression means you *attack* the source of your anger — bullying a subordinate or insulting a customer. It's that old fight-or-flight pattern I talk about throughout this book (see Chapter 4, for example).

Person versus organization

Employees also differ in terms of where they direct their CWB. About 50 percent of the time, people are apt to retaliate against a *person* — insulting a fellow worker about their performance. The other 50 percent of the time, people take their anger out on the *organization* — destroying property. Either way, it disrupts the workplace and takes away from the bottom line.

Aggressive employees are three times more likely to retaliate against people with whom they work, whereas avoidant employees are more likely to satisfy their anger by engaging in CWB directed toward their place of employment.

Which of these profiles do you fit? Do some self-examination and ask yourself why — "Why do I always attack my team members when I get frustrated or irritated?" or "Why do I always run away from my anger and the issues that underlie it?" Avoidance usually results from fear. What are you afraid of — losing your job, losing control of your temper after you get started, what? Attack typically implies that you are dealing with an enemy. Are your co-workers really your enemies? Is this work or is it war? Is it because you have a combative personality and, thus, everything inevitably becomes a war?

Understanding the aggressive personality at work

Some people have more of an aggressive style of interacting with the world than other people do. By *aggressive,* I don't necessarily mean that you intentionally attack or seek to harm others, just that you seem to move against the world as opposed to going with the flow. Whether this is good or bad depends on which type of aggressive personality you are.

Katherine, a 34-year-old, up-and-coming junior executive in a nonprofit organization, is a classic example of what I call an achievement-driven personality. She goes well beyond just being achievement oriented. She's *driven* — all her energies work toward achieving success in her career. Katherine is extremely task oriented, has a really competitive nature, and is forceful when it comes to pursuing goals. She is direct in her communications — including how she expresses anger — leaving little doubt as to where she stands on issues. Those who work with her admire her determined spirit. She's not a talker — she's a doer! The only time she gets angry is when she becomes frustrated by obstacles that slow her down in her efforts to be efficient and get the job done. If you can keep up with her, she's your best friend and easy to work with and for.

Kelly, on the other hand, is more combative in how she approaches work. She, too, is highly competitive, but she tends to come across more confrontational in her dealings with others. If something goes wrong, she's in your face in a heartbeat! She's impatient, intense, and she can be quite demanding of those she works with — "Get that report to me by the end of the day and no excuses!" Ask anyone in the office and he'll tell you what a dominant personality she has. She's the type who has the first — and last — word on every subject. And, yes, she's angry a lot. But, her anger — unlike Katherine's — is not linked to frustration; rather, it simply serves as fuel for satisfying her combative personality. Kelly reminds me of a legendary football coach who was once described as "a guy who could walk into an empty locker room and start a fight!"

Both styles of aggressiveness are linked to the Type A behavior pattern, which typifies a preponderance of employees in western industrialized countries (like the United States). The good news, however, is that the link is strongest for the achievement-driven, rather than the combative, style. This possibly explains why the vast majority (84 percent) of Type A's don't succumb to early coronary heart disease and other stress-related illnesses. On the other hand, if you're one of those combative, angry Type A's, you may be a health accident waiting to happen! (To prevent this, consider the advice offered in Chapter 10 on how to become a Type B.)

Knowing Where to Look

Not everyone is susceptible to counterproductive work behavior. Clearly, if you're experiencing toxic anger — that is, intense anger than occurs on a daily basis (see Chapter 2) — you're a prime candidate. I estimate that somewhere between 25 and 40 percent of the work population fit this profile — a significant problem!

The disgruntled employee

Employees likely to engage in CWB often exhibit one or more of the following signs of disguised anger:

- ✔ They seem disinterested in their work.
- ✔ They're generally disagreeable at work.
- ✔ They show clear signs of distress.
- ✔ They're discouraged about how their careers are progressing.
- ✔ They keep their distance from other team members.
- ✔ They're highly distrustful of their superiors.
- ✔ They frequently appear distracted while completing a task.
- ✔ They show disrespect to those higher up in the organization.
- ✔ They're disenchanted about the mission of the organization.
- ✔ They verbalize disappointment about issues of salary and promotion.
- ✔ They're pretty much disgruntled, disgusted, and disheartened by everything that goes on during the workday.

As I suggest in my earlier book *ANGER-FREE: Ten Basic Steps to Managing Your Anger* (Quill, 2000), most people don't go around telling everyone within earshot that they're angry, pissed, or even annoyed. Most people express their anger in more subtle, politically correct terminology — but it's anger nevertheless.

Aaron, a 58-year-old urban planner, was definitely a disgruntled employee — and he made no bones about it. For 22 years, he had worked at a job he thoroughly enjoyed and that consistently rewarded him for his efforts. Then he decided to accept a preretirement package. For a long time, Aaron had wanted to move his family to a warmer climate and phase himself into full retirement. At first, his plan seemed to be working . He moved south and took a job with a salary comparable to what he had previously. But then, after two years, the company unexpectedly reorganized and laid off a large number of employees — including Aaron. Despite all efforts, the only job he could find in that location that fit his résumé paid him much less than he felt he was worth. He took the job, hoping that if he worked hard and gave his employer his usual 120 percent, he would eventually receive a substantial increase in compensation. But, as it turned out, that wasn't in the cards, because his educational background — an associate's degree — prevented him from moving up in pay grade. He was at odds with company policy. Given his age, he couldn't afford to just quit, and he didn't want to move his family again. Aaron was stuck! All he could do was spend his time complaining of just about everything — no matter how insignificant. His complaining, as you can imagine, did not sit well with his employer, who finally advised him to either stop complaining or leave.

Aaron was at a crossroads. He needed help immediately — not five years of on-the-couch therapy. So, I suggested he do the following to manage his anger (and you can do the same in *your* life):

- **Accept the reality of the situation.** To a large extent, Aaron was disgruntled because he refused to accept that he was dealing with an "immovable" object — company policy. Complaining was his way of trying to pry his employer loose from that policy — to make an exception in his case.

- **Stop personalizing the situation.** Aaron was angry because he believed the policy was directed at him. I asked him, "Do all the other employees have to abide by this policy?" His answer, without hesitation, was yes. So, I reminded him, "This really isn't about you at all. It's just the way they do business." He agreed.

- **Write down your feelings.** To defuse some of the anger that Aaron was carrying around — which was leaking out in the form of complaints — I recommended that he take 20 minutes a day and write out his anger (see Chapter 9).

- **Pull back on your efforts.** Aaron needed to stop giving 120 percent to his employer — working overtime without pay. His only rationale for this was that it was a means to an end — the end being a pay raise. I reminded him that his employer wasn't exploiting him, he was exploiting himself — and, that's not healthy!

- **Engage in some positive thinking.** Aaron's anger was also the result of the fact that this whole situation was constantly on his mind. The psychological term for that process is *rumination*. Because Aaron admitted he had little success in distracting himself from this problem, I suggested instead that he simply find something else — something positive and something that he had some control over — to ruminate about. (Chapter 4 offers some possibilities.)

- **Find some benefit in what you do.** I advised Aaron to think about his current job and come up with something positive. In other words, "What are you not complaining about? Salary aside, what works for you?" Aaron needed a more balanced view of his employment situation to ease away some of his angry feelings.

- **Get some exercise.** Regular exercise is a good way of "exorcising" not only physical toxins in the body but also emotional toxins like anger. Forty-five minutes in a gym three day a week can do wonders for your disposition.

- **Forgive, forgive, forgive.** Aaron was carrying around what I call *yesterday's anger,* and it was becoming burdensome both to him and his employer. The only way I know to unload this burden is forgiveness (see Chapter 13). Aaron needed to forgive himself for taking early retirement only to find himself in this mess, and he needed to forgive his employer for having what he considered an archaic promotion policy.

By following these suggestions, Aaron got "unstuck," not from the financial realities of his job, but from the negative emotion — anger — that accompanied it. He still had to watch his pennies, but he was no longer a disgruntled man.

The self-centered employee

Some years ago, I had the distinct pleasure of meeting a delightful, energetic psychologist, Dr. Lisa Penny at the University of South Florida, who educated me about the relationship between big egos (the technical term for this is *narcissism*), anger, and counterproductive work behavior. As it turns out, the bigger your ego (that is, the more self-centered you are), the more easily angered you are at work and, in turn, the more likely you are to engage in CWB. Although no one likes to be constrained at work — interrupted by others, inadequately trained, lacking the resources you need to complete the job satisfactorily — self-centered employees take these constraints personally (Why are you doing this to *me?*) and react with anger.

How do you know if you fall into this category? Here are some clues:

- **You tend to be self-absorbed in what you're doing and unaware of (and unconcerned about) what your colleagues are doing.** You aren't a team player.

- **You tend to have a clear sense of entitlement.** For example, you might say things like, "You *owe* me respect" and "I have a *right* to that raise or promotion."

✔ **You can't put yourself in the other guy's shoes whenever there's a conflict of some sort or difference of opinion.** You just keep reiterating what *you* want, how *you* see things, and why *your* solution is the right one.

✔ **You tend to be grandiose — feeling as though you're somehow special when it comes to working with others or completing a project.** You expect your co-workers to defer to you because of your power, brilliant ideas, and charismatic personality.

✔ **You tend to exploit others at work — that is, always use others to meet your agenda regardless of the cost to your fellow employees.** And, to add insult to injury, you get angry if your co-workers don't *appreciate* the fact that you chose them to exploit!

✔ **You tend to *self-reference* a lot.** The words *I, me,* and *mine* seem to permeate your speech no matter what the topic.

What if you're tired of being so self-centered? What do you do to change? Here are a couple of strategies:

✔ When you find yourself thinking like a self-centered employee ("Why are these people in *my* way?"), counteract that by thinking instead, "I'm sure these folks have important things to do, just like I do. The problem is we're both trying to do them at the exact same time. Maybe if I help them, they'll help me."

✔ Stop *demanding* that your co-workers do what you want — this goes along with a sense of entitlement — and instead *request* that they do what you want. You'll be surprised at how much more receptive they are!

✔ Spend more time trying to look at things from other people's perspective. Become more attuned to the people around you — to what they're thinking and feeling.

✔ Remember that life is a two-way street. The more understanding and sympathetic you are to those you work with, the more they respond that way to you. Not a bad deal, huh?

✔ Just as your mother taught you, always say "please" and "thank you" with every exchange during the workday. It's the glue of a civilized workforce.

Where do these people come from?

Self-centered employees are more likely to be first-born or only children. They're more likely to be male. They're more likely to have fathers who encouraged them to be independent while growing up. Their fathers were also more likely to use monetary rewards to get them to comply as children. Who wouldn't feel special if she actually got paid for doing the very same things other kids do without being compensated.

Improving Your Negotiating Skills

Most of what you do when you get to work each day involves some type of negotiating. Negotiation is nothing more than an effort between two or more employees aimed at resolving a conflict of interests. I'm always amused when I'm consulted by companies to coach managers and executives to make sure "everyone is on the same page." Companies seem to think that it's normal for their employees to be like-minded and are always surprised (and sometimes downright angry) when this isn't the case.

Negotiations always involve emotions — because the negotiators are human beings. But that's only a problem if the emotions in play are negative. If negotiators are in a positive emotional state — excited, optimistic — they tend to be cooperative and conciliatory. This more often leads to a win-win solution, where both parties come away feeling like they've gotten something they wanted. If either or both negotiators, however, are in a negative emotional state — angry, pessimistic — things tend to be much more competitive and neither party is comfortable making concessions. If no one concedes, you're at an impasse. No one walks away a winner!

Negotiators respond to their opponent's emotions. The best way to ensure a positive outcome is to start with a smile. That, believe it or not, sets the tone for everything that follows. Start with a look of irritation on your face and you'll have a hard row to hoe. Begin by emphasizing some point of possible agreement (hard to do if you're angry — but worth the effort); doing so sets a positive tone before getting down to differences of opinion. Remind yourself that, even though the other parties are your opponents, *they are not the enemy* (one of the ten anger-freeing thoughts listed in Chapter 25). And, last, if you must be angry when you enter into some type of negotiation, try to express your anger constructively (details in Chapter 11).

Creating a Positive Work Environment

Anger at work is not isolated to one particular employee, one specific exchange or circumstance, or one identifiable issue — for example, work overload. Individual emotions originate within the general context of the overall work environment. And that context (or climate) varies considerably from one work setting to another. Walk into any work situation — from a factory floor to a corporate boardroom — and after about five minutes observing people at work, you can tell whether the climate is hostile (people at each

other's throats), sad (too many lost opportunities, too much turnover in per-
sonnel), tense (lots of uncertainty), or cordial (We love it here!). You don't
have to be a rocket scientist — it's that easy.

Dr. Barbara Fredrickson at the University of Michigan and her colleague Dr.
Marcial Losada of the Universidade Catholica de Brasilia, Brazil, have come
up with a fascinating theory about how workplace emotions affect employee
productivity. Instead of concentrating on one specific emotion — anger —
they look at the positive and negative nature of emotions and, much more
important, the relationship between the two, which they refer to as the *positivity ratio.* So far, they have found that:

✔ For employees to flourish in their work, the ratio of emotions expressed
   in the workforce overall must be approximately 3-to-1 in favor of positive
   feelings.

✔ If that 3-to-1 ratio isn't reached, workers tend to flounder — describing
   their work lives as empty and unsatisfying.

✔ Too much positivity, on the other hand, can also be a problem — a
   minimal amount of *negativity* is necessary to avoid work patterns
   from becoming inflexible, stagnant, boring, and overly routine (which
   in turn can lead to irritability among employees). But having enough
   negativity isn't something that most companies need to worry about!

✔ The negativity must be appropriate — that is, employees may not
   express contempt for one another or act out in rage — in order for it
   to be beneficial (see Chapter 11 and find out how to use anger constructively).

✔ The expression of positive emotions must be genuine rather than forced.
   (Memo to all employees: From now on, every one of you will have a
   smile on your face at all times!)

In the following table, I list a number of emotions that you may have
observed where you work. Circle ten of those that you feel best and most
accurately describe the emotional climate of your work situation *in the past
week.* It doesn't matter which column you circle from — you choose ten emotions total. Then calculate the positivity ratio by dividing the number of positive emotions by the number of negative emotions (for example, if you have
three words circled in the Positive column and seven words circled in the
Negative column, you do this simple calculation: 3 ÷ 7 = 0.43). Is your positivity ratio above or below 2.9? If the ratio is 2.9 or below, you — and everyone
else you work with — is much more likely to get angry at work. If the ratio is
at least 3.0 (but less than 11.0 — this is an example of too much positivity),
your workplace has a healthier environment.

Positive Emotions	*Negative Emotions*
Amazed	Afraid
Amused	Agitated
Appreciative	Alarmed
Cheerful	Angry
Content	Anxious
Curious	Ashamed
Delighted	Bitter
Enthusiastic	Bored
Excited	Depressed
Generous	Frustrated
Grateful	Guilty
Happy	Irritated
Hopeful	Petrified
Joyful	Regretful
Kind	Resentful
Loving	Sad
Optimistic	Sorrowful
Satisfied	Unhappy
Thrilled	Worried

If you're an employer, here some tips on how to create a more positive work setting:

- ✔ Recognize an "Employee of the Month" based not on productivity, but rather on how positive the person relates to customers, clients, and co-workers.

- ✔ Offer small rewards for displaying a positive attitude at work — tickets for the family to attend a theme park, a gift certificate to a restaurant, or tickets to a local comedy club.

- ✔ Celebrate every employee's birthday, and have the birthday guy or gal bring sweets for the entire office staff.

- ✔ Instead of observing dress-down Friday, have "lighten-up" Fridays where everyone at work is on their most positive behavior.

The Dutch have it right

I spent a year working in the Netherlands and was fascinated by the many differences between U.S. culture and theirs. For example, a Dutchman takes the initiative for making sure his birthday is a huge, continuous celebration. All day long, he tells everyone with whom he comes into contact "It's my birthday today!" And, at work, he brings cake and assorted sweets for the entire office staff. The more he likes himself and the more reason he has to celebrate his birthday, the bigger the cake! Unlike Americans, who wait for others to remember their birthday and take responsibility for whatever celebration comes their way — and then get depressed when no one acknowledges it — the Dutch leave nothing to chance. What a sensible and civilized tradition!

If you're an employee, try to the following to make your work environment more positive:

- ✔ Begin each workday by greeting your fellow employees by saying, "Have a great day!"

- ✔ Interject some humor into the workplace dialogue. Laughter communicates to your co-workers that you mean no harm.

- ✔ Always apologize when you do something that you know offends a fellow employee. Not only will you feel better but, as it turns out, saying you're sorry also defuses the tension in the other person and makes it harder for her to hold a grudge.

- ✔ Make a friend at work. Surveys show that having a friend at work — particularly if it's your best friend — greatly increases the odds that you'll enjoy going to work and be more satisfied with what goes on there.

Making Civility the Norm

At work, niceness counts. Treating your fellow employees in a civil manner — fair, respectful, courteous, pleasant — virtually assures that you'll be treated with civility yourself. The reverse is also true — be rude and hostile to others and they will, in turn, act that way to you (or go out of their way to avoid you!).

Anger is often the byproduct of being on the receiving end of incivility. And incivility typically leads to some form of counterproductive work behavior.

How big a problem is workplace incivility? Huge! Approximately 90 percent of all working people believe a lack of civility at work is a serious problem — even though it doesn't rise to the level of workplace (physical) violence. Incivility is a major reason for turnover, with approximately half of the employees who have been targeted for uncivil treatment contemplating looking for another job and one in eight actually quitting.

If you're an employer and you want to ensure that civility is the norm, follow these suggestions:

- Make it clear — from the top down — that uncivil behavior will not be tolerated (no matter what was allowed in the past) and that no exceptions will be made in terms of job status.

- Introduce training in civility as an integral part of recruitment and orientation.

- Have written policies on what constitutes civil and uncivil behavior and what consequences are attached to the latter. Invite input from all employees.

- Make civility counseling a vital part of the human resources program.

- Survey employees periodically on the status of civility in your workplace.

- Institute a peer-review system for recognizing and sanctioning uncivil behavior.

- Emphasize *constructive* criticism, *constructive* anger expression, and *constructive* competition.

If you're an employee and you want to make civility the norm where you work, do the following:

- Make "Do unto others as you would have them do unto you" your personal mantra at work.

- Be constructive in your criticism of fellow employees — tell them how to do what they do better!

- If you think your workplace is too uncivil, initiate some positive change — don't wait on the other guy.

- Make it clear to all those you work with that you expect to be treated in a civil manner at all times and don't be afraid to provide corrective feedback when it's called for.

- Remind yourself and others at work that civility isn't about who's in charge or who's right — it's about mutual respect.

- ✔ Always allow your fellow employee to save face by addressing any problems or criticisms in private. It's less intimidating and leaves him less embarrassed.

- ✔ Be optimistic and always assume the best when it comes to the efforts of those with whom you work. Give them the benefit of the doubt until you have proof to the contrary.

- ✔ If you have to be critical of a fellow employee, show her the courtesy of saying what you have to say face to face — and if you can't say it to her face, don't say it at all!

Speaking Up, Not Out

Anger always speaks out — if not in actual words, then through efforts on your part to "act out" what you're feeling. Acting out feelings is what counter-productive work behavior is all about.

Better than speaking *out* is speaking *up* — saying what's on your mind and in your heart. Psychologists refer to this as *assertiveness.* The assertive employee provides face-to-face, one-on-one feedback that affirms his needs ("I need to be treated with more civility around here"), authenticates his emotions ("Yes, I'm angry and I think I have a right to be"), acknowledges the positives as well as the negatives of the situation ("You know I like working here, but . . ."), and assumes a positive outcome — all without being in the least bit aggressive.

Assertiveness is more about action than attitude. On the contrary, if you don't often stand up for yourself, you end up being perceived by those you work with and for as weak (a pushover, the proverbial doormat) and someone not to be respected or taken seriously — which invites others to treat you badly. Rarely do you hear someone at work say, "Boy, I really admire her — she's such a mouse!"

So how exactly are you supposed to speak out in an assertive manner? Follow these tips (and head to Chapters 4, 5, 8, and 11 for even more info):

- ✔ **Take ownership — always start with the word *I*.** For example: "I need to talk to you about something that is bothering me." "I need to give you some personal feedback about this morning's meeting." "I'm not sure you understand where I'm coming from."

- ✔ **Open with a positive statement.** For example: "I think you know how much I like working here, but. . . ." "I think it's fair to say that you've always been fair with me in the past, but. . . ."

✔ **Stop bobbing and weaving and get to the point.** Be specific about what it is that is bothering you — making you angry. Don't just say "I'm angry!" Tell the other person exactly why.

✔ **Appeal to the other person's empathy.** For example: "I'm not sure you appreciate the impact your words earlier had on me." "I want to think you weren't intentionally trying to make me mad, but. . . ." "If I were to talk to you rudely, I'm not sure how you would feel, but it really upsets me."

✔ **Avoid four-letter words.** No one likes to be cussed at, not even the person who cussed at you. Besides, the message gets lost when surrounded by expletives.

✔ **Be persistent.** Don't expect one assertive act on your part to change the world. Change the dialogue first and the world will follow. Trust me.

Chapter 21

At Home

C an families have conflict without combat? Absolutely. In this chapter, I tell you what a healthy family does to minimize destructive anger — the kind that, all too often, ends up in domestic violence. Don't worry . . . it can be as simple as sitting down together at dinner every night.

Take the Smiths as an example. Mother, father, and teenage daughter — they're a family in trouble. Anger is at the center of almost every interaction the Smiths have throughout the day. They fuss, they yell, and they use force to get whatever they need from each other. They feel hopelessness about their future as a family. The mother continues to seek a peaceful solution to family conflict, but the father has given up. He spends most of his time away from home and loses his temper when he's there. The daughter battles with both parents over almost everything.

Long ago, the Smiths decided their daughter's anger was the problem that needed to be fixed. They've taken her to one mental health professional after another, all to no avail. What the family *hasn't* done is examine their own dynamics — the style with which they communicate and deal with one another. What this family needs is what I call "anger management times three."

Anger within families involves power struggles; it's the antithesis of coopera-tion. It wastes family resources — energy, time, money — and can leave a residue of hostility and resentment. Family members become so concerned about winning battles that they lose sight of the fact that, together, they're losing the war. Relationships become fragmented — every man for himself. They can no longer trust or count on each other for support. They've become a family in name only.

In this chapter, I give you some practical tips on how *not* to end up like the Smiths. I talk about how families can use anger constructively (see Chapter 11) to form more intimate, loving relationships (see Chapter 22). And I show you how to minimize anger through effective parenting.

It Takes Two to Tango: Avoiding Angry Dialogues

When an angry family member confronts you, the easiest thing to do is respond in kind — answer anger with anger. What ensues is what psychologist and author Harriett Lerner calls the "dance of anger" (in her best-selling book by the same name). I liken it to the tango — a dance characterized by its drama and passion.

If you don't want to dance the anger dance, you have two options:

✔ **You can simply opt out — in effect saying, "Thanks, but I'll pass."** Teenagers, for example, often initiate an angry exchange with parents as a means of releasing pent-up tension, mostly relating to difficulties they're having with their peers. And what do most parents do? They jump right in with both feet — first, by telling their kid, "You shouldn't feel like that" and, when that doesn't work, by getting angry themselves. The best course of action: Be sympathetic but don't engage with the other person's anger. Let his anger be his anger — don't make it yours. It'll die down quicker that way.

✔ **You can engage in another type of dance, one with less drama — you can begin by validating the person's emotion and then give him a chance to work through it.** Consider the following example:

Parent: Hi. How was school?

Teenager: Leave me alone. God, every time I walk in the door, you're always asking me how I feel!

Parent: You sound like you're angry.

Teenager: I am. But I don't want to talk about it, okay?

Parent: That's fine. But if you do, I'm here. I feel that way myself sometimes — just want to work things out myself.

Teenager: (voice louder) Well, I'm not you! Besides, you wouldn't understand. You never do.

Never laugh at an angry loved one

Some people have a hard time expressing their anger out loud, so the last thing you want to do is laugh when she does find the courage to say "I found that annoying." When you laugh at someone who's expressing her feelings, you're being dismissive and showing contempt. This is the most destructive type of communication between family members. Having someone listen to you when you're angry is not only important, it's essential to good family relationships. If we listened to each other more when we're annoyed, maybe we wouldn't have to listen so much when we're in a full-blown rage.

Parent: (not raising voice) Of course, you're not me — I wasn't suggesting that you were. You have your own way of dealing with your anger. I was just being sympathetic.

Teenager: It's that stupid Jen — she thinks she's so much better than me. I could just kill her; she makes me so mad.

Parent: So you're angry with Jen. What did she do this time?

Now, the two are engaged in a dialogue about anger rather than an angry dialogue.

Managing Anger from the Top Down

Family members — parents and children alike — learn by example. If a child sees his parents rant and rave, cuss, and hit one another in anger, he'll learn to handle anger poorly himself. Similarly, if parents allow their child to throw an angry tantrum every time she doesn't get her way, they in turn act the same way — they've learned to act like their child.

Parents are the ones who set the tone for the home environment, and they need to take primary responsibility for ensuring that anger is expressed in a civil and constructive way. (You may be able to hold your kids responsible for cleaning their rooms, but you can't hold them responsible for the anger in your household.)

Unfortunately, my parents were poor role models for reasonable anger — my mother was a yeller and my father was a hitter, and neither one could keep from bringing out the worst in the other. Not wanting to be like either of them, I ended up going to the other extreme and became instead a pouter and a sulker. (Now you know where my fascination with anger comes from.)

Won't somebody listen?

One of the most effective methods of defusing toxic anger in adolescents, I've found, is just getting them to talk about their feelings and being a good listener. That's why in my anger-management classes in schools, I don't come in with an overly structured curriculum. Instead, I start by going around the circle, asking each kid, "How are you? How has your anger been since I saw you last?" and then going from there. After the kids begin to trust me, they open up and tell me all sorts of things they never tell anyone else. Try to be that kind of listener for your own kids — you may be surprised by what they share with you.

The home environment is a learning laboratory, a classroom where all the important lessons of life, and survival, are taught. Chief among these is the lesson on how to survive —and even benefit from — conflict between family members. Conflict is inherent in all families simply because its members have different interests, personalities, temperaments, values, wants, likes, dislikes, anxieties — all of which have to be negotiated if the family is to operate in relative harmony. The major distinction between healthy and unhealthy families is how they choose to resolve these conflicts — not whether they have the conflicts in the first place.

So if you're the parent, how do you set a healthy tone for your family's conflicts? Here are some tips for managing the anger that results from family conflict:

✔ **Be accepting of conflict and anger.** Don't disapprove of or dismiss conflicts between family members or try to distract people's attention away from problems. *Remember:* Anger is a signal that something is wrong and needs to be resolved. You *want* those signals — if you didn't have them, or didn't heed them, the anger would only grow.

✔ **Talk about anger comfortably.** Don't make anger a taboo topic that becomes yet one more "elephant in the living room" — something everyone knows is there but no one talks about.

✔ **Distinguish between different levels of anger and conflict.** You want to help your family differentiate between being irritated, being "just plain mad," and being in a rage (check out Chapter 2). The first two are okay — the third is not.

✔ **Keep your cool.** You don't help children keep their cool by losing yours! You're the adult — even if you don't feel like you have much ability to keep your cool, you can bet that you're better able to keep your cool than your kids are able to keep theirs.

✔ **View anger and conflict as an opportunity for new learning.** Step back, look at each other, and find out something about the other person — the result is a greater sense of intimacy (sharing of one's real self!).

✔ **Don't punish — instead, problem-solve.** Instead of fussing at each other for being angry, ask each other two simple questions:

- What are you angry about?

- What would you like to do about it?

The first question defines the problem; the second question defines the solution. If the other person knows what the problem is, but doesn't have a solution, help him find one — and one that doesn't involve acting out his anger is some hateful and vengeful way.

✔ **Seek win-win solutions.** No one likes to lose — certainly not someone who's already angry. She just gets angrier! What you want is to find a solution to family anger that leaves everyone feeling that they got something positive out of the exchange — if only the fact that they were actually *heard* for a change. Here's where a nonaggressive approach works best — an approach that is not competitive ("I win, you lose!") or confrontational and where one person in the family doesn't try to dominate the others.

Choosing the Unfamiliar: Changing Your Family's Patterns

Albert Einstein said, "Insanity: doing the same thing over and over again and expecting different results." Human beings are creatures of habit, and so are family units. Over time, families develop certain predictable patterns of behaviors — family dynamics — that have a life of their own. Families have decision-making patterns, problem-solving patterns, patterns that define how we react to major changes in life circumstances, and patterns in how we react to each other emotionally.

After these patterns are established, families tend to act them out reflexively, mindlessly — even if they don't work. Families tend to do today exactly what they did yesterday — even if it's not necessarily effective. In fact, I think that at least *part* of the anger that family members feel is because they're aware that their patterns don't work.

So, why not choose the unfamiliar for a change? Here's an example: When my kids still lived at home and we took long driving vacations, it was inevitable — predictable — that my son would get angry because we were playing music my daughter liked on the radio, my daughter would get angry because we were playing music my son liked, and I would get irritated because the two of them were bickering back and forth constantly. Nothing my wife or I did seemed to satisfy the kids — we were stuck! Then one day — somewhere between Virginia and Florida — I got a brilliant idea: This family would do something it had never done before. We would each — all four of us — get to choose what we all listened to for 30 minutes at a time and continue rotating that until we arrived at our destination. Guess what? No one objected. From that point forward, there were no more hostilities about the radio — everybody was a winner. It may sound like a little thing, but believe me it made a *big* difference in the emotional climate within the car.

Make a list of your own family's situations where anger is most likely to occur. Think about how each member of your family reacts in that particular situation. Now, think what you can do to change how you react. The next time that situation occurs, take the initiative to choose the unfamiliar. Don't be afraid to be creative. Surprise the rest of the family by doing something unpredictable, and then watch how they respond — sometimes all it takes is one person changing the routine, and everyone else follows suit. Pretend you're a scientist conducting an experiment on how to create family harmony. If one thing doesn't work, try something else — keep experimenting until you find what you're looking for.

This isn't just something that parents can do. As a kid (especially a teenager), you know the dynamics of your family, you know what sets them off. Why not take the initiative, try something different, and see what happens?

Looking at Your Parenting Style

You have your own style of dressing or decorating your house or signing your name — and you have your own style of child rearing. How you raise your kids doesn't just affect the intensity of conflict in your family — it affects their emotions, their grades in school, whether they start smoking, whether they engage in risky sexual behavior, among other things.

There are four main styles of parenting. See if you can find yourself in one of these styles (and keep in mind that you may be a mix of more than one):

- ✓ **Authoritative style:** If you're an authoritative parent, you're highly involved in your children's lives and you're not afraid to exert reasonable control over their behavior. You're fully aware of what your kids are doing and who they're doing it with. You have a physical presence in their lives and you engage them in activities that generate a sense of belonging and togetherness. Above all, you foster a sense of *autonomy* (the ability and freedom to self-govern), which increases with age, and you present a clear message that with freedom comes responsibility. You rarely, if ever, use punishment — threats, arguments, ultimatums — to keep your kids in line.

What can you expect from your children? They'll be cooperative, in a positive mood, do well in school, have high self-esteem, evidence self-control, and persist at tasks.

✔ **Permissive style:** If you're a permissive parent, there's no question that you love your children. There's also no question that you want to be their best friend. To ensure that, you put few demands on them, impose few limits on their social and emotional behavior, and essentially leave the parenting up to them. You give them a lot of freedom and allow them to be autonomous in areas where they're incapable of succeeding. You don't set curfews for your teenagers — you feel that they know when it's time to come home.

Permissiveness sounds good on paper, but kids raised in permissive homes tend to be impulsive, temperamental, defiant, rebellious, and antisocial, and they show little evidence of self-control. Their relationships with parents tend to be hostile/dependent — they can be highly dependent one minute and terribly demanding the next.

✔ **Autocratic style:** Autocratic parents tend to be angry themselves. If you're autocratic, you make a lot of demands on your children and yell, criticize, and punish them when they fail to live up to your expectations. When it comes to talking with your children, there is no give-and-take between your ideas/needs and theirs — your basic philosophy is "It's my way or the highway!" You're definitely not a good listener. And autonomy is out of the question.

Your kids live in fear and tend to suppress or act out their negative emotions. Whether you realize it or not, they view you as harsh, cold, and rejecting. Like you, they often resort to force — aggression — to get their way. Boys, especially, evidence high levels of anger outside the home — at school and with peers.

✔ **Unengaged style:** Unengaged parents are parents in name only. If this is your parenting style, when asked where your children are and what they're doing, you immediate response is, "I don't know. I'm not sure." And that's the sad truth of it. You tend to be *un*accepting of your children, *un*aware of what's going on in their lives, *un*available to them day and night, *un*involved — whatever they're doing, they're doing with people other than you.

Children raised by unengaged parents are extremely alienated — from adults and peers alike. They frequently use anger to keep others at a distance. They're emotionally volatile — prone to rage. And they have very limited social and problem-solving skills. Bottom line: Children who raise themselves without love do a poor job of it.

When it comes to minimizing anger in the home — both yours and that of your children — the best parenting style to employ is the authoritative one. Take Ross and his wife, Jane, for example. They have two children, both teenagers. They encourage their kids to be involved in all sorts of activities — school and community sports, choir, band, synagogue — and they're there to support them in every instance. Each evening at the dinner table, the topic of conversation involves everything from world events to "Who are you spending time with these days?" Ross and Jane invite their children to talk about their feelings, their problems, even difficult topics such as the recent suicide of a kid at their high school. Ross and Jane argue with their kids at times, but they're always respectful of their kids, and their kids are respectful of them in turn. As often as possible, decisions about family life are made as a family — even though Ross and Jane have the final say. Apparently, their kids like and are comfortable in their home environment — they're always bringing friends home and including them in family activities. Do Ross and Jane ever get angry with their kids? Sure. Do their kids ever get mad at them? Of course. But these times are few and far between and the anger never leads to disruption, disrespect, or violence.

Josh, a friend of Ross and Jane's son, has a much different relationship with his parents. Josh's parents have always been hard on him, demanding that he do well in school, fighting with him constantly over who his friends are, insisting that he participate in activities that interest them, and restricting his movements as much as possible. (In other words, they're autocratic.) Josh ends up emotionally conflicted — he both loves and hates his parents. That's why he stays away from home as much as he can, but at the same time constantly talks to anyone who will listen about his unreasonable parents. Josh is an intelligent kid, but he does poorly in school — to get back at his parents. He smokes, drinks, and has wrecked his car on more than one occasion. He and his parents are caught up in a vicious cycle of anger with no end in sight.

Is the autocratic style the worst-case scenario when it comes to parenting? In a sense yes, but actually it's no worse than the other two (permissive and unengaged).

Can't you understand why I'm so angry?

I surveyed the kids in my high school anger-management classes as to how they were being raised. Sadly, but not surprisingly, only 18 percent saw their parents as having an authoritative style. The vast majority instead described their parents as unengaged (32 percent), autocratic (32 percent), or permissive (18 percent). And, everyone — including their parents — want to know "Why are these kids so angry?"

Parenting isn't a static process. Early on, of course, children need a lot of direct control, if for no other reason that to keep them safe. One of my neighbors told me how he had a "discussion" with his 2-year-old son about the harm that could befall him if he stuck his finger in an electrical socket. He said that he had explained to his son the difference between AC and DC current so that he would appreciate how electricity worked. He then asked me what I would do if my son, Chris, went to stick his finger in the wall socket. "Oh, that's easy," I said. "I would just smack his hand and say *no!*"

Later on, as kids grow up and can watch out for themselves a bit, it makes sense for you to loosen up — exerting more indirect control or influence over they way they think, feel, and behave. Teenagers, for example, should be part of the family discussion about curfews, sex, drugs, alcohol, cigarettes, the difference between right and wrong, and so on. As a parent, you want to encourage them to have an opinion about what goes on in the world around them and what part they want to play in that world. Progressively allow them to make important decisions or they'll be indecisive or make poor decisions the rest of their lives. (I often see this in kids — smart kids — who go away to college after being raised by autocratic parents. They spend most of their first year doing all the things they were never allowed to do — or even talk about — while they were at home; sometimes with disastrous results.)

Of course, after your children become adults, it makes sense to become a more permissive parent. After all, where do you get off telling your 33-year-old how to live his life? Continue to be interested in their welfare, but be available as a consultant or counselor, and supportive of their efforts to succeed in life. When it comes to telling them what to do — forget about it!

The most effective parents are the ones who know when and how to transition from one parenting style to another as their kids grow up.

Video games and anger

One thing families can do to minimize angry, aggressive behavior in their children is to restrict the amount of time their kids are exposed to video games, especially violent ones. A study of 227 college students at a large Midwestern university found that aggressiveness — a person's overall tendency to act in a hostile way toward others — was highly correlated with the amount of time he spent playing both violent and nonviolent video games. Exposure to video games was also linked to delinquent behavior such as purposely damaging property and attacking someone with the idea of seriously hurting him. These relationships were strongest for males, in large part, because they tend to spend more time playing video games than females do.

Have a family meeting and review the various parenting styles. Ask each family member to write down the style they believe fits each parent. Is there consensus or a diversity of opinion? Let each person give examples of why she rated each parent the way she did. Don't comment until everyone has had his say, and then open the floor for general discussion. Remember not to get defensive — that will defeat the whole purpose of the exercise. You may be surprised by what you discover.

The Power of One

Dr. Robert Maurer's book *One Small Step Can Change Your Life* has a simple, yet profound message: When you want to make important changes in your life, think small. My translation of that is what I call the "power of one." Beginning today, commit yourself to doing one — and only one — thing to create an anger-free environment at home. It really doesn't matter what that one thing is, as long as it has some potential for creating family cohesion and harmony and you're willing to stick with it long enough to realize some change. In the following sections, I give you some places to start.

One meal a day

Psychologists repeatedly find that families who share one meal a day together get along better than families who don't. Granted, getting everyone in the family together in one spot, at one time, for one purpose can be a daunting task in today's stressful world — but there's no mistaking the fact that it's a key to family unity and a feeling of connectedness between family members.

Our time together . . .

My father didn't get too many things right as a parent, but one thing he did that was good was insist that our family spend the whole day together working in the yard every Sunday. My older brother hated it (which made me happy!), but he had no choice — so he worked side by side with the rest of us edging the driveway, mowing, pruning shrubs, all in the hot Florida sun.

I always thought it was a special day — a time for just the Gentrys. It was one of the few times we got to see my father when he wasn't tired, fighting with my mother, or angry. We worked together and, afterward, played and ate together. It was a good time all around!

Sharing a meal together is not about food — it's about community. It's a time when the family members can:

- ✔ Revisit their biological roots

- ✔ Share a positive moment

- ✔ Express ideas and emotions

- ✔ Negotiate changes in family rules

- ✔ Get things off their chest (see Chapters 5 and 8)

- ✔ Reinforce each other for individual achievements

- ✔ Plan future events

- ✔ Have spiritual time together

- ✔ Talk about current events

- ✔ Learn about family history

- ✔ Learn to see things from the other person's perspective

Family members won't be likely to drift away and become isolated — and thus become literal strangers — when they interact with one another in this intimate for-members-only way on a daily basis. And there's less likelihood of toxic anger occurring in a situation where people know one another in the way that daily meal sharing allows.

One evening a week

Try sharing one evening a week with your family. You can accomplish the same things you do by eating one meal a day together — only in more depth. You can use this time to address unresolved family tensions — or just to enjoy each other's company.

Rudy, a middle-aged man who is being seen for anger management involving domestic abuse, has started having family meetings once a week to talk about his anger and its impact on everyone else in his family. These evenings are difficult for Rudy because, for many years, he denied that he had a problem with anger. It's also tough on him because he has inflicted so much emotional harm on his wife and kids. Rudy began the first family meeting by acknowledging to everyone that he has a problem with anger and by sharing what he's learning about himself in treatment. His teenage son opened up about how afraid he has been of Rudy his whole life and how that has forced him to connect only with his mother. He went on to say how he and his sister are constantly vigilant whenever Rudy is around and how tense and frightened they become when they realize their dad will be coming home soon.

Finally, his wife shared how she has hidden things from her husband all of their married life — important things, personal things — for fear that he would erupt in rage. After two hours of intense family discussion, Rudy was reduced to tears and had a profound sense of remorse. "Good," I tell him. "You *should* feel bad about using your anger all these years to hurt the people you love — and that's your incentive to stick with the anger-management program." Facing up to his problem and allowing his family to speak out is probably the greatest gift Rudy has ever given his family — or himself.

One day a month

Spending one day a month together as a family is hardly a big investment of time in order to create a healthy emotional climate — it's only 3 percent of the year! This day can be the time when the family gets out of the box and ventures off into some new area of interest or experience — for example, river rafting, visiting a local museum, hiking, taking a 20-mile bicycling trip, or attending a sporting event. Rotate the responsibility for deciding this month's agenda among family members so that everyone has an equal opportunity to involve the whole family in something that interests and excites them.

Enjoy the time together — because joy is the emotional antithesis of anger!

One week a year

Families who vacation together stay together. It's amazing what one week a year together can do to revive family ties, cement relationships, reconnect you to your biological roots, and remind you of all the many good times you've had over the years. It's a time of family revitalization! It reminds you that, no matter how busy your life throughout the remainder of the year, you're never really alone — your family is there to support you. One week a year is a time for family healing and rehealing — of replenishing positive emotions and letting go of grievances from the past (see Chapters 12 and 13). It's a time when the past, present, and future come together as one, offering you an opportunity to appreciate the coherence that family has brought to your life.

Recently, I met a man who, at age 62, still gets together every year with his entire family — children and grandchildren — for a family vacation. He said they used to do this at their house, but they found that there were too many distractions — everyone was running off somewhere, meeting other people. So they decided to begin vacationing at some new site — Montana, Hawaii, Florida — each year so they would be forced to spend all their time together.

The lessons of Roseta

Over 40 years ago, Professor Steward Wolf and his colleagues became intrigued by the absence of heart disease in a small Italian-American community in eastern Pennsylvania — Roseta. Rosetans had a death rate from heart disease that was less than half that of nearby communities and the United States as a whole. Ironically, people in Roseta appeared to have the same amount of heart disease as their neighbors — they just didn't *die* from it. Even more ironic was the fact that Rosetans, as a group, tended to be overweight, smoke heavily, and have high cholesterol levels, as well as being sedentary — all classic risk factors for fatal heart attacks. So, what was their secret?

The secret was that they — the entire community — were, in effect, one big happy family, distinguished by their close family ties, mutual support, strong religious beliefs, a feeling of reverence for the elderly, and social *interdependence* (everyone depending on each other in healthy and meaningful ways). Rosetans were a cohesive group with a strong group identity, strong group allegiances, and a common set of values that ultimately led, to quote Dr. Wolf, to an "unshaken feeling of personal security and continuity" both of life and purpose.

Sadly, Dr. Wolf lived long enough to witness the decline and fall of Roseta's old-world traditions and sense of family. Individual achievements took the place of community activities; material gains became more important than spiritual and moral values; and residents became much less connected in their day-to-day lives. Guess what happened? In no time at all, Rosetans began to catch up with the rest of the country in terms of fatal heart attacks. They had clearly lost their advantage!

"New-world" relationships in Roseta involved very angry people. Maybe their real secret was not the cohesive family structure within the community, but the freedom from anger they all enjoyed as a result. Because anger is a major risk factor for heart disease (see Chapter 3), it seems likely.

How many old-world behaviors typify your family? For example, does your family:

- Work together on collaborative projects?
- Attend religious services together regularly?
- Value family unity over material success?
- Show respect for the elderly?
- See each member as an integral component to the overall health and well being of the family?
- Work to protect each other from unhealthy outside influences?
- Support each other in times of unusual stress?
- Support each other during times of family conflict?
- See anger as an impediment to family cohesion?
- Feel responsible for the emotional health of other family members?

Wouldn't this make a great topic of discussion when your family shares its one meal together each day or at one of your evenings together each week? Give it a try.

Chapter 22

In Intimate Relationships

*M*illions of people live with, love, and suffer at the hands of an intimate relationship with an angry spouse, child, parent, sibling, or close friend.

Becky's teenage daughter can be cooperative and charming at times, but then again she can fly into an uncontrollable, violent rage. On more than one occasions, Becky has had to call the police for help — a difficult thing for her to do, because she loves her daughter deeply. Becky is afraid of her child's temper, and for good reason. Becky clearly has been the victim of what I call a "loving-but-angry relationship" — her love, her daughter's anger.

Elaine has a similar relationship with her second husband. On the one hand, she's quick to defend him by suggesting that "he's not violent or anything like that." But, then, she goes on to describe how irascible he is and how often he hurts her feelings when he yells at her and says things that make her feel stupid. "He's not dumb, you know," she protests. "He just has a bad temper." Like Becky, Elaine is a victim — and a depressed one at that.

This chapter addresses issues of anger management within a variety of intimate relationships. Here you discover how to avoid becoming part of an angry couple. You see how to set healthy boundaries, how to communicate anger without being contemptuous, and how to think your way into healthier relationships. This chapter also exposes the mental traps that keep you in harm's way while dealing with those you love the most. Most of all, this chapter helps you realize that abusive anger is one thing, but being a victim is another.

The Loving-but-Angry Relationship

When you think of domestic violence, what comes to mind? If you're like most people, you immediately conjure up an image of a husband and wife engaged in an angry, violent exchange. But what if you're having that same exchange with your elderly father, who has belittled and berated you your entire life? Would you call that domestic violence? I would. And, what if you had the same kind of exchange with your sister or close friend? Would you regard that as domestic violence? I would.

My point is that, as a society, we need to broaden our definition of domestic violence to any type of close, intimate relationship that is based on love with some angry person. These relationships are the most difficult ones in which to manage anger because you can't walk away from them (at least not easily) and because you probably have a different standard for what is acceptable behavior for loved ones versus strangers (in other words, you'll tolerate more from your loved ones than you will from strangers).

Intimate partner violence

The term *intimate-partner violence* (IPV) is relatively new. It is used to characterize any act that results in a person being hurt physically, emotionally, or sexually by someone the person is dating; victims of IPV can be men as well as women.

IPV is presumably motivated by anger. Large-scale studies of IPV suggest that it's an all-too-common experience among high-school-age girls, affecting one in five. Hardly what you'd expect to encounter within the context of your first love.

How does IPV affect people? Victims of IPV are more at risk for a variety of self-destructive behaviors, including:

- Heavy smoking
- Binge drinking
- Drunk driving
- Cocaine use
- Unhealthy weight control (diet pills, laxative use)
- Early-onset sexual behavior (under age 15)
- Unsafe sex (multiple partners, nonuse of condoms)
- Unplanned pregnancy
- Suicide

Not a pretty picture.

No one is exempt

My wife chairs the local America's Junior Miss program, which offers the highest caliber of high school senior girls an opportunity to compete for college scholarships. These girls are truly exceptional in terms of intelligence, talent, poise, physical fitness, and their ability to communicate effectively with adults — not the sort of young women you'd expect to have been exposed to intimate-partner violence.

Yet, when I asked them about their experience with IPV, I found that:

✔ Forty percent had already been involved in a loving-but-angry relationship.

✔ Twenty-five percent were in a current relationship with someone who had a bad temper.

✔ Twenty-seven percent had been physically abused (hit, shoved, or slapped) by someone they were dating.

✔ Over 50 percent had been subjected to significant verbal abuse.

✔ Almost 60 percent knew a peer who had also been the victim of IPV.

And, these were the girls who came from "good" homes, who were the best and the brightest, and who were most likely to succeed in life. If you had any doubts about the prevalence of IPV among teenagers, these numbers should provide all the proof you need.

The angry marriage

Marriage is perhaps the most intimate relationship of all. Ideally, it is one that is based on trust, mutual respect, complementary interests, shared values, and abiding love. Many marriages, however, are far from ideal. A couple who began as blissful newlyweds ends up in an angry marriage.

By "angry marriage," I don't mean a couple who occasionally shares an angry moment. What married couple doesn't? An angry marriage is one in which anger defines both the emotional tone of the relationship as well as the couple's *primary* style of interacting with one another.

To test whether you and your spouse qualify as an angry couple, ask yourself the following questions:

✔ Do you and/or your spouse get angry at least once a day?

✔ Would you rate the intensity of your anger (or that of your spouse's anger) a 7 or higher on a 10-point scale, ranging from 1 (very mild) to 10 (very intense)?

✔ Once provoked, does your anger (or your spouse's) last for more than a half-hour?

✔ Have either you or your spouse ever pushed, shoved, or hit one another when you were angry?

✔ Has your anger (or your spouse's) ever left you (or your spouse) feeling anxious or depressed?

✔ Would you say that you (or your spouse) have become a much angrier person since you got married?

✔ Do you or your spouse find yourselves worrying about each other's temper?

✔ Do you frequently use inflammatory language (cursing) to communicate with your spouse (or does your spouse frequently use such language to communicate with you)?

✔ Have you or your spouse ever treated each other with contempt — belittling, demeaning, or devaluing each other?

✔ Are you (or is your spouse) beginning to question whether you love your partner?

✔ Do you (or your spouse) find yourselves answering anger with anger most of the time?

✔ Do you (or your spouse) feel unsafe in your marriage?

✔ Do you or your spouse always have to have the last word in a disagreement?

✔ Do you and your spouse demand a lot of each other?

✔ Do you or your spouse feel entitled to certain things in your marriage?

✔ Would you (or your spouse) describe your marriage as competitive?

✔ Would you describe yourself or your spouse as an impulsive person?

✔ Do you or your spouse tend to dominate one another in conversations?

✔ Do you or your spouse engage in road rage?

✔ Have you or your spouse ever thought about or actually sought counseling for problems arising out of anger?

If you answered yes to three of more of these questions, you should consider you and your spouse an angry couple. How do you change this? Take advantage of the solutions offered in the remainder of this chapter, as well as throughout the book.

Parent-child anger

Parent-child relationships provide a natural venue for anger. As a parent, your job is to shape your child into becoming a decent, civilized adult (see Chapter 21) — an awesome task at best! Among other things, this means that you have to place limitations and restrictions on your child's behavior, which may frustrate your kid and make him angry. The kid's job — at least as some kids see it — is to fight the parent every step of the way, which makes the parent angry. And so it goes around and around for about 20 years in normal families.

In some cases, however, this interaction between parents and children (called the *socialization process*) gets out of hand. The anger between the parent and the child becomes too intense, lasts too long, and is expressed in hurtful ways.

The entire time I was growing up, my father was an angry man — the type I describe in Chapter 2 as suffering from episodic rage. One minute we were engaging in family fun, and the next minute he was ranting and raving in a threatening manner. All along — even into my adult years — I kept wondering what I was doing that made him so mad. And then one day, long after he had died, my mother gave me the answer I had been waiting for: "You know, your father never wanted children," she said. "But I did." Why was my father so angry all those years? Because we were here — not because we did anything to provoke him, simply because we were born.

Parents are not the only ones who have anger fits. Many parents are on the receiving end of child anger and abuse. One mother brought her teenage son to see me for anger management. She described the impact of his behavior this way: "You have the whole spectrum of emotions. You become very angry yourself; you get hysterical; you feel absolutely devastated at times; and you have enormous feelings of guilt. I find myself asking over and over, 'What have I done to create this?'"

Mature is as mature does

In a healthy, seasoned, mature marriage, each partner exercises self-control. This is the key to marital stability. The husband doesn't leave it up to his wife to set limits on his unreasonable anger and vice versa. In immature marriages, partners proceed full-speed ahead with their emotions and end up doing a lot of damage to the relationship. This may explain why marriages today last only about five years on average — a sad but compelling statistic.

Sibling anger

Anger between siblings goes all the way back to the days when Cain and Abel had the whole world to themselves. As the story goes, Cain got angry and killed Abel in a fit of jealousy — Cain thought Abel was God's favorite (as older siblings are prone to think when it comes to their younger siblings).

How often is that same family dynamic played out in families today? Too often. In recent years, a lot of attention has been directed at bullying and the harm it causes those who are its victim — low self-esteem, depression, substance abuse, poor school performance. Most of the emphasis seems to be on bullying in the context of peer relationships outside the family — particularly at school.

But bullying doesn't begin there — it starts in the home and moves into the schools and onto the streets later on. One young man in my seventh-grade anger-management class proudly acknowledged week after week how he angrily beat his younger brother to a pulp over the smallest disagreement. He openly admitted that he got pleasure out of hurting his brother and felt no remorse whatsoever over the damage he caused. What became of this young man? He ended up in my high school anger-management class three years later, this time on a court order for assault behavior. And, guess who the victim was? His brother!

If You're the Angry Loved One

All the various anger-management strategies outlined in this book apply to you. What's *different* about anger in intimate relationships is the fact that you're dealing with loved ones rather than strangers or casual acquaintances. The fact that you're angry with the people you love can actually be an incentive — you have more to lose than you do if you're too angry at work. At work, you can get fired, but if you're angry with your loved ones, you can lose the most important people in your life.

In the following sections, I let you know what may happen if you let your anger continue, and I give you some tips if you're the angry one in your intimate relationships.

You may become the person you fear and hate

People are changed by intimate relationships — sometimes for the better, sometimes for the worse. Regrettably, in a loving-but-angry relationship, you can — and often do — end up acting just like the person you fear and hate. You may not start out the relationship being an angry person, but over time, you develop into one in an effort to defend yourself and level the playing field. This transformation doesn't happen overnight, but it does happen.

Amanda, a young married woman in her late 20s, found herself experiencing fits of rage every few days. Her husband, whom she had assaulted more than once, was afraid of her. Her family urged her to get help. Finally, she did. In one of our early sessions, I asked Amanda about her parents — what kind of people were they? Instantly she replied, "My mom, she has a worse temper than I do." She recounted how her mother had always been overly critical and how she would get very angry when Amanda didn't do things perfectly. "You mean she acted just like you do with your husband," I observed. Amanda appeared stunned by what I said — it was obviously something she had never thought of before. Without realizing it, Amanda had become the person she loved (but also feared) the most — her mother. And she had transferred what she had learned in one intimate relationship (mother-daughter) to another (husband-wife). By making this observation, I had given Amanda a choice: Repeat the cycle of intimate-partner violence, or make a change.

Two wrongs never make a right

In an intimate relationship, one angry person can be a problem — but two is a disaster! I know you think you'll feel better if you answer anger with anger, but you're wrong. As Dr. James Averill, a psychologist at the University of Massachusetts, has noted, less than 20 percent of folks report feeling "triumphant" after expressing anger, as contrasted with 60 percent or more who are left feeling hostile or depressed. An exchange between two angry people is definitely a no-win situation.

I can't tell you how many men I've counseled who ended up in legal trouble because they reacted to an angry wife (or ex-wife) in anger. The following conversation typifies what I'm talking about:

Client: I messed up again. I got arrested and charged with assault and battery. I can't believe I was so stupid.

Me: How did that happen?

Client: It was weird. I was having an enjoyable dinner with some friends when my wife [they were separated] called and wanted me to come pick up the kids right then. She sounded upset.

Me: So, what did you do?

Client: I excused myself and left the restaurant, even though my friends urged me not to. I went to the cemetery where my wife wanted to meet me.

Me: Cemetery? Why there?

Client: I have no idea, but I went there anyway. As soon as I got there, my wife charged at me angry, yelling, and screaming. I told her to back off, but she just got more agitated. I took the kids and was putting them in the car, when my wife got in my face — and I just got angry and pushed her away. Then I got in my car and drove off.

Me: Then what happened?

Client: When I got home, the police were waiting for me. They'd gotten a complaint from my wife that I had just assaulted her. So, they took me in and booked me.

Me: So, what's the lesson learned here? About anger, that is.

Client: First of all, I should have stayed at the restaurant and finished my dinner with my friends. Second, I should never have agreed to meet her in a place where there are no other people around — no witnesses. Plus, I should have kept my cool even though my wife had obviously lost hers. Then I wouldn't be in all this trouble.

Me: Right!

Establishing healthy boundaries

Boundaries are limits. They tell you when you've gone too far. They also tell you when your anger is out of bounds. One way to think about rage is that it's anger that has crossed the line — the point beyond which you cannot control it. Emotional, physical, and sexual violence should also be considered as out of bounds. The difference between my father and me is not that he had a bad temper and I don't — it's that when he got angry, he hit my mother, whereas (I can proudly say after 40 years of marriage!), no matter how angry I've gotten, I've never laid a hand on my wife.

Here are some examples of what I mean by establishing healthy boundaries on anger:

✔ **When your anger gets too intense, stop whatever you're doing and walk away.** The easiest way I know to gauge this is to rate your anger on a 10-point scale. If you're a 7 or above, that should be your cue to walk away.

✔ **Commit yourself to the idea that physical violence is *never* acceptable.** I made this commitment when I was a small child, watching my parents hurt each other in anger day after day.

✔ **Set a limit on how much anger you're willing to express toward a loved one.** When you feel like you're progressing from anger into rage, *stop!* From that point on, what's more important is what you *don't* do than what you do. This is a perfect time to go for a long walk, exorcise your anger at the gym, or practice the tips in Chapter 6 on how to keep your cool.

✔ **Demand that others respect you as much as you respect them.** If you can restrain your anger toward your loved ones, insist that they do likewise — or leave the situation immediately! As I point out in Chapter 21, it takes two to tango. You can avoid an escalating angry dialogue by disengaging at just the right time.

✔ **Tone it down. *Remember:*** No matter what you're trying to communicate to a loved one when you get angry (which may be something that person needs to hear!), the message gets lost when the volume goes up. (See how yelling also affects your health in Chapter 5.)

✔ **If you're getting too angry, let your loved one have the last word, which effectively puts an end to your anger and his.** This is one thing that is definitely under your control.

✔ **Don't be afraid to call a timeout when you're getting too angry.** Say something like, "Okay, this is as far as I want to go with this. I think we're getting beyond the point where my anger is constructive. But, I'd like to come back and discuss this more later on."

Forgoing reciprocity

We live in a tit-for-tat world. If someone close to you hurts you, it's only natural to want to hurt him back. You push my buttons and I'll push yours! Unfortunately, that is exactly how exchanges that begin with one or both parties getting irritated end up in domestic violence. This need for this *emotional reciprocity* accelerates the process of toxic anger. It adds fuel to the fire.

Responding in kind when someone gets angry with you is a reaction — and a *reaction* is any behavior that is highly predictable, mindless, impulsive, and typically leads to negative consequences. What you want to do is *respond* to your loved one's anger, not react to it (see Chapter 6).

If You're on the Receiving End of a Loved One's Anger

If you're on the receiving end of the anger, the most important thing you can do is to stay out of harm's way. Your job isn't to fix your loved one's anger — that's your loved one's job (see the preceding section).

Most people who are on the wrong end of a loving-but-angry relationship think they have only three options:

✔ Hope and pray that the angry partner will change.

✔ Seek professional help to undo some of the damage done by the abusive anger.

✔ Terminate the relationship altogether.

I'm offering you a fourth viable option: You can start acting in ways that don't lead to victimization. In the following sections, I show you how.

Eliminate the mental traps

If you're in a loving-but-angry relationship, you probably got stuck there through a series of mental traps. What kind of traps? They're traps that have to do with two equally strong emotions: love and anger. What's in your mind — firmly held beliefs about love and anger — keeps you from achieving what matters most: a relationship that is both intimate and safe.

To counteract the mental traps in the following sections, you need to practice what psychologists call *cognitive restructuring*. That is, rewire your thinking about the relationship between love and anger. Start by challenging any of the false beliefs listed in the following sections. For instance, if your mind tells you, "If my husband loves me enough, he'll stop being so angry," restructure that thought by saying to yourself, "My husband definitely has an anger problem. He needs help. I can't be the one to fix him — he needs to be responsible for that. Whatever is causing his anger, it's not me. The answer to his anger is inside him. And loving me can't make all that right."

The belief that you can eliminate someone else's anger

In my experience, the most pervasive mental trap of all is the idea that a loving relationship will make the person you love less angry. Nothing could be farther from the truth. You can't do anything to make your loved one less angry — it's what your loved one does that counts! And if you're the angry one, believe me, the other person can't rid you of your anger — it's all up to you.

Tina fell into this trap for years, trying to fix her female partner's intermittent-rage disorder with love and support. As Tina said, "Living with her was like living on top of a volcano — you never knew when she was going to erupt next." In the end, all Tina got for her efforts was a trip to the emergency room, a fractured skull, a ton of medical bills, and a restraining order against her lover.

The belief that anger is fleeting but love is forever

A second mental trap has to do with the belief that anger comes and goes, but love is forever. No way. For a large — and perhaps growing — segment of the population, anger is anything *but* fleeting (for some statistics, see Chapter 2). Anger is a chronic condition — and a toxic one at that. Trust me, anger will be around long after the love is gone.

The belief that if he loves you, he'll change

Another myth about anger and love is that if the angry person loves you enough, he'll change. Not really. Although love for another person can be an incentive for becoming anger free, by itself it isn't enough motivation to alter long-standing, complex emotional patterns that have a life of their own. As I argue throughout this book, there are many facets to effective anger management and no one simple solution.

Don't make the other person's anger the test of how much he loves you. Assume that he loves you — he just doesn't know how to control his temper.

The belief that all you need is love

The Beatles may try to convince you otherwise, but you need a lot more than love. Many people believe that as long as two people love each other, nothing else matters. Some people still believe that even after they're released from an emergency room after being assaulted by the person they love.

Tina, the young woman I mention earlier, took a while to get her mind right. The fractured skull wasn't the first significant injury she had sustained at the hands of a loved one — but it was the last. This loving-but-angry relationship wasn't the first Tina had — but it was the last.

Lots of things should matter in your life in addition to love — energy, health, your career. (See how anger poisons your life in Chapter 3.)

I'm off to play the violin

One of my favorite anger-management clients, a downtrodden woman in her mid-40s, spent most of her time, when she wasn't working, at home taking angry abuse from her husband. She had come to dread weekends, because she would be exposed to 48 hours of relentless, angry criticism.

At one point, I reminded her of the joy she used to experience in playing the violin and suggested she take lessons again as part of her anger-management program. She did and that has become her sanctuary — a few hours away from her husband's anger. She's also started going out with friends from work, riding her horse again, and going back to church, all of which takes time away from her husband's anger. He's not too happy with all this, but she is — and so am I!

The belief that anger is just a sign of caring

The last mental trap is the one that tells you, if someone you love is angry with you, it means she actually cares. I love it when I hear stories about parents or spouses who engage in outrageous behavior (including violence) toward someone they supposedly love, all the while saying, "I'm doing this for your own good." Rubbish! Angry people care about *themselves* — what they want, what they expect, what they demand, what they think — not you. They're expressing anger for their own good — to let off some steam, to relieve tension, to protest what they regard as unfair treatment. If they actually cared about you — your welfare, your safety, your sanity — they would take whatever immediate action was necessary to short-circuit their anger (see Chapter 4).

Stop being part of the problem

If you can't be the solution to your loved one's anger, don't be part of the problem. Relationships are two-way streets. Your loved one's anger affects you, and your behavior in turn affects his anger. What you don't want to be is an *anger facilitator* (the person who makes it easier for the other person to move ahead with his anger beyond the point of no return).

When someone who is obviously in a state of rage says, "I'm warning you — don't say another word!," take her at her word and shut up. If a person who is well on his way to losing his cool says, "Get out of my way — I've got to get out of here!," move aside or you'll very likely get hurt. It doesn't pay to push someone who's already angry.

Here are some other ways you can stop being part of the problem:

✔ **Don't apologize for someone else's anger.** That's just another way of helping him not take responsibility for his own emotions. Instead of saying, "I'm sorry I made you mad," tell him, "I can see you're angry about something. Do you want to talk about it?"

✔ **Don't keep silent about someone else's bad behavior.** People who exhibit unreasonable anger need corrective feedback. They need to hear when they're getting too loud or acting in ways that make others afraid. If you're quiet and you let things slide, the other person may think her behavior is just fine and dandy.

✔ **Don't minimize the problem.** When one of my clients is relating an incident where she became angry and rates the intensity of her feeling at that moment as an 8 on a 10-point scale, I simply say, "Okay, you weren't angry. You were way beyond anger — you were in a rage." My clients don't like being told they were in a rage, and suddenly they want to argue with me that they were *only* angry. It's their way of pretending that what they were feeling was normal. But I don't let them off the hook.

✔ **Get a life of your own.** Too many people make their loved one's anger the centerpiece of their lives. You put everything else on hold while you try to fix the other person's anger. Instead, follow your own interests. If you have buddies you play basketball with or friends who meet to chat about the latest Oprah book, you'll have someplace to go, something to do, when your loved one flies off the hook.

✔ **Don't help the other person save face.** People who have too much anger need to face up to their problem. Stop coming up with excuses for the other person's outrage.

✔ **Stop being your partner's excuse.** Virtually all of my anger-management clients begin by describing all the other people who "make me angry." I ask them, "Why did you get angry in that situation?" and they answer, "My wife did. . . ." I always say, "I didn't ask about your wife — I asked why you got angry in that situation." Inevitably, they repeat, "I told you, my wife. . . ." I don't let them off the hook. I keep repeating my question until they quit using other people to excuse (take responsibility for) their anger. Nothing much can happen until they take responsibility for themselves.

✔ **Pretend your loved one is a stranger.** I asked one mother who had suffered repeated physical and emotional abuse at the hands of her teenage son, "If this were a youngster from down the block, would you let him hurt you like this?" "Absolutely not," she replied without hesitation. "There's no one else on this earth that I would stay around for more than a minute or two if they treated me like my son does." So, I suggested that, from that point on, she think of her son as a stranger — and behave accordingly. That was the beginning of her recovery.

✔ **Stop paying the bill.** I'm a firm believer that mature, responsible people pay the consequences of their behavior. I never have quite figured out why some parents I know paid all the speeding tickets their teenage kids got any more than I understand why they bear the cost of replacing broken doors, smashed telephones, wrecked cars, all destroyed by these "loving" children. The logic here is simple: If you pay, you're the responsible party. If they pay, they are. That's the message you want to send, right?

Inoculate yourself

Psychologist Donald Meichenbaum at the University of Waterloo pioneered a technique called *stress inoculation training* (SIT) that has real promise for people who find themselves stuck in a loving-but-angry relationship. Although Meichenbaum was primarily interested in helping clients cope effectively with overpowering anxiety, you can use it to protect you from your loved one's anger. Think of this as an alternative to answering anger with anger.

As with other types of inoculation — polio, smallpox, flu — stress inoculation training will increase your resistance to the stress (and potential harm) of being on the receiving end of someone else's anger. SIT is a proactive technique, which includes three basic steps:

1. **Become more aware of how you typically react to your loved one's anger.**

   Nancy, for example, would be relaxed until she heard her husband's car turn into the driveway. Immediately, she would tense up and brace herself for his inevitable anger. She would think to herself, "Please, Lord, don't let him get mad at me today." And she was already prepared to take the blame for his irritation ("I just can't seem to do anything right.").

2. **Cope with the arousal — the fight-or-flight response — that accompanies angry encounters with your loved one.**

   To reduce her anticipatory tension, Nancy tells herself:

   I can handle this — it's not like I haven't been up against his anger before.

   Easy does it. Don't panic.

   I'm not going to take this personally. His anger is about him, not me.

   I just need to relax, relax, relax.

3. **Generate a situation-specific solution.**

Here's where Nancy has to consider her options. Should she react as usual (by getting tense when his car pulls in the driveway)? Or is there some other coping strategy that would be more effective when her husband begins to lose his temper? For example, she might simply acknowledge his anger ("I can see you're angry again today."). Or she could question his anger ("It must be awfully uncomfortable being that angry. Is it?"). She could set some limits on his anger ("I don't think I want to stay around and listen to this."). She could attempt to elicit some empathy from her husband ("Have you any idea whatsoever how your anger affects me?"). Or she could offer her husband a Life Saver to both get his attention (so he can practice some anger management) and to sweeten his disposition (see Chapter 4).

Refuse to play the role of the victim

I was struck recently by the story of a man who had risen from the ranks of the homeless to that of a wealthy, successful businessman in a relatively short period of time. At one point, he and his son had slept in a subway bathroom night after night because they had nowhere else to go. When asked during a television interview how difficult it was for him to regain his integrity after living in such horrendous conditions, he replied, "I think you misunderstood me — I said I was homeless, not hopeless. My son and I never lost hope or our integrity. We always knew we'd eventually find a place to live."

When in doubt, try humor

I remember once being in a social situation where another man was doing all he could to hassle me. He directed one hostile, sarcastic remark after another toward me, hoping I would react in kind. He was one of those folks who just love a good fight.

At first, I was quiet and tried to just ignore what he was saying. But he just kept on until I could feel myself getting angry. And then I resorted to the one thing that has helped me deal with adversity my whole life: humor. I began making jokes about the situation we were in and everyone around me (except him) started to laugh. The more he fussed, the more I joked. It wasn't long before he got quiet and basically retreated from the conversation. Not long after that, he up and left the situation altogether. Humor had won the day!

And so it is (or should be) when you're confronted by a loved one's anger. Clearly, the anger is a major problem — but it isn't a reason to become a victim. To keep from being a victim, try the following:

- ✔ **Hang on to your sense of hope.** When you're faced with an angry loved one, it's easy to fall into a trap of hopelessness. To keep hope intact, try spending some time with a supportive friend who can remind you that you're not a worthless person.

- ✔ **Do something, anything, to avoid feeling a sense of helplessness.** For example, practice the stress inoculation technique I described earlier in this chapter.

- ✔ **Use the support resources at your disposal to keep yourself safe.** If you need a "safe house," this is not the time to be bashful — call a friend and ask for sanctuary. Call a lawyer and ask for advice. Call the police, if necessary, and ask for protection.

- ✔ **Be assertive.** Find your voice and speak up for yourself. Remind yourself that you have a right to be treated with respect and restraint — and the last thing you need is to be someone else's verbal or physical punching bag! There's a big difference between telling your angry loved one, "I can't stand it when you treat me like this!" and saying, "I won't stand for that kind of behavior anymore." *Can't* has to do with ability; *won't* indicates a sense of will.

- ✔ **Be honest with yourself — admit you have a problem.** As long as you deny the reality of a loving-but-angry relationship, you're stuck. You have to acknowledge a problem before you can hope to solve it. This book is about solving problems associated with anger — yours and the other person's — but you can't make any progress until you face up to the truth.

If reading this chapter (or the book as a whole) does nothing more than keep you from being a victim of another person's anger, then it's worth the price of admission!

Part VII
The Part of Tens

In this part . . .

I offer ten quick strategies for managing anger yesterday, today, and tomorrow. I show you ten ways to empower your children to effectively manage their angry feelings without resorting to punishment. I give you ten techniques for anger-free driving (road rage isn't about the road, it's about you!). I provide ten simple thoughts you can keep in mind at all times to eliminate toxic anger and help you find inner peace.

Chapter 23

Ten Ways to Raise a Non-Angry Child

*B*eing a parent is no easy job, especially when it comes to your child's emotional development. All children start out life angry. If you're a parent, you know all too well the angry cry that your baby lets out when she's hungry, lonely, or in pain. Anger is her way of telling you, without using words, "I need something!" The louder the cry, obviously, the stronger and more urgent the need. Your job — at least as your baby sees it — is to satisfy that need, whatever it is. You are — like it or not — the key to managing your baby's anger. But, if you try the techniques in this chapter, that won't always be the case.

In this chapter, I show you ten ways to shift that responsibility for managing anger to your child — much the same as you teach her to ride a bike, play soccer, or read. You discover how to be her emotional coach — showing her the rules for appropriately expressing her anger and teaching her the skills she needs to achieve success in this important area of her life. Think of it this way: If you help your child manage her anger while she's still a kid, she won't need this book when she's a grown-up!

Being an Emotional Coach

You love your child, you care about his well being, and you want him to be successful in life — unless your name is Miss Hannigan and your kid is named Annie, I can make these assumptions about you. Unfortunately, just because you love your child doesn't mean you're prepared to be an emotional coach. Fear not: You can be a great coach for your kid. Just keep the following tips in mind:

✔ **Make raising a non-angry (or at least reasonably angry) child, who will eventually develop into an emotionally mature adult, a primary goal.** Most parents have goals for their kids — but these goals tend to have more to do with education, sports, and being popular than they do with personal traits or emotions. Many parents assume the latter will come naturally — unfortunately, they're wrong. Make raising a non-angry child a formal part of your job description as a parent from day one and keep it in mind at all times — even when you're frustrated and ready to tear your hair out!

✔ **Be active and hands-on when you're interacting with your child.** Can you imagine a baseball coach who sits quietly in the dugout and lets his players figure out how to play the game all by themselves without any instruction or practice? Of course, you can't. So, how in the world can your kid learn to manage complex emotions like anger on his own? He can't — and he won't! Coaching requires active involvement on your part. Your kid needs your support, your guidance, your wisdom, your knowledge, your patience, your acceptance, and your skills. Coaching is not about being permissive (overindulgent and inattentive) or indifferent (emotionally detached).

Talk openly with your child about your feelings — including anger — and help him understand that emotions are a normal part of being human. Use the information in Chapter 2 to help your child appreciate the distinction between different levels of anger (for example, anger versus rage). Find ways to illustrate for your child the difference between *being* hurt (an emotion) and *doing* hurt or harm (a behavior) to himself or others. And then make it absolutely clear that the former is acceptable, but the latter is not.

✔ **Be proactive.** Typically, parents wait for children to misbehave — for example, throwing a temper tantrum in a grocery store — and then they punish them after the fact. This style of parenting is reactive parenting at its best (or worst, depending on how you look at it): "You were terrible in the store, so you go to your room for the rest of the day." Coaching is proactive. For example, when you're about to enter a store, you remind your child, "We're about to go into the grocery store. Remember the rules we've talked about? Make sure Mommy can always see where you are, don't run off, and if Mommy says you can't have something and you get upset, tell Mommy how you feel instead of kicking and screaming. If you don't follow the rules, we'll go straight home. But if you behave yourself, we'll stop by the park afterwards and play on the swings! Okay?" That's being proactive.

✔ **Accentuate the positive.** I know an anger-management specialist whose approach makes good sense. He not only tells his clients what *not* to do when they become angry — interrupt, point, threaten, curse, break things — he offers them a list of positive behaviors that involve self-restraint. That's coaching!

Reward your child — with praise, not cookies — when she asks for something rather than demands it. Teach her how to be considerate of others and then reward her when she shows you that she's learned that lesson. Emphasize the importance of apologizing when you've acted badly — teaching your child to say "I'm sorry" is teaching her to take responsibility for her own behavior.

✔ **Focus on solutions rather than problems.** I'm afraid most children (certainly most teenagers), if asked, would agree with the statement "Parents preach — coaches teach." Kids don't need adults to tell them they have problems; what they need (and desperately want) is for someone to tell them what to *do* about those problems. Saying to an angry kid, "Stop yelling — you're upsetting everybody," doesn't address his problem (whatever occasioned the outburst). Telling him to stop yelling also doesn't provide him with a solution that goes beyond simply venting his rage.

Instead, say to your son, "I can tell by how angry you are that you're having a problem. It would help if you could tone it down a little so I can understand what the problem is — then maybe I can help you. I'm sure it's something that we can work out if we can just get past your anger. Now, what were you trying to tell me?"

A win-win solution

For years, Frank and his daughter would get into angry exchanges as soon as he walked in the house after a long day. He would ask, "How are you?" She would reply with an angry tone. He would respond in kind. And, they were off to the races in something that always ended badly.

One day, Frank decided he didn't want to play this game anymore, so — as the parent — he took responsibility for finding a way out of this no-win situation. He realized that he and his daughter were both trying to achieve the same end — to have the last word. Because of her youth, he knew she had more energy to fight her way to the finish but less wisdom and willingness to change than he did.

From that day forward, Frank always let his daughter have the last word (win), but he reserved the right to decide when that was (win). As soon as he saw the conversation heading down the wrong road, he immediately signaled a timeout and disengaged. She followed suit, and they no longer escalated into fights.

In calmer moments, Frank made sure his daughter got the coaching lesson: Anger only begets anger, and cooler heads prevail whenever there's a conflict. Sounds like a win-win solution to me.

Children who start out life noticeably impulsive and excitable are difficult to coach, and they require more parental effort (read: tough love) than those whose temperaments are more thoughtful and calm. You may have several children, each with a different temperament.

Starting Early and Talking Back

It's never too early to begin raising a non-angry child. The emotional dialogue between parents and children begins when children are around 3 months of age, when infants start "speaking out" through emotions about what they want. That's when you need to start talking back. Children are smarter than you think — they respond to comforting words, "You're upset I know, but it's okay," and a comforting tone before they even learn to talk. (See Chapter 5 for a discussion of the importance of "toning it down.")

Your soothing words and calm tone tell your child that you're comfortable with emotion — yours and hers. The last thing you want to teach her is that you're afraid of her anger. That will either cause her to suppress her feelings (in an effort to not upset you), or worse yet, empower her to misuse anger as a means of controlling you and everyone else around her. These are not the lessons that will lead to emotional maturity.

When a colleague of mine who treats emotionally disturbed kids heard I was writing this book, he told me, "Be sure and tell your readers that you can take the most disturbed 7-year-old child and, with enough professional help, turn him completely around. But, it takes three times more effort and skill to see improvement in a minimally disturbed teenager. Those first few years are a window of opportunity — and they're so important."

Creating Teachable Moments

Don't wait for situations to come up that anger your child. Take the initiative and create opportunities so that he can learn to cope with negative feelings — I call these *teachable moments*. Here are some possibilities — choose one and give it a try:

> ✔ **Play a game with your child and purposely don't let him win.**
> Afterwards, ask him, How do you feel when you lose? Are you angry? How do you think other people feel when they lose? Are they angry? What do you think we should do about your angry feelings? What do you

think we should do about other people's angry feelings? There are no right or wrong answers here. The point is just to get a conversation going between you and your child so that you can both start thinking about anger and how to manage it when it happens.

- ✔ **Present a situation to your child that involves the violation of some moral principle — fair play or honesty.** Ask him how he thinks the person who is being treated unfairly or lied to feels. Does he think that person would get mad? Does he think the anger the other person is feeling is justified? Ask the child what he thinks should be done about these feelings. For example, what if other kids refused to let your child join in a game they were playing or what if your child's older brother took something of hers and then lied and said he didn't take it?

- ✔ **Ask your child to pretend that he's angry and then pretend to hurt someone else's feelings.** What would he say to the other person to hurt her? Ask your child, How do you think your angry words would make that person feel? How would you feel after you said those angry words? Are you sure you want to hurt someone just because she made you angry?

Children's books about anger are great teaching aides. Typically, they contain one or two lessons about how to manage anger (for example, you'll get over being angry when you find something to enjoy or you'll stop being angry when you find something to do that parents can say yes to rather than no). Some of my favorites include: *I Was So Mad,* by Mercer Mayer; *When I Feel Angry,* by Cornelia Maude Spelman; *When Emily Woke Up Angry,* by Riana Duncan; and *Poems About Anger by American Children,* edited by Jacqueline Sweeney.

Being a Positive Role Model

A colleague of mine who has a lot of experience working with troubled children heard I was working with angry adolescents. He advised me to pose the following question to these angry, delinquent youngsters when I first met them: "Who else in your family is as angry as you are?" Without fail, the children immediately identify one or both of their parents — most often the father.

You can't teach what you can't do! If you can't control your own temper, how can you expect you child to? Like it or not, you're your kid's primary role model, good or bad, during his formative years. So, when it comes to coaching, you have to start with yourself.

If you're unsure whether you're a good emotional role model, ask yourself the following questions:

- Do you get irritated or angry at least once a day?
- Would you rate the intensity of your anger 7 or above on a 10-point scale?
- When you're angry, do you stay that way for more than 30 minutes?
- Have you ever pushed, shoved, or hit someone in anger?
- Have you ever threatened or cursed someone in anger?
- Would you say you are angrier than many people you know?
- Do your loved ones seem to worry about your temper?
- Have you ever lost a job because of your temper?
- Have you ever lost a friend because of your temper?
- Have you ever spent money repairing something because of your temper?

If you answered yes to even *one* of these questions, you may not be the best role model for how to handle anger well. But look at the positive side: Managing anger can be a learning experience for both you *and* your child. You can learn as you teach.

I heard you

Some years ago, I was asked to make a community presentation called, "Dealing with the Angry Child," as part of a larger program aimed at helping parents cope with their kids' attention deficit-hyperactivity disorder (ADHD), drug use, and academic failure. To my surprise, the room was packed with distressed looking parents, all of whom seemed eager to hear what I had to say.

As I spoke, I paid particular attention to one man who stared at me continuously throughout my presentation with what I would call a serious and somewhat hostile expression on his face. Afterwards, as parents stopped to thank me for my remarks, he passed by without comment, his expression unchanged.

Several days later, I was gassing up my car alongside three other men when one of them — the man I'd seen at the presentation — loudly exclaimed, "Doc, I heard what you said — you know, about angry children having angry parents and how we should look at ourselves as well as our children. I went home and thought about that and decided you're right. I have to work on my anger before I can help my son with his. Thanks."

Wow. Who would have thought he got the message?

Adults who do *not* have a bad temper tend to remember their parents as being loving, warm, close, easygoing, calm, and relaxed. If you want your kid to grow up to be an adult without a bad temper, try to be all these things, and you're on the right path.

Putting the "I" in Emotion

Always correct your child when she says something like, "He made me angry." Instead, teach her to say, "*I* got angry when he. . . ." This is what self-control is all about — taking responsibility for our own feelings. Until your daughter learns that no one else can *make* her angry, she won't achieve emotional maturity. Children need to understand as early as possible that no one has the power to make them feel anything — not fear, not anger, not sadness, not pride, not even joy — that power resides solely in themselves.

As your kid's coach, try to express your emotions the same way: "*I* get frustrated when you don't obey me."

Labeling Feelings Appropriately

Before your child can express his feelings in an appropriate and constructive way, he needs an emotional vocabulary. You need to teach him to describe — as clearly as possible — how he feels and then help him find the right label to fit that emotion.

Young children are often unable to differentiate emotions except to say, "I feel bad" or, "I feel good." Your job is to help your kid fine-tune those feelings so he can better appreciate his unique reaction to the world around him.

Consider the following conversation between a mother and her 5-year-old son:

Mother: Honey, is something wrong?

5-year-old: I don't feel good.

Mother: Do you mean you're sick? Or are you upset about something?

5-year-old: I'm upset.

Mother: Okay, tell Mommy how you're feeling. What does your upset *feel* like?

5-year-old: I don't like this stupid puzzle. I can't make the pieces go together.

Mother: So, you're angry. You feel angry because you can't figure it out.

5-year-old: Yeah, I'm mad. I hate that stupid puzzle.

Mother: I understand. Sometimes people get angry when they can't make something work. Sometimes I feel the same way you do.

5-year-old: You do? You get upset, too?

Mother: Yes, I get angry just like you.

As your child gets a little older, you need to teach him to distinguish between different levels of anger — mild, moderate, and severe. An easy way to do this is have him rate the intensity of his feelings on a scale from 1 to 10 (more about this in Chapters 2 and 6). A rating of 1 to 3 equals irritation; 4 to 6 equals mad; and, 7 and above equals rage. If your son rates his anger as a 7, your response should be, "Honey, you're not just angry, you're in rage. Why are you that angry?"

Identifying Causes

Don't be satisfied by having your child identify what she's feeling; ask her why she's feeling that way. At first, identifying the cause of their anger can be difficult for children — it's difficult even for adults — because they aren't used to tying their emotional reactions to what's going on around them at the time.

Don't tell me how I feel

Thirteen-year-old Jennifer was in a bad mood as she sat in the kitchen watching her mother fix dinner. Trying to help, her mother said, "You don't have to be so irritable. I know you're tired and hungry. Supper will be ready shortly." Jennifer exploded, "Don't tell me how I feel! These are my feelings. *I* know how I feel — *you* don't!" Was she right? Absolutely. Did her mother mean well? Absolutely. But her mother still should've asked if Jennifer was upset, and if Jennifer said yes, her mother should've asked why. Then she should've left the rest of the conversation — or lack thereof — up to Jennifer. As it turned out, Jennifer wasn't tired or hungry — she was upset (angry) about something another girl had said to her that morning at school. Who knew?

Your child may feel anger because

✔ **Someone (or something) has hurt her self-esteem.** Youngsters are apt to become angry when someone criticizes, demeans, or otherwise attacks their self-esteem. If someone — including you — calls your child "stupid" or "an idiot," she'll probably feel angry. She may also feel angry when she fails at something (for example, she fails a spelling test in school); she may say something like, "The teacher thinks I'm dumb!"

✔ **She's gone through some kind of physical abuse.** Children get angry when they're physically attacked — hit, shoved, pushed — or even when they're threatened by the possibility of being harmed in some way. (Who can blame them?) *Remember:* Physical abuse can come in the form of the bully on the playground — it doesn't have to be an adult harming your child for it to be abuse.

✔ **She's not getting something she wants.** All kids want things in life, and when they're prevented from achieving or obtaining those things, they become frustrated and then angry. Anger is their way of protesting, their way of saying, "I'm not getting what I want!" Your child's anger can be especially intense if she feels entitled to the thing in question or if she's the type of child who has difficulty in delaying gratification ("I want what I want *now!*").

✔ **Her moral principles (yes, she does have them) have been violated.** Just like adults, children have values and beliefs about how the world should work — the world should be fair, people should tell the truth, people should be kind to someone who's hurt. If circumstances violate those values, they often get mad — "That's not fair!," "You're lying!," or "Leave her alone — can't you see she's not feeling well?"

✔ **She feels helpless.** One of the main reasons children get angry has to do with situations in which they feel out of control, helpless, frightened, and vulnerable. Kids may, for example, get angry when their parents fight a lot because they're afraid that one parent will hurt the other or the family will break up. Adolescents may become very angry when a fellow student commits suicide or dies of cancer — things over which they have absolutely no control.

You may often *think* you know why your child is angry or upset, but most of the time you're wrong. Don't assume. Ask.

Teaching Problem Solving

Children have trouble coping with emotion. Coping is a skill that your child has to learn — and you can be a huge help to your child when it comes to teaching coping skills.

Your child needs help dealing with the *feelings* themselves (anger) as well as the *causes* (frustration). You can begin by asking your child, "What do you think we should do about your anger?" or, "What is it that you're angry about?"

If you start by focusing on the feeling itself, you can try to help him choose from a number of strategies that work:

- Distracting himself (shifting his focus onto something else, preferably something positive)

- Creating some distance from the angry situation (going for a walk or drive)

- Relaxing away the tension he feels (taking ten deep breaths)

- Changing his emotional tone (laughing)

- Using his imagination to find a safe place in his mind to escape his anger

If you decide to focus on what *caused* his anger, have him consider strategies such as:

- Confronting the person with whom he is angry (in a nonaggressive way)

- Sharing his concern about that other person with a neutral party

- Resigning himself to the fact that some things just can't be changed

- Changing how he looks at the other person's behavior

- Giving in to his anger and doing what the other person asks (I call this the *"whatever" response*)

- Asking for help in dealing with the problem

Teaching your child to vent his anger by yelling or hitting something like a punching bag or a pillow might provide some temporary relief, but in the long run it only leads to more anger and ultimately to an increase in aggressive behavior.

Choosing the Third Alternative

Human nature is such that we all start out life — as children — reacting to our own anger by either fleeing or fighting. The *fight-or-flight response* is part of our animal heritage. *Flight* means simply that a child runs away from the source of his anger (and the anger itself) and chooses not to deal with it — to let it pass. *Fight* means exactly that — the child attacks the source of her anger directly, either physically or verbally. In a study of eighth graders, for example, I found that 26 percent of children would just "walk away" when confronted with another child's anger and try to avoid the situation altogether. Forty-five percent fought back — answering anger with anger. And 29 percent indicated they would "walk away initially, but return later to discuss the problem" — that's the third alternative, the one that I recommend.

Learning the Difference between Wanting and Getting

It's normal — in fact, it's downright healthy — to want things in life. But, children need to be taught as early as possible the difference between *wanting* something and *getting* it. This important distinction is especially hard for young children to grasp and that's where you — the parent — come in. Spoiling a child basically means that you teach the child "what he wants, he gets, always." Spoiled children have a fierce sense of entitlement ("I'm special, I'm all powerful, and no one can tell me no"), which quickly leads to anger when their wants are not immediately satisfied.

I was having lunch in a fast-food restaurant once, when in came a father, mother, and two kids. While the father and son ordered the food, the mother and daughter went to get a table. The daughter went straight to a table by the window, but the mother said, "Let's sit over here. The sun's too bright there." The daughter exploded, angrily shouting, "I'm sitting here. I want to be in the sun. You can sit where you want!" Without a word, the mother — head down with a look of defeat on her face — moved to the table by the window. When the father came with the food, he asked his wife, "Why are you sitting here? There's too much sun." The mother replied — head still down — "Just sit here. Let's not have an incident."

Do your child a big favor — say *no* once in a while. Eventually, your kid will hear no from someone, and she needs to know how to respond when she doesn't get her way.

Chapter 24

Ten Ways to Combat Road Rage

*I*f you're one of those road warriors who drive with vengeance and anger in their hearts, you're in luck: This chapter gives you ten helpful ideas to use to combat road rage. With the tools in this chapter, all you'll need to do next time you get behind the wheel is fasten your seat belt, check your mirrors, put your hands at the 10 o'clock and 2 o'clock positions, and go!

Don't Rush

When I was young, my Uncle Aubrey used to take a bunch of us kids on trips to see interesting sights and expand our horizons. He was a great guy, but boy did he drive slowly. We were always saying, "Aubrey, hurry up — we want to get there!" His answer was always the same: "Boys, if you're in a hurry, you need to leave a half-hour earlier." And he was right.

If you're driving aggressively and getting impatient with everyone else on the road, chances are you feel that you're in a rush. Much like the Mad Hatter in *Alice in Wonderland,* you're thinking to yourself, "I'm late, I'm late, I'm late, for a very important date!" You didn't allow yourself enough time and now time is your enemy.

When your mind gets in a rush, your body follows suit. Everything increases — blood pressure, heart rate, muscle tension. You're poised for action and ready to jump on whomever gets in your way. And you use anger to *clear* the way!

That's why I took the job

My wife and I had just left New York after a three-day visit with a large health organization that was recruiting me to join their research faculty. Because of mechanical failure in our plane, we were forced to land at an airport 45 miles away from our destination. When we arrived at the other airport, we had to rent a car to get back home. I was exhausted after days of negotiating and power lunches and in no mood for hassles like this.

I flew into a rage in the airport and drove out of the rental lot with a vengeance.

But, then, as we drove through the rural countryside and saw the Blue Ridge Mountains,

something miraculous happened: I began to relax and my rage quickly subsided. What a peaceful, serene journey that was!

Years later, when someone asked me why I decided to turn down the New York job — where I would have commuted to and from the city by subway every day — and instead moved to Virginia to start a private practice, I thought a minute and said, "Actually, I think it was that unexpected drive from the airport — what a transforming experience."

Twenty-five years later, I still enjoy that drive.

Stop rushing and start relaxing. Calculate how long it will take you to drive somewhere and add an extra 10 minutes for every 15 to 30 minutes of driving time. Or see if you can drive without looking at the time — before you put your key in the ignition, put your watch in your pocket, and stick a piece of masking tape over your car's clock. (And don't cheat by listening to a radio station that tells you what time it is.)

Loosen Your Grip

How hard do you hold the wheel when you drive? If you're an aggressive driver, you're probably using the "death grip."

Loosen your grip and you'll be amazed at how much more relaxed you feel while driving. Hold the steering wheel like you would hold a soft-boiled egg or a child's hand — gently. The change in physical tension is instantaneous. The relaxation you experience in your hands travels up your arms into your shoulders and neck, and down into your lower back — throughout your entire body, just like that. Give it a try.

Focus on the Journey rather than the Destination

Aggressive drivers have tunnel vision. They're focused on only one thing — where they're going, the destination. If you're an aggressive driver, if anybody gets between you and your destination, there's hell to pay. You're staring straight ahead. Your mind is way out front, down the road, around the next turn before you get there. You're on a mission!

If this sounds familiar, you're missing the big picture: the journey. And life — even driving your kids to school or running to the grocery store — is all about the journey. Destinations come and go, but the journey is continuous. Relax into the journey — look around at the people, scenery, and events that you're passing, and you'll probably be a whole lot less angry.

Be the Other Driver

Are you the person who roars past the little old man driving under the speed limit, shaking your fist and screaming for all the world to hear, "They shouldn't let old farts like you drive!" and "Get out of the way, you old fool!"?

Well, consider this for a second: One day, if you're lucky and your road rage doesn't kill you first, you'll *be* that old guy. That's right — that will be you, slumped down in the seat, white hair hardly visible above the wheel, staring straight ahead, oblivious to everything around you, and driving 35 in a 55-mph zone. Try to visualize yourself as the other driver. Put yourself in his shoes. And then ask yourself, "How would I want other drivers to act toward me?" Not with rage, I'm guessing.

Here are some anger-freeing ways to think about slow drivers:

- ✔ "Wow, that's great that he can still drive at his age."
- ✔ "I hope I'm still that independent and able to get around on my own when I'm that old."
- ✔ "Maybe that's the secret to growing old gracefully — driving slow."
- ✔ "I bet he feels a whole lot more relaxed right now than I do."
- ✔ "He doesn't look angry — maybe there's a lesson here."

Take the "I" out of Driver

To paraphrase that great American philosopher, Woody Allen, "We're all bozos on the same freeway." Driving should be about *us,* right? Not just about *you?* Of course, road-ragers would disagree: "Get out of *my* way, damn it!" "You're holding *me* up — *I'm* going to be late for *my* appointment." "*I* hate drivers like you." "You're not going to pass *me* — no way."

Make driving more about the other guy:

- ✔ "I'll slide over and let *him* pass. *He's* in more of a hurry than I am."

- ✔ "The way *she's* driving, *she* must really be enjoying her day."

- ✔ "Wow, what an angry fellow — I wouldn't want to be in *his* shoes."

- ✔ "I used to drive like *she* does, but thank God I don't any more."

- ✔ "I'm sure *they* have somewhere important to go, too."

Drive with humility. Be ordinary — don't think of yourself as someone who's entitled to special consideration out there on the highway. Avoid stereotyping your fellow travelers — women drivers, old drivers, teenage drivers, Yankee drivers, redneck drivers, truckers. Don't set yourself apart from the pack. Just be one of the bozos and relax.

Look on the Bright Side

Every problem has a silver lining. If someone ahead of you in traffic slows you down, you end up feeling less rushed. That's good. If you tend to speed a lot and suddenly find yourself stuck behind a slower driver with no opportunity to pass, maybe he's keeping you from getting your next speeding ticket. That's good. If you see another driver doing something that you regard as "just plain ignorant," that makes you a smarter driver, right? That's good. If it takes you longer to get somewhere than you had planned, you end up having more time to relax and enjoy your own private thoughts along the way. That's good. You can use this kind of logic with just about every situation.

The next time you feel yourself on the verge of rage, ask yourself: "What good can possibly come from this?" When you come up with an answer, you can relax.

I'm just ordinary

A middle-aged client of mine, who was referred to me for anger management, recently came to a startling conclusion about himself that, he said, greatly reduced his day-to-day anger — on the road, at work, at home. Here's what he said: "It suddenly dawned on me — I'm just an ordinary guy who lives on a cul-de-sac like a lot of other guys. Yeah, I have a good job and a management title, but I'm still just an ordinary guy. All this time — years — I thought I was someone special and I got angry when other people didn't treat me that way. No more."

Repeat after Me: They Are Not the Enemy

Rage is an emotion that people reserve for their true enemies. Enemies are those folks that you believe mean to harm you deliberately and intentionally. "That S.O.B. tried to hit me just now!" He's out to get you — plain and simple. So, you protect yourself with rage.

Problem is, those other drivers aren't your enemies. They don't even know you — they're strangers. Truth is they're not thinking at all about you — they're thinking about themselves. There's no grand conspiracy operating here! Granted, they may be a nuisance sometimes, but your enemy? Nah.

Here's the litmus test: You're driving down a stretch of highway with no cars anywhere around you. Up ahead, you see a truck on the side of the road, waiting to enter the lane of traffic. Just as you get to where the truck is, the driver suddenly and without warning pulls out in front of you, causing you to hit your brakes and veer into the left lane.

Why did he endanger you (and himself) by doing that rather than waiting until you passed? Did he do that on purpose? Was he waiting for the right moment to whip out in front of you, hoping to startle you and maybe cause you to crash? Or is it just that he just doesn't know any better — he doesn't have a clue about safe driving? If you choose the first answer, I guarantee you'll experience road rage. If you choose the second answer, you won't.

The choice about how to respond to a situation is always yours!

His wife says . . .

I'd been working with an angry man and his wife for about a year, and things were steadily improving. "We're good, things are good," they both agreed. "And what do you attribute that to?" I asked. The wife spoke up immediately and said, "It's that card you gave my husband — the one that says, 'They are not the enemy.' He carries it with him all the time. I think he's beginning to realize that, while he may have problems with our daughters and me, we really aren't his enemies."

Stop Catastrophizing

So the woman in front of you is slowing you down — it's not the end of the world. So that guy is stuck in the passing lane, holding everybody else up — it's not the end of the world. So the person in front of you doesn't move as soon as the light changes to green — it's not the end of the world. Or is it?

Is your world that fragile and tenuous? Do you actually view the everyday hassles of driving as a series of unending catastrophes — sudden, unexpected events that cause *great* harm? Are they on par with finding out that you have cancer? That you just lost most of your retirement money because of a major correction in the stock market? That your lovely daughter wants to marry a drug dealer? Now, I grant you — *those* are catastrophes!

Richard found out the hard way about the perils of catastrophizing. He was stopped at an intersection when a young woman pulled up from behind and tapped Richard's new car on the bumper. It wasn't much of a tap, but she did make contact. He jumped out of his car, ran to where she was sitting in her car, and launched into a tirade of threats and cussing. The police arrived soon after, and, much to Richard's surprise, arrested him for assault in public. It turned out the girl called the police not only to report the accident but also to report Richard's angry behavior. He had to go to court, retain an attorney, and was found guilty. He ended up in anger management, rather perplexed, still rationalizing his rageful behavior "because she hit me, damn it!"

The next time you find yourself getting outraged while driving, ask yourself the following ten questions:

- Is this worse than a terrorist attack?
- Is this as bad as a category-5 hurricane?
- Is this the hill you want to die on?
- Is this really worth ruining your day by losing your cool?

✔ Is this worth having a heart attack over?

✔ Is this worth all the energy it will take to be rageful?

✔ Has this happened to you before and did you survive it?

✔ On a scale of 1 to 10, is this really a 100?

✔ Are you bigger than this — or, is this bigger than you?

✔ Is this a sign that the end of the world is at hand?

If the answer to these questions is a resounding yes, then by all means rage on. If not, you can relax.

Stop Being So Rational

I can hear you now. "What in the world is he thinking, pulling out in front of that other car? He should know better than that. God, that's dangerous." Or, that old frustration: "Why can't she pull over and get in the non-passing lane if she's only going to go the speed limit? She's not supposed to be in this lane. What an idiot!"

The mistake here — which leads to your anger — is that you're trying to understand why other people drive the way they do. My advice: Stop trying and just accept things as they are, not how you want them to be or think they should be. Driving behavior in humans is no more rational than any other aspect of life. Why do people vote the way they do? Why do people eat the way they do? Why do people do drugs?

All you're doing is (literally) driving yourself crazy. Expect less and relax more.

Settle for Just Being Irritated

Anger occurs at three different levels of intensity. As I cover in Chapter 2, these levels include

✔ **Irritated:** Ratings of 1 to 3 on a 10-point intensity scale. Other adjectives you can replace for *irritated* include *annoyed, bothered,* or *fretted.*

✔ **Mad or angry:** Ratings of 4 to 6 on a 10-point scale. You can also think of this as *infuriated, incensed,* or *exasperated.*

✔ **Rage:** Ratings of 7 to 10 on a 10-point scale. Synonyms include *furious, berserk,* and *irate.*

No one is asking you to feel *nothing* when you get frustrated while driving. The problem isn't that you get angry; the problem is that you get *too* angry (experiencing rage). Why not settle for just being irritated or even mad? That way you're still in control of your actions even though you're obviously not a happy camper. After all, no one ever gets arrested for "road irritation," or we'd probably all be in jail.

Everything is a matter of degree, and anger is no different. Why not tone it down and relax?

Absolute rubbish

Some years ago, I attended a workshop on road rage sponsored by an auto club. A panel of so-called experts — all engineers — concluded that the two main reasons people experience rage are: (1) There are simply too many cars on the highways, and (2) The entry and exit ramps on major roadways are too steep.

This, of course, assumes that all drivers are normal people who have complete control over their emotions. I can hear the defense lawyers now, "Your honor, my client is not guilty — the road make him do it." Absolute rubbish! The reason people experience road rage is because they don't know how to manage their anger.

Chapter 25

Ten Anger-Freeing Thoughts

Anger management is a case of mind over matter. What you have in your mind matters — it spells the difference between being full of anger versus anger-free. In this chapter, I offer you ten thoughts that will help you manage anger — yesterday, today, and tomorrow.

No One — Absolutely No One — Can Make You Angry without Your Consent

Every time I hear (and I hear it a lot!) someone say "He or she made me mad," I want to run up and tell that person how absolutely wrong this is. When people say that, it's just their way of trying to make other people responsible for their emotions. No circumstance, person, or event has that power over you. You aren't a car that can be started by another person's key — and you should be glad about that!

What *is* true is that external events can (and do) provide you with opportunities to become angry. The unfortunate part is that people embrace this opportunity all too readily. You can, if you want, choose not to lose your temper. Either way, the choice is entirely yours.

The next time — and there will be a next time — you find yourself facing an opportunity to become angry, remember this comforting thought: No one can make you angry — no matter how hard he tries — unless you decide to let him.

Anger Boomerangs — And So Does Love

You've probably heard numerous sayings like "What goes around comes around" and "You reap what you sow" — most of them coming out of the mouth of one of your parents. Annoying as those sayings may be, they do serve a purpose: They remind you that life is, by and large, a two-way street. There is a certain reciprocity to human emotion; in other words, anger begets anger, fear engenders fear, and one act of kindness is often followed by another. People respond in kind to whatever you throw out there. Throw out anger and you get back anger. Throw out love and you get back love. Emotions work just like a boomerang.

If you want others to treat you positively, begin each day by asking yourself the following questions:

- ✔ Who can I care about today?

- ✔ Who needs my understanding, not my judgment?

- ✔ How many kind remarks do I want to offer others today?

- ✔ To whom can I be sympathetic?

- ✔ How many people can I hug before the sun goes down?

- ✔ How often can I say *please* and *thank you*?

- ✔ How happy are people when they see my smiling face?

Then see how difficult it is for you to get angry.

It's Only Money

The whole world is one giant, global economy. In the end, whether you real-ize it or not, most things come down to money — money gained and money lost. Far too often, you may find yourself upset — angry — because some-thing goes wrong and it has a monetary consequence. If the cost is minimal, you get irritated. If the cost is more than you can (or want to) bear, you fly into a rage.

What you need to consider, however, is that it's only money. It's not the end of the world or civilization as we know it. It doesn't mean that your life is ruined forever. It's only money.

Years ago, when I was not as good at managing anger as I am now, I used to get mad when one of my kids called to say she had been involved in an automobile accident. My first thought — I'm sorry to say — was, "How much is that going to cost?" And, my first question to my kid was, "How's the car? How much damage was there? Is it drivable?" (Interestingly, this is exactly how my father used to react when one of *his* kids had an accident.) Then one day it hit me: The more important question — the one I should be asking — is "Are you okay? Are you hurt? How are you?" The rest is only a matter of money and metal!

It's all about priorities. What I discovered was that my love and concern for my children was far more important than the "cost" of *anything*.

Other People Are Not the Enemy

From an evolutionary standpoint, anger serves a purpose. It is a means to an end — survival. Emotions were built into your nervous system to help you adapt to life so that you can live long and well. Anger has a single purpose — to protect you from your enemies, those who threaten your very existence. But who are these enemies and how many do you have?

If your kid comes home with a D on his report card, is he your enemy? If your wife isn't as interested in sex as you'd like her to be, is she your enemy? If someone ahead of you in the express-checkout line at the grocery store has 11 items rather than 10, is she your enemy? Is everyone who gets in your way, inconveniences you, or beats you at poker your enemy? If so, then you're going to be angry a lot!

Reserve the status of "enemy" for those people who truly threaten your physical safety. Think of the rest of them as *people* — son, daughter, spouse, person who doesn't see fit to obey the rules in the checkout line — not enemies. Unless the lady in the checkout line pulls out a gun and asks you for your wallet, she's just an annoying person, not an enemy — and not worth getting angry over.

Life Isn't Fair — Not Even at the Top

Sometimes humans are funny creatures. When life goes the way you want it to, you call that fair. When it doesn't, you call that unfair. You decide what's fair and what's unfair. In other words, you're the ultimate judge. How you think about what happens to you is what determines how angry you get. Every time you think "unfair," there's the anger!

I ask you the question I asked myself one night when I went to check on my son and found him sleeping soundly with a look of contentment on his face: "Is it fair that I have two beautiful, healthy children, while my sister had a son who died at 13 from cancer?" My argument: Having healthy children is no more fair than having unhealthy children. The difference is in our minds. And no one ever gets angry because life is fair in a way that favors him.

So, maybe the answer is to stop thinking about whether what comes your way today is fair or unfair and just deal with it as best you can — without being judgmental, which is where the anger comes in. Try it.

Also, remember to be grateful even when life doesn't go the way you want it to.

Energy Is a Terrible Thing to Waste

Have you ever heard that old saying that "Energy is wasted on the young"? The same can be said of anger. It takes energy for you to be angry, it takes energy for you to stay angry, and it takes energy for you to do all the things you do to express or relieve anger. Too much anger can leave you utterly exhausted.

Are you sure you want to devote so much energy to one emotion — or, for that matter, to emotions in general? You don't have an unending supply of energy — you can use it up like any other resource. Where you spend your energy pretty much defines your day. If you put most of it into tasks, at the end of the day you feel productive. If you put most of it into anger, at the end of the day you feel angry, defeated, exhausted, and unproductive.

As long as you're alive, you're spending energy on something. The question is: "What are you spending it on?" Is your energy working to benefit you — to improve your lot in life — or it is simply wasted? You get to choose.

Maintaining vitality in old age

Research shows that as people age, they consistently report fewer episodes of anger, less intense anger, and that they get over anger more quickly. Maybe that's because the angry people die off early. Or maybe it's because those who survive have discovered one of the great lessons of life: It takes energy to preserve life. And you have a lot less energy at your disposal in the second half of your life as you do in the first half. So, people are forced to become good stewards of energy as a way of ensuring vitality.

Don't Kid Yourself: We're All Bozos

Woody Allen was right — we're all bozos. The minute you forget that, you're in trouble. Thinking of yourself as superior to other people is an open invitation to anger. Anger tends to flow downhill toward those you regard as inferior — as sillier, stupider, and less contentious than you are. You tell yourself: "They — the lesser people — deserve what they get when they make me mad."

Besides anger, the second major cause of counterproductive behavior in the workplace — malicious gossip, refusing to help a co-worker, outright theft — is what psychiatrists call *narcissism* (more about this in Chapter 20). The narcissistic employee is one who has a grandiose view of herself — she sees herself as a "special" bozo, a bozo whose opinions should carry more weight than others, and a bozo who feels that all the other employees are just there to cater to her needs. In other words, the *queen* bozo!

The same is true in marriage. According to marriage expert Dr. John Gottman, as soon as contempt enters the relationship, the marriage is doomed. Contempt goes along with a feeling of superiority and it goes way beyond ordinary criticism of your partner — the intent behind it is to demean, insult, and psychologically harm your so-called loved one.

Settle for just being an ordinary — nothing-special — bozo. Then you can relax.

This Isn't the Hill You Want to Die On

Just as in war, as you struggle your way through life, you must invariably decide which objectives — hills, goals, or issues — are worth dying for and which ones matter less. The more things matter — the more of an emotional investment you have in something — the angrier you get when things don't go your way. And, as my former colleague Dr. Redford Williams at Duke University so poignantly put it, "Anger kills!" So, it pays to be selective in the battles you choose to fight.

Reserve the right to fight just one major battle a day, and live to fight another day!

There's Nothing You Can Achieve in Anger That You Can't Achieve without It

Anger can be used constructively in some instances (see Chapter 11), but anything you want to achieve in life can be yours without anger.

How I stopped hating insurance companies

In my experience, insurance companies hate to pay mental-health providers. They would rather pay thousands of dollars for a major back operation than a few hundred bucks for our efforts to teach a client how to live successfully with pain.

Over the years, I've had many angry conversations with claims agents who balked at paying my bill. And, although I won all these battles, I found myself getting mad just thinking about making one of those calls.

What I've discovered in recent years, however, is that things go much better — the conversations are shorter and more pleasant, and I get paid quicker — when I don't lead (or jump in) with an angry, defensive attitude. Now, when the insurance rep says, "I can't pay this bill," instead of hollering into the phone I simply reply, "Oh, I'm sure you can. You work for a big company and I bet you can do just about anything you set your mind to. What I need from you is to tell me how I can help you pay my bill. I know your time is valuable, and I don't want you to spend any more of it on my problem that need be. So, what can I do to help?" Believe it or not, this strategy works! And I no longer hate insurance companies.

Somewhere along the line, people forged an association between getting mad and getting things done. And now the anger comes automatically when we're faced with obstacles, challenges, and problems. It's what experimental psychologists call *superstitious reinforcement* — in other words, we think anger is vital to our day-to-day survival when it's really not.

Try to remember the last time you got angry. What was the problem that led to your getting mad? Could you have dealt with this problem in any other way without needing to be angry? Be honest. Did your anger help or hinder your ability to resolve the problem? I'm willing to bet it was a hindrance.

At some time in the history of mankind, anger no doubt served a purpose — mainly through its connection with physical survival. But in today's world, anger has nearly outlived its usefulness. Too often, anger is nothing more than a bad habit that is passed down from one generation to the next.

When You're Dealing with People, You're Not Entitled to a Damn Thing!

If you discover one thing from reading this book that will help you manage anger better, I hope it's this: You're not entitled to anything. I believe that a sense of entitlement is the root cause of much of the anger in today's fast-moving, complex world.

According to the dictionary, an *entitlement* is anything you have legal claim to — like the title to a piece of property. Historically, it was something that English kings granted noblemen for their loyal service. And yet today, if you're like me, you apply the concept to just about every facet of your everyday life.

Here are some common examples of things people have a false sense of entitlement to:

- ✔ A spouse who always agrees with them
- ✔ Children who always obey them
- ✔ Consideration from everyone, all the time
- ✔ Continuous employment
- ✔ Peace of mind
- ✔ A world where everything is fair
- ✔ Cheap gasoline
- ✔ Prosperity
- ✔ The respect of their peers
- ✔ A stable economy
- ✔ Freedom from oppression
- ✔ Having their ideas, beliefs, and opinions valued by everyone
- ✔ A good night's sleep
- ✔ A promotion at work
- ✔ A car that always starts first thing in the morning

The problem with a sense of entitlement is that it conveys a sense of obligation, certainty, and predictability — for example, your adolescent kids will, without question, always do what you ask of them because *they owe you* that courtesy for bringing them into this world. And what happens if they don't see it that way? You get angry.

Forget the entitlements and instead negotiate successfully for what you want (not demand) out of life — a raise, a promotion, respect, love, and recognition. It makes life flow a whole lot easier.

Index

BUSINESS, CAREERS & PERSONAL FINANCE

0-7645-5307-0

0-7645-5331-3 *†

Also available:

- Accounting For Dummies †
  0-7645-5314-3
- Business Plans Kit For Dummies †
  0-7645-5365-8
- Cover Letters For Dummies
  0-7645-5224-4
- Frugal Living For Dummies
  0-7645-5403-4
- Leadership For Dummies
  0-7645-5176-0
- Managing For Dummies
  0-7645-1771-6

- Marketing For Dummies
  0-7645-5600-2
- Personal Finance For Dummies *
  0-7645-2590-5
- Project Management For Dummies
  0-7645-5283-X
- Resumes For Dummies †
  0-7645-5471-9
- Selling For Dummies
  0-7645-5363-1
- Small Business Kit For Dummies *†
  0-7645-5093-4

HOME & BUSINESS COMPUTER BASICS

0-7645-4074-2

0-7645-3758-X

Also available:

- ACT! 6 For Dummies
  0-7645-2645-6
- iLife '04 All-in-One Desk Reference
  For Dummies
  0-7645-7347-0
- iPAQ For Dummies
  0-7645-6769-1
- Mac OS X Panther Timesaving
  Techniques For Dummies
  0-7645-5812-9
- Macs For Dummies
  0-7645-5656-8

- Microsoft Money 2004 For Dummies
  0-7645-4195-1
- Office 2003 All-in-One Desk Reference
  For Dummies
  0-7645-3883-7
- Outlook 2003 For Dummies
  0-7645-3759-8
- PCs For Dummies
  0-7645-4074-2
- TiVo For Dummies
  0-7645-6923-6
- Upgrading and Fixing PCs For Dummies
  0-7645-1665-5
- Windows XP Timesaving Techniques
  For Dummies
  0-7645-3748-2

FOOD, HOME, GARDEN, HOBBIES, MUSIC & PETS

0-7645-5295-3

0-7645-5232-5

Also available:

- Bass Guitar For Dummies
  0-7645-2487-9
- Diabetes Cookbook For Dummies
  0-7645-5230-9
- Gardening For Dummies *
  0-7645-5130-2
- Guitar For Dummies
  0-7645-5106-X
- Holiday Decorating For Dummies
  0-7645-2570-0
- Home Improvement All-in-One
  For Dummies
  0-7645-5680-0

- Knitting For Dummies
  0-7645-5395-X
- Piano For Dummies
  0-7645-5105-1
- Puppies For Dummies
  0-7645-5255-4
- Scrapbooking For Dummies
  0-7645-7208-3
- Senior Dogs For Dummies
  0-7645-5818-8
- Singing For Dummies
  0-7645-2475-5
- 30-Minute Meals For Dummies
  0-7645-2589-1

INTERNET & DIGITAL MEDIA

0-7645-1664-7

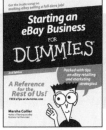

0-7645-6924-4

Also available:

- 2005 Online Shopping Directory
  For Dummies
  0-7645-7495-7
- CD & DVD Recording For Dummies
  0-7645-5956-7
- eBay For Dummies
  0-7645-5654-1
- Fighting Spam For Dummies
  0-7645-5965-6
- Genealogy Online For Dummies
  0-7645-5964-8
- Google For Dummies
  0-7645-4420-9

- Home Recording For Musicians
  For Dummies
  0-7645-1634-5
- The Internet For Dummies
  0-7645-4173-0
- iPod & iTunes For Dummies
  0-7645-7772-7
- Preventing Identity Theft For Dummies
  0-7645-7336-5
- Pro Tools All-in-One Desk Reference
  For Dummies
  0-7645-5714-9
- Roxio Easy Media Creator For Dummies
  0-7645-7131-1

SPORTS, FITNESS, PARENTING, RELIGION & SPIRITUALITY

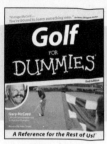

0-7645-5146-9

0-7645-5418-2

Also available:
- Adoption For Dummies
0-7645-5488-3
- Basketball For Dummies
0-7645-5248-1
- The Bible For Dummies
0-7645-5296-1
- Buddhism For Dummies
0-7645-5359-3
- Catholicism For Dummies
0-7645-5391-7
- Hockey For Dummies
0-7645-5228-7

- Judaism For Dummies
0-7645-5299-6
- Martial Arts For Dummies
0-7645-5358-5
- Pilates For Dummies
0-7645-5397-6
- Religion For Dummies
0-7645-5264-3
- Teaching Kids to Read For Dummies
0-7645-4043-2
- Weight Training For Dummies
0-7645-5168-X
- Yoga For Dummies
0-7645-5117-5

TRAVEL

0-7645-5438-7

0-7645-5453-0

Also available:
- Alaska For Dummies
0-7645-1761-9
- Arizona For Dummies
0-7645-6938-4
- Cancún and the Yucatán For Dummies
0-7645-2437-2
- Cruise Vacations For Dummies
0-7645-6941-4
- Europe For Dummies
0-7645-5456-5
- Ireland For Dummies
0-7645-5455-7

- Las Vegas For Dummies
0-7645-5448-4
- London For Dummies
0-7645-4277-X
- New York City For Dummies
0-7645-6945-7
- Paris For Dummies
0-7645-5494-8
- RV Vacations For Dummies
0-7645-5443-3
- Walt Disney World & Orlando For Dummies
0-7645-6943-0

GRAPHICS, DESIGN & WEB DEVELOPMENT

0-7645-4345-8

0-7645-5589-8

Also available:
- Adobe Acrobat 6 PDF For Dummies
0-7645-3760-1
- Building a Web Site For Dummies
0-7645-7144-3
- Dreamweaver MX 2004 For Dummies
0-7645-4342-3
- FrontPage 2003 For Dummies
0-7645-3882-9
- HTML 4 For Dummies
0-7645-1995-6
- Illustrator CS For Dummies
0-7645-4084-X

- Macromedia Flash MX 2004 For Dummies
0-7645-4358-X
- Photoshop 7 All-in-One Desk Reference For Dummies
0-7645-1667-1
- Photoshop CS Timesaving Techniques For Dummies
0-7645-6782-9
- PHP 5 For Dummies
0-7645-4166-8
- PowerPoint 2003 For Dummies
0-7645-3908-6
- QuarkXPress 6 For Dummies
0-7645-2593-X

NETWORKING, SECURITY, PROGRAMMING & DATABASES

0-7645-6852-3

0-7645-5784-X

Also available:
- A+ Certification For Dummies
0-7645-4187-0
- Access 2003 All-in-One Desk Reference For Dummies
0-7645-3988-4
- Beginning Programming For Dummies
0-7645-4997-9
- C For Dummies
0-7645-7068-4
- Firewalls For Dummies
0-7645-4048-3
- Home Networking For Dummies
0-7645-42796

- Network Security For Dummies
0-7645-1679-5
- Networking For Dummies
0-7645-1677-9
- TCP/IP For Dummies
0-7645-1760-0
- VBA For Dummies
0-7645-3989-2
- Wireless All In-One Desk Reference For Dummies
0-7645-7496-5
- Wireless Home Networking For Dummies
0-7645-3910-8

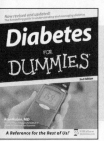

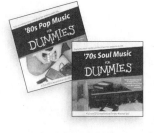